Hertfordshire
COUNTY COUNCIL
Community Information

1 0 MAR 2001

- 7 JUL 2001

2 5 FEB 2000

Ask 7/60

1 4 SEP 2001

2/2 DC

7/12

1 6 DEC 2000

5th Jan 2001

- 1 FEB 2001

Please renew/return this item by the last date shown.

So that your telephone call is charged at local rate, please call the numbers as set out below:

	From Area codes 01923 or 0208:	From the rest of Herts:
Renewals:	01923 471373	01438 737373
Enquiries:	01923 471333	01438 737333
Minicom:	01923 471599	01438 737599

L32b

D0186064

Norman Painting

—

Reluctant Archer

Granta Editions

Publisher's Note

It has been impossible, in most cases, to trace
copyright owners for the illustrations used in this
book. If any copyright owner wishes to contact
Granta Editions we will insert proper
acknowledgements in any subsequent edition.

Acknowledgement

The author and publisher are grateful to
Mrs Kathleen Tynan for granting permission to
reproduce the letters by Ken Tynan on pp28–29

First published in Great Britain in 1982 by
Granta Editions Ltd, 7 Brooklands Avenue,
Cambridge CB2 2BB
In association with Client & Co, Herts

Copyright © Norman Painting 1982

ISBN 0 906782 06 6

Edited by First Edition, Cambridge
Design and production in association with
Book Production Consultants, Cambridge
Typeset by Glyn Davies Typesetting, Cambridge

Printed and bound in Great Britain by
Biddles Ltd, Martyr Road, Guildford, Surrey

Contents

Dedication

TO
my dearest DIANA,
one of the most loving people I know

TO
my friends pictured within,
and many more unknown and unnamed

TO
my sister who watched and waited when I
was at either side of death's door
and who visited me devotedly

TO
all my friends and colleagues in the BBC
for their tolerance and affection

AND
for preventing this book being published
posthumously and without the final section

TO
Dr P.W. Fisher
and the dedicated team of the Intensive Care Unit
of the Horton General Hospital, Banbury, and
many other members of the Hospital Staff,
especially Dr P.M. Khan for his patience and humanity

I not only dedicate this book
but am profoundly grateful to be alive to do so.

Preface

In the year in which this book is first published, the BBC is 60 years old. The author of this book has been actively involved with broadcasting for 37 of those years, as the following pages indicate. Although radio filled much of his life, there were many other things in it too, and it is also part of the purpose of the book to give an account of them.

The two great egoisms are writing an autobiography and having children – assuming, that is, that both acts are deliberate: it is possible to be indiscreet with both pen and penis.

I have, at the time of writing, no children; and I doubt if I would have written this book, if the idea had not been suggested to me. But I am glad that it was, because much of what I say has been at the back of my mind for some years. It is not a rags-to-riches story, rather from-fried-herrings-to-smoked-salmon, but it happened, and the story of my student days was not at the time a usual one.

If I seem to say too little about my childhood it is, paradoxically, because there is so much to say! I am actively working on a separate account of those years that I can recall so easily, so vividly, and in such detail.

The plan of this book is probably simpler than it may at first appear to be. Chapter 1 goes from birth to graduation at the University of Birmingham. Chapter 2 covers my Oxford years. Chapter 3 is an account of a remarkable student tour of America. These first three chapters are written more or less in sequence; but in the remaining chapters chronology is abandoned. My life has been so enjoyably full because of the diversity of its activities; and each of these is treated separately, in order to build up a detailed portrait. So Chapter 4 gives an account of early broadcasts, starting during student days in the mid-forties. Chapter 5 describes my training as an interviewer, also starting in the late forties. In Chapter 6, my career at the desk as a writer is outlined, and Chapter 7 illustrates my involvement in music; both these chapters have to go back to my childhood in order to tell a complete story.

Appearing on the screen came comparatively late and Chapter 8 is therefore concerned with fairly recent years.

Having read the first eight chapters, the reader may well have a better understanding of my reluctance, over 30 or more years, to devote so much of my time and energy to one programme, *The Archers*. A sympathetic reader, if convinced by these arguments, should by this point have a clear portrait of the author in mind: the final chapter adds the finishing touches, warts and all.

There are indeed rather more than finishing touches in this final version: for, shortly after the main part of the manuscript was completed, the author sustained a series of heart attacks, including a massive one and even momentary complete cardiac arrest. He is now on the way to complete recovery and, apart from a new final section, the book remains basically as originally intended: not an intimate portrait, not a full-length nude, but a formal head and shoulders, dealing mainly with the author's public, not his private, life.

If, in this self-portrait, the artist has revealed himself as a maturing, fun-loving, ruminative, busy and forward-looking man, then he may not be too far from having painted a recognizable likeness.

August 1982   N.P.

CHAPTER 1

Childhood and youth:
sketching the background

I slipped into the world like a smile, according to my mother, and who would know better? It was St George's Day – Shakespeare's birthday – and that year it fell on the Wednesday of Easter Week.

I was both wanted and welcome: there had been two daughters before me, only one of whom had survived. During her pregnancy my mother had seen a musical comedy, and had secretly wished that her baby might grow to be involved in the theatre – an odd thought, perhaps, for one of her completely untheatrical background.

She little dreamt that her child, against all his own inclinations and intentions, would find himself in the record books as the world's most durable radio actor! For that is what I must be, if *The Archers* is, as it seems to be, the world's longest-running daily radio serial.

My father on the other hand, once the novelty of having fathered a son had worn off, was less enthusiastic about my interest in music, acting, and poetry than my mother, and would have welcomed a greater keenness in soccer, railways, and digging the garden.

The days of my childhood were, on the whole, happy. As there was a gap of more than six years between my sister and myself, I spent a great deal of time alone. I had schoolfriends, of course, but my constant companion was a dog, a Jack Russell smooth-haired terrier, called Spot. I was very much the outdoor boy with a dog, a bicycle and a passion for swimming in rivers. I especially enjoyed the Avon near a place called Blackdown, just outside Leamington.

The shadow of mortality scarcely fell over those early days, except, before Spot came on the scene, in the death of my black retriever puppy, Prince, the anguish of which remains with me still. Even recording it here has brought back the pangs of that Sunday morning when I could have been no more than ten. I was also, as now, a persistent worrier, and often spent whole weeks in desperate anxiety over childish fears, which could be dissipated by a word of reassurance as quickly as they had appeared.

My father earned very little as a railway signalman. Throughout the greater part of my childhood his wages were 55 shillings (£2.75p.) a week. My sister had moved on to a secondary school at 11+, and her education had proved such a strain on family finances that when I was awarded not a free place but a special place at Leamington College, my father insisted that this could not be afforded. Long arguments followed. My mother pleaded, and succeeded: I went to Leamington College for Boys. But there was one point that I remember well. When, tired of hearing my parents wrangle, I had said: 'I'll go to the Central School. I don't *want* to go to the College!', my mother knew this was untrue, and persisted in her argument that I should be given the same chance as my sister. I now realize that this was the first step upwards; but I was then so weary of the endless talk at home of finding ways and means of economizing that I was unwilling to add to the problems.

My days at the college were happy ones. The headmaster, Arnold Thornton, had not blinked when, at my first interview with him, I had announced in answer to his question about what I wanted to do that I wished to become an actor, or a writer. He was a keen amateur performer himself, and was an attentive audience when, at his request, I recited for him Walter de la Mare's 'The Listeners'.

The college was not a place of rule-books and examination fever. Wide interests were encouraged, and what I lacked on the playing field I made up for in the printing room, the school orchestra and, inevitably, the school plays. It's true that to everyone's surprise (my own included) I did once score a try on the rugger field; and once at cricket I bowled a hat-trick. It seemed, though, that having proved I could, I no longer had any interest in continuing these activities.

The orchestra was different. We entered a schools orchestra competition at Queen's Hall in London, adjudicated by Thomas F. Dunhill; and, as the test pieces (The Minuet from Haydn's 'Surprise' Symphony and an arrangement of Mendelssohn's 'On Wings of Song') were scored for strings, woodwind and piano, I was recruited to play the piano part. I also joined a swing music group, playing such classics as 'Basin Street Blues' and 'Bob White What're ya Going to Swing Tonight?' at school concerts.

The real attraction for me, though, in school entertainments was the plays. I still have the programme for the first play I had performed. I not only wrote the thing, I directed, and played a main part in it, thus setting a pattern I was to follow later . . .

Then a shadow fell over my young life. At long last my father had been promoted. His salary was increased from 55 shillings (£2.75p.) a week to 75 (£3.75p.): however, he was to be based not in Leamington Spa, but Nuneaton. I had known Nuneaton from occasional short visits, as my grandparents lived there. Architecturally, the town seemed to lack character, and certainly had none of the space, elegance and lightness of Leamington. It was a marketing town in a mining area, but with good farming land around it.

My new school was to be very different, too. Leamington College had come down in the world from being a minor public school (where Lytton Strachey was a pupil, and where Dr Joseph Wood had been headmaster before leaving to be headmaster of Harrow) to being a spaciously-housed secondary school. King Edward VI at Nuneaton was an old grammar school, with a flourishing reputation for boys winning scholarships to the older universities – though Leamington College, in spite of its relaxed style of teaching, was not far behind. I remember that we were given a holiday when D.J. Enright, now well-known as a poet and critic, won a Cambridge scholarship. Another of its old boys was soon to become world famous: Sir Frank Whittle, pioneer inventor of the jet engine. At that time, the most famous old boy of my new school in Nuneaton was Robert Burton, the seventeenth-century author of *The Anatomy of Melancholy*. It now has another: the internationally-known agriculturalist, Sir Henry Plumb, who, then in the form below me, gave few hints of his future brilliance.

It was an awkward time to change schools, and at first I rebelled. For one term I moved in with our one-time neighbours, the Guests, in Leamington. I became a guest of the Guests, and merely went to my new home at weekends. Then I tried commuting, rising early, running across country that had been known to George Eliot to catch a train for the hour's journey to Leamington. This soon proved too exhausting, and reluctantly I gave in. I had just one year before taking School Certificate, what is now known as 'O'-levels.

King Edward's was a tense, highly disciplined school. The buildings were cramped and overcrowded in marked contrast to the lofty hall and refectory and brightly-decorated classrooms of Leamington College, but there was a sense of tradition, and academic hard work. My school-fellows seemed earthier, not so

3

well-spoken and more given to rugger and fisticuffs.

There was to be a play produced in my first term, though, and my eyes lit up. It was Sheridan's *The School for Scandal* and at first I was cast as Lady Sneerwell. I may not have promised well as a drag performer; or the boy originally cast for Joseph Surface may not have inspired confidence. Either way, the casting was changed, and I, though an unknown newcomer, was given the important part of Joseph Surface. The result was a glowing school report at the end of term, and immediate promotion at the end of the school year to sub-prefect. I learnt something that was to be of enormous value to me, later: by joining the cast of a play, I could make both friends and a reputation.

I also swam for my school; indeed, at the first school swimming gala I attended, I established a record for the breast stroke which was unbeaten for some years. This taught me something else: that significant events in life are often flukes. My achievement came about because I'd arrived late, was annoyed with myself, rushed into my costume, dived in and swam with such fury I broke the record!

I reached the age of 15, did well in my 'O'-level equivalent, and, at the beginning of my second year at King Edward's, entered the sixth form. It was then that my father announced that he could not afford to keep me at school for much longer, certainly not until I was 18. All my day-dreams of a university career collapsed like a pricked balloon. Books on careers from the local library were sought out and studied: there didn't seem to be many openings for someone who acted, wrote, and played the piano a little.

I was certain of one thing regarding my career: I could never face a nine-till-five office job, nor could I endure travelling daily a long distance to my work. One term doing an hour's journey night and morning had made that clear.

Librarianship seemed a possibility. It would mean dealing with books and with people; the hours were varied; and one could qualify by correspondence while earning some cash. Not that the money I earned amounted to much I discovered, when, against my headmaster's hopes and advice, I had left school and had started work as a junior assistant in the local library. Until I reached the age of 16, my take-home pay was well under one pound; and my first annual increment took the figure to only slightly over that sum. But I was at least contributing a mite towards the family income, rather than diminishing it.

I think the only reason I was sad to leave school was that it meant the end of my university hopes. Otherwise, I revelled in the sense of independence. For a reason I do not know, I developed an urge towards self-sufficiency: I made my own bed, designed my own room, perfected my cooking, spent hours writing sub-Masefield poems about roughing-it on sailing ships. I did not, in fact, break my ties with school. I joined the Air Training Corps, played rugger for the Old Boys, and took my limited holidays at the school's harvest-camps.

Moreover, inevitably there was a play. Or rather this time, it was a pageant, and it called on most of the available talent from the town, whether or not those concerned were in favour of the reason for the production or not. The pageant was written by one of my *Children's Hour* heroes, Dr L. du Garde Peach, and had been commissioned by the Co-operative Wholesale Society (CWS). I was offered, and accepted, the part of Speaker, who was a kind of narrator. The pageant was given some hundreds of simultaneous productions all over the country to celebrate the centenary of the CWS, and the part of Speaker was played in London by Wilfred Pickles. The BBC announcer Alan Howland (with whom I was later to work in radio) first accepted the part and then declined it when he found the script somewhat leftish. On the other hand, I, seeing how starry the part was, had no second thoughts at all – after all, my father was a Labour councillor, even though I did go on theatre trips with the Young Conservatives . . . (Unlike Philip Archer, I have as little interest in party politics as in sectarian religion.)

Playing the Speaker, apart from being great fun and a tremendous boost to my ego – I don't thing it was too bad a performance either – stood me in good stead very shortly afterwards, when I went cap in hand to the local authority, asking for help to get to university. Half the council had been my fellow-actors, many of them playing bit-parts or merely walk-ons or chorus; and most of the town had turned out to see the show, as we played to packed houses.

There was one person in the audience, though, a certain William White, who was unknown to everyone at the time. It was to be 30 years before I met him face to face in the flat of my radio 'mother', Gwen Berryman, who had become friendly with him. He was by now very well-known indeed and, before our first meeting, I was racking my brains as to what I could possibly say to him. I needn't have worried. He entered the room, hand outstretched for a firm handshake: 'I've been dying to meet you for years', he said. 'Co-op Hall, Nuneaton . . . You in that Greek tunic, with all those girls . . . I've followed your career ever since.

The wireless and all that, you know. But I've often thought what a loss it is to the theatre, you being in *The Archers*!'

His name, bless his heart, is now Larry Grayson; and his comments in that opening speech showed a genuineness and generosity that I now know are typical of the man. I later discovered that his sisters knew my mother and they had many acquaintances in common among local people. As Dame Anna Neagle has said, 'He enjoys his success enormously, and he deserves every bit of it.' Very true. He had a very long and tough climb to the top, seeing at times the less acceptable and certainly the most unglamorous side of show business. But he remains serene and unembittered. If anyone has a right to be bitchy, he has; but he's just the opposite.

As my 18th birthday approached, I began to see boys who had been with me in the sixth form during my brief one term there, and whose parents weren't that much better off than mine, winning open scholarships, bursaries, and exhibitions to university. Exploiting my position as librarian, I researched the question fully, finding out every possible means of obtaining grants or scholarships. I seemed in those difficult un-state-aided days to be totally unqualified for help.

I wrote dozens of letters, which I carefully typed out and sent off in my own name, or occasionally had signed by my father. I even sat at short notice an examination for which I was completely unprepared, with predictable results. I had been away from school for three years, and was that much behind. It is true, I had half-heartedly been studying for my librarianship exams, some of which I had passed, especially those concerned with literature; but studying like this could not compare with the intensive cramming which was part of the school's policy for its sixth-formers. Part of the sixth-form course at Nuneaton was to acquire sufficient Latin to pass the Oxford and Cambridge entrance exams. I had always been good at Latin, but hadn't studied it since my Leamington College days.

I persuaded my old headmaster to see me. I told him I wanted to go to university. He at once pointed out that Oxford and Cambridge weren't possible as I had no Latin. I refrained from saying that that was because of his policy; I had arrived at his school with excellent Latin. But, he went on, there were other universities, and he might be able to say a word to get me a small grant from the local authority.

For a moment or two I was deflated; Oxford had always been my dream. On the other hand, extensive reading had opened my eyes to the existence of other universities, many of which had great qualities . . .

Then, by chance, I went to make up numbers on a coach tour organized, I think, by the WEA to Birmingham University. There must have been a lecture of some sort, but I forget which. What I shall always remember is going in to the beautiful concert hall of the Barber Institute, for a short recital by the Professor of Music, Victor Hely-Hutchinson. He played Mozart; and all these years later I have only to hear or play a certain sonata in F major, especially the Maggiore and Minore sections, and I am transported back to that afternoon. I walked out into a fresh breeze after rain; the lawns sloped sharply away until they met the blue-grey gloom of Selly Oak. But there, high up above it all, I seemed like a visitor to the Promised Land. Inwardly I said: 'I'd give anything to come here.' In a matter of months, I did.

It was not only Victor Hely-Hutchinson's playing which so enchanted me, nor the whole atmosphere of what I later found to be the most opulent corner of the university in those days. He had an added glamour: he was a BBC name, someone whose music I had heard on the wireless. The initials 'BBC' have always been magic to me.

There were other attractions about the University of Birmingham, though. It seemed to connect directly with those stimulating figures of the thirties, whose work I found especially exciting: W.H. Auden, Louis MacNeice, Walter Allen – they were still talked about as belonging to the Birmingham scene. MacNeice had been a lecturer in classics at the university. I was later to persuade him to come back and talk to The English Club, but though I met him many times in later years, he always greeted me as if I were a complete stranger; I must have made very little impression on him. W.H. Auden lived nearby in Solihull with his family; and his father, Dr G.A. Auden, was the university doctor. I remember him one chilly autumn morning putting an ice-cold tape-measure round my naked chest and asking blithely, 'What is your favourite period of English literature?' When I gasped and remained speechless, he beamed happily and said, 'It is rather refreshing, isn't it?' He was a nice man. Auden and MacNeice published a travel book called *Letters from Iceland*, which contained their supposed 'Last will and testament'. Many of its comic 'bequests' were to 'beneficiaries' whom I was to encounter during the next few years. The novelist Walter Allen had been born and educated in Birmingham, at King Edward's Grammar School and at the university and, in addition to his novels and book-reviews, was writing radio features, in which, a few years later, I found myself appearing.

My plan for a university education was ingenious. It was not my own, but had been suggested by my headmaster. He had discovered all the signs were that, as the Second World War was still in progress, I could expect to be called up for military service in mid-October. He counselled me to resign from the library, to enrol as an undergraduate and be called up as a student. Then, he argued, at the end of the war I should be – as he had been at the end of the First World War – 'showered with money', as he put it, because my university education had been interrupted.

Never have boats been burned with greater eagerness. I applied for extended leave of absence from my post as junior assistant librarian, found myself appallingly gloomy digs in darkest Edgbaston and, with my life savings of 17 pounds and all the hope in the world, together with a grant of 40 pounds from the local authority, I enrolled as a student on a four-year course in English Language and Literature, leading to a degree of Bachelor of Arts with Honours. The course was, in theory, to take four years, as, not having been at school for sixth-form work leading to what was then called Higher School Certificate (now known as 'A'-levels), I was required to complete an intermediate year, studying three additional subsidiary subjects. With great panache, knowing the whole thing was, if you'll forgive the pun, academic, I chose French and Philosophy in addition to English and the obligatory Latin.

Sure enough, within a couple of weeks or so, I was called to a War Office Selection Board. I had a credit in maths (i.e. the equivalent of an 'O'-level). 'Right! Royal Artillery! Next!'

It was all going according to plan, except that I'd given no thought to which branch of the service I would prefer to serve in. Another couple of weeks found me in the Sibree Hall, Coventry, going through my army medical. I came out of that hall with very mixed feelings. I was not to be called up, at least not for a while, as I had been put into medical category three. My eyesight was not up to scratch, and my feet, it transpired, were flat. The news about my feet astonished not only me, but all who knew me. And it certainly did not preclude my taking part in many long route marches during the next few years. As an arts student, I was required to undergo military training at the university in a kind of extended Officer Training Corps, called during the war, the Senior Training Corps (STC).

The plan had gone seriously awry. Not only did I have no

money – books and enrolment fees had taken most of my capital – but I was committed to passing an exam within three terms in English Language, English Literature, French, Latin and Philosophy. I had not studied Latin since Leamington; I had achieved quite good results in French at Nuneaton; my Library Association exams had widened my knowledge of English Literature; but Philosophy I had never studied systematically at all. I was hopelessly behind my fellow-students.

None of this seemed to worry me in the slightest. University life was carefree, and surely there were ways and means of supporting myself? I soon found out how I could eat rather better than my fellow-students. I got a job washing-up in the university refectory. This gave me a shilling (5p.) an hour and the pick of the menu. May Florrie, the manageress, and Winnie and her colleagues in the refectory be forever blessed! I made them laugh, and they took to me. I ate like a king – or at least like a member of the Senior Common Room. Not for me the rissole, and the potato cheese: I had soup, a joint and two veg, and a pudding, every lunchtime.

I soon graduated from dishwashing to writing cheques: the students would file in front of me with their laden trays and I would pontificate on the nutritional value (or usually otherwise) of what they had chosen to eat. Too much starch; not enough protein; no vitamin C. Not that I was paid to do this – my job was merely to write down the amount, so that they could pay Doris as they left. Doris sat at the cash-desk at the end of the refectory, regaling the world with one of the sweetest, sunniest smiles I've ever known. It was years before I saw with a shock, when during an emergency she left her cash-desk to call someone urgently to the phone, that she was terribly handicapped and walked with crutches.

My tutor, Elsie Duncan-Jones, had whispered that there might be money available for me from the vice-chancellor's fund, but as I was an unknown quantity, she would have to wait until I had written her an essay or two before she could confidently recommend me. After my first essay she answered my eager-eyed enquiry with the comment, kindly spoken but devastating, that she was a little disappointed. I could see my university career ending with the first term – I who once had thoughts of going to Oxford!

Once more drama came to my rescue. I joined the university dramatic society. It was known to all as BUDS – the Birmingham University Dramatic Society. (The music society, which I also joined, was known as the University of Birmingham Music Society for reasons which most of us spotted at once.)

The first term was always marked with what were called freshers' playshops – one-act plays, or single acts from longer plays, put on by freshmen. I appeared in two of them: as the old actor in Emlyn Williams's *The Light of Heart* and one of the terrible twins (called Philip oddly enough) in Shaw's *You Never Can Tell*. Dear John Waterhouse, the adored acting-head of the English Department, singled out in his review the two actors who had given outstanding and widely contrasted performances – they were both me.

I saw my tutor in the corridor the next day: 'I heard about your brilliance in the playshops, Mr Painting. I've written to the vice-chancellor!'

Dr Raymond Priestley, the Vice-Chancellor (he had yet to be knighted at this time), received me with as much courtesy and consideration as if I had been an ambassador, not a poor student begging for a crust. He had travelled as geologist with Scott to the Antarctic; but it was many years before I learned that he'd taken with him, as his one book, Spenser's *Faerie Queene*, with its full depiction of romantic chivalry. He was a very gentle gentleman himself, with that impressive humility you only find in the really great, and with the great man's other hallmark: the ability to listen to one, and look at one, as if there were no-one else in the world at that moment.

He asked me about my predicament, and made sympathetic noises as I told my tale. I mean precisely that. He made sympathetic noises: little grunts of understanding. Eventually, he said that my case would be considered; but in the meantime, how was I to live? Would extra fire-watching help?

I must explain that during the war, every public building which would normally be empty during the night had to be patrolled, so that action could be taken if there were an air-raid. Teams of fire-watchers signed on each evening at an air-raid warden's post, and were given simple training in fire-fighting, especially for dealing with incendiary bombs, and then were sent on regular patrols of the building. If one signed on at the university warden's post by 7 o'clock and stayed the whole night, the reward was the sum of four shillings and sixpence (22½p.). If one did not appear until 8, then the figure was three shillings (15p.) but in either case, one had a camp-bed to sleep on and a roof over one's head, plus a supper of coffee and sandwiches. Most people volunteered for duty one night a week; but, as one undergraduate had discovered, if you volunteered every night, you had no need of other lodgings.

The vice-chancellor hastily said that in principle he frowned on this, especially as the student concerned (who must remain nameless as he has since gone on to be internationally famous) had brought so many of his personal belongings into the warden's post that the place was like a slum. I rushed to explain that I only needed to be there for Monday, Tuesday, and Wednesday: I could go home most weekends from Thursday to Sunday. (At this time, the university was only partly residential – not that I could have afforded the cost of living in one of the halls of residence.)

Putting me on my honour not to add to the untidiness of the place, and if possible to improve it, the vice-chancellor gave me permission to do fire-watching for three nights a week. But when, shortly after, I received a letter telling me that a grant was being made to me from the vice-chancellor's fund (of, I think, 40 pounds) I was over the moon. I busily knuckled down to the serious business of enjoying myself.

In spite of wartime conditions, of shortages, rationing, gloomy news and the fact that the university building in Edmund Street, where I spent much of my time, was not the most cheerful of places, they were heady, racy golden days. It was not exactly a time of wine, women and song: I could afford to drink little in those days; music has always played a great part in my life; and as for women . . . increasingly I became one of a shrinking minority of men among several thousand women students. There was never a dull moment.

My undeniable success in the freshmen's plays was quickly consolidated by an appearance in Tchekhov's *Three Sisters*. I soon became part of the scene, where university drama was concerned. I joined various clubs: music, The English Club, and so on; and became a member of the student governing council. Life suddenly extended, expanded, became richer, more varied, more colourful, more exciting. I enjoyed my academic work as much as all the other activities. Studying English Literature was pure pleasure; learning French was fun (though I never seemed to find time to read all the set books); and the one-year course called 'Introduction to Modern Philosophy' stimulated me to explore avenues of thought completely new to me, and incidentally disciplined the mind so that specious arguments and false logic were quickly spotted, and nailed. A year working on Plato's *Republic* also subjected me to an influence which I still feel.

There was, however, one weak spot. If I had not lived in such a state of youthful euphoria, I might have seen warning lights. I had always loved Latin, and at school was usually in the first three or four in class. That was some years ago, though; and I had done no systematic revision. I suppose I felt in my enjoyment of every moment that I could walk on water. I couldn't. I passed all my exams at the end of the university year, except Latin. However, I would be able to take it again at the end of the long vacation, so all was not quite lost. It was essential to pass at the next attempt, or my career would reach a premature end. I had, though, to live during the vacation; and also contrive to find money to finance the following three years – assuming that I was successful in my second attempt at Latin. As I was only on leave of absence from my post as librarian, I was able to return for most of the vacation and earn a little money. My hard work at Latin became more of an intention than a real fact. One of my colleagues was sent to a crammer's; but that cost more than I could afford. I took the exam again. This time I did worse than I had three months previously. A university career for me had been a dream: my own stupidity had now rudely awakened me.

There were several mitigating circumstances. I had been a model student in my work on other subjects, and in my participation in a wide range (perhaps too wide!) of undergraduate activities. I had also had a poor start, having left school at 15, so missing sixth-form work; and during the past year I had, in addition to normal university activities, been compelled to attend army training parades several days a week, and some nights, for guard duty. I had also elected, for financial reasons, to report for fire-watching duties every night that I was in Birmingham, when I was not on STC guard duty.

My head of department, John Waterhouse, made an impassioned appeal on my behalf; and, although he risked the friendship of his colleague, the professor of Latin, he won the day. I felt then, still feel, and always will, that I can never repay the debt I owe John Waterhouse. But for him, the course of my life might have been completely different. It is not surprising that my regard for him and his wife Elspeth grew to being only just this side of idolatry. He encouraged my acting, my writing, my poetry-reading, my music; he drew out whatever personality I had. If it is true, as Elsie Duncan-Jones wrote to me when I left, that I am sure of a place in the university's hagiography, then the credit for that must go to John Waterhouse – the same man whom Auden and MacNeice remembered in their 'Last will and testament' in *Letters from Iceland*, when among the bequests appears:

Item to dear John Waterhouse a gymnastic
Exercise before breakfast every day
(A better cure for the figure than wearing elastic)

And a grand piano under a flowering tree
To sate his versatile and virile taste
From the Hammerklavier to the Isle of Capri.

The next three years were packed with incident. I became fascinated by Anglo-Saxon, but was appalled at the amount of poetry I needed to know for my final exams. So I enlivened my own interest by making modern verse translations. Although only part of the epic, *Beowulf*, was set for examination purposes, I translated the whole poem into verse. With my friend, Ted Doherty, I also translated *The Women of Troy* by Euripides, and the dramatic society staged it. On another occasion, Ted and I showed versatility if not brilliance (at least not on my part) with a spirited rendering of a two-piano version of Brahms's Handel Variations, at a university concert.

The system of spending Monday to Thursday at the university, and Friday to Sunday at home, worked well. I appeared to do no work in the first half of the week, apart from attending lectures. I could be seen in the union drinking coffee and holding court; or speaking as a councillor at guild council, the student self-governing body; or chairing meetings of various clubs; or, most common of all, rehearsing some play or other. The real reading, the translating, and the major task of writing the weekly essay were all done at my parents' home at Nuneaton, where my lifestyle was almost monastic.

In this way there was even time to write a three-act play with another undergraduate, Gordon Thomas, which we staged for degree day. It was a rip-roaring redbrick version of *Charley's Aunt*, with three aunts, and drew enthusiastic praise from the not-always-easy-to-please critic of the *Birmingham Post*, T.C. Kemp, and also from our patron, Sir Barry Jackson.

Most of my energy was devoted to the dramatic society and nearly every term saw me involved in a new production. Only twice did I play anything that wasn't a major part: as a cockney actor in Jerome's *Passing of the Third Floor Back* and as Abel Drugger in *The Alchemist*. The latter part had been made famous by Garrick, though; and I was, in fact, the director of that production.

I played Tobias in Bridie's *Tobias and the Angel*; Hercule Poirot in Agatha Christie's *Black Coffee*; the Robertson Hare part in Ben Travers's farce *Rookery Nook*, which I also directed; Gaffer Pearce in Masefield's *Tragedy of Nan*, and most audaciously of all, Lear in my own production of Shakespeare's *King*

13

Lear. My compulsory army training and an almost daily swim kept me enormously fit; I couldn't afford to drink or smoke much; and there was never a single moment in a single day that wasn't occupied.

The outstanding student in the arts faculty when I first came to university was Ted Downes, now known the world over more formally as Edward Downes, translator of opera libretti and conductor at Covent Garden, Sydney Opera House, and most of the world's great opera houses and concert halls. Ted was rebellious, ebullient and highly talented. He announced one day that he was giving up the piano (at which we all thought he was a virtuoso) and taking up the French horn. He reasoned that pianists were two a penny: a struggling musician would have more chance as a wind-player. He learnt the French horn in three months, and gave a recital at the Barber Institute with Professor Victor Hely-Hutchinson. He also very kindly found time to give me an occasional piano lesson. We acted together in *Three Sisters*; and he wrote, and performed at the piano, some splendid and witty music for *Tobias and the Angel*, but alas! I think it was never written down.

Ted nearly poisoned me on one occasion. It was the dress rehearsal for *Three Sisters* and, insisting that he needed to practise pouring wine in the party scene, he had persuaded the stage manager to fill the decanter with the only liquid on hand, which was diluted paint. Ted told everybody not to drink the stuff, but merely mime it – everybody that is, except me. When the moment came, I threw myself into the part, raised my glass, and drained it. There was a sudden hush: I thought someone had dried. Then Ted gasped that it was paint, and probably poisonous. I whispered that the play must go on, and anyway, it was too late; and so far as I remember that was the last of it. I had a stronger stomach in those days . . .

Ted took his predicted brilliant first, and gained with it enough grants and scholarships to ensure his immediate future. Before he left for the Royal Academy of Music, he passed on to me the gist of a conversation he'd had with my tutor. Ted had remarked that he thought I was now toying with the idea of an academic career; whereupon my tutor had immediately commented that I needed to do a great deal more hard work if that was the case. I quickly got the message.

I had one more year before graduating. This time I'd learnt my lesson: I organized and disciplined myself, preparing for finals. The last weeks of a warm and sunny May saw the end of lectures and the beginning of that tense time of revision before the exams started. I remember meeting one of the girls from my year at the main entrance, staggering in with a pile of books on her way to the library. She couldn't believe that I wasn't going there, too, but instead, was on my way to row a little boat on Harborne Reservoir. It wasn't that I was over-confident – far from it – but I took the view that if I didn't know my stuff by then, I certainly could't mug it all up in a few days. I knew that I had worked hard and systematically; and indeed, as I lay drifting in the boat, I was mentally revising, standing back from the four years of reading and writing, and trying to sort out my thoughts. I used these occasions of apparent leisure to memorize key quotations, too. I also knew by now that the external examiner the year before, Professor F.P. Wilson of Merton College, Oxford, had surprised several members of the teaching staff by extracting my papers from the pile and writing across one of them: 'This man can write.'

Once the last exam paper was written, I found relaxation in hard work of a different kind – rehearsing for the degree day play. Plays for the end of the academic year were always much lighter than in the other terms, and this year I was playing Poirot in Agatha Christie's *Black Coffee*. Also taking part was a comparative newcomer to the English Department, Gareth Lloyd Evans, who was both lecturing and doing research for a higher degree after graduating at Bangor, North Wales. (He was soon to marry one of the girls from my year, and eventually become the doyen of the Shakespeare Institute at Stratford, Reader in Dramatic Literature at the University of Birmingham, biographer of J.B. Priestley and a drama critic of *The Guardian*.)

He played a sort of low-key secretary, who was, in fact, the murderer; and at a certain point in the play he had to hand to me, as Poirot, a slip of paper containing a missing formula. As rehearsals went on it became increasingly clear that Gareth, as a member of the teaching staff, had a pretty good idea what marks I'd gained for each of the papers in my finals. He then teasingly suggested that my results were in his pocket, written on a slip of paper. Whenever we came to the point where, as the secretary, he had to hand the paper to me as Poirot, he held on to it, and put it back in his pocket! We had become in the past year very good friends; and yet, though he teased me, he never gave me the slightest hint of whether I had done well or badly.

Then came the day when we were asked to report to the English Department in case we were required to be given a *viva voce* examination. I met my tutor and a dear friend of mine, also waiting for her results, Gwen Rooke (my life has been peppered with Gwens!)

Gwen asked: 'It is true that one's only called to a *viva* if one's a borderline case, isn't it?'

With a complete poker face, my tutor said that it was, and looking me straight in the eye said: 'You've certainly fallen slap in the middle of a class. There's nothing borderline about your results!'

My heart sank. In those days, though, my spirits never seemed to be able to stay down for long. I revived at the prospect of a student coach-trip to the Shakespeare Memorial Theatre that night, to see Peter Brook's production of *Love's Labour's Lost*.

Gareth and I sat in the front row of the dress circle, trying to concentrate on the play. But I knew that the exam results were almost certain to be published at about seven o'clock. In the interval, Gareth agreed to come with me to a phone box some distance from the theatre, so that I could ring the university. With trembling hands, I lifted the receiver, and asked for the number. After an age, I heard it ringing . . . and ringing . . . and ringing . . . It was clear that there was to be no answer.

Gareth said that we ought to be getting back, as the play would have started again.

As we ran across the lawns back to the theatre, Gareth said: 'Hell! The results must be out by now. Congratulations, chum. You've got a first! The only one in your year!'

The play had started again. We trod on people's feet struggling back into our seats. I could scarcely breathe. Hot tears of relief and amazement burnt my cheeks. I saw little of the play. The trust that people had put in me, with so little to go on, had been justified. I felt I could look my books in the face. More than this, I knew that as I was the only first-class degree with honours in my year, I had to be – as it later proved – a strong, indeed unbeatable, candidate for several prizes and scholarships. And for me this meant one thing . . . Oxford!

What did I want from Oxford? Why was it so special? I doubt if I could have explained at the time. For what I wanted from Oxford was Oxford itself: the essential, quintessential, Oxford, of ancient architecture, of mediaeval streets, of college gardens with the afternoon sun slanting shadows over their ineffable lawns, of student society with its social and mental challenges, of that maturity and elegance of setting which had been missing from the twentieth-century red brick enclaves of a modern university like Birmingham. It was not necessarily something finer or better: it was something different, something adding a further dimension to my experience of a student life.

But I was not so naive I could not also see that a higher degree from Oxford might well open doors to a more assured academic life, if that was what I finally chose. As a don, I knew quite well, I would still be able to indulge my passion for the theatre, as writer, director and, even, as actor. At Oxford, Professor Nevill Coghill, and at Cambridge, Professor George Rylands, were well-known examples of this type of don. And I did have genuine academic interests. I was deeply involved mentally and emotionally with Anglo-Saxon poetry; and I was becoming daily better informed in a completely different field: archaeology.

The future beckoned brightly but ambiguously: there seemed a tantalizing richness of choice. The one thing I never in my most fanciful moments envisaged was that, within a year or two, I would be committed to a course that led to more than 30 years as an actor and writer in radio soap-opera!

Significant events in life, as I said before, are — like winning the breast-stroke swimming record — very often flukes.

CHAPTER 2

Oxford: touching in the highlights

So, at last, the gates of Oxford were open to me. All those years before it had seemed more remote than Shangri La, but now I was there. Later on, I said, 'It took a little time, but I went the pretty way.'

Of course, Oxford is in many senses a mirage, a myth, a legend. At first, the Oxford I'd come for was not to be found – the Oxford of the golden afternoons of Lewis Carroll, the Oxford of the high jinks of *Charley's Aunt*, the Oxford of the poets, and the seventeenth- and eighteenth-century eccentrics. But eventually I found my Oxford: on summer evenings in college gardens during undergraduate performances of plays; or strangely, on dark wintry afternoons when the rain outside washing those ancient stones would soon give way to warm panelled interiors with tea and cinnamon toast.

I remember on one occasion, when several of us were chatting in Peter Parker's rooms in Lincoln College, how Peter suddenly stopped, and said: 'Listen! This is the moment!' It was dusk and he put on an amber lamp over his desk. Then we heard the bells of Oxford all chiming, but not quite together, in that same disordered unity that one finds in the architecture of Venice. But that was later. At first, the magic of Oxford eluded me.

Indeed, my first two days there were among the loneliest of my life. The usual notifications to freshmen, telling them where to report and what to do at the beginning of their first term, for some reason went astray. I had been accepted at Christ Church on condition that I would find myself lodgings out of college. This I had done and I had notified the authorities of my address, but somehow I wasn't summoned to college matriculation and the other formalities of admission, so I don't appear on the photographs of freshmen; nor did I meet any of my contemporaries on the first days of term. Far from meeting any of them, I wandered the streets of Oxford lost and bemused.

It all seemed very different from the last four years at the University of Birmingham. Almost from the start I had been, in most senses, at the centre of the stage. Now I was unknown, alone, and lonely.

I don't think I did then look back: that is not a natural reflex for me. But if I had, I could have reviewed many memories. Of four crowded undergraduate years of virtually unalloyed happiness. Of cold and foggy journeys in winter to a gloomy Gothic Birmingham; of sunny days on the lawns at Edgbaston out of the city. Of dances at the women's hall of residence, with dance-cards and delicious refreshments. Of the heavy Victorian Gothic of the Edmund Street building where I spent half my time, and of the thirties redbrick Tudor and light oak panelling of the union building at Edgbaston. Of hours on guard in the basement of the Edwardian main building of the university, and its great hall where the Chancellor, the Rt Hon. Anthony Eden, had admitted me to my degree. Of daily tram-rides along the Bristol Road from the city centre to Edgbaston, for the university was very much in two halves in those days.

I might have looked back a mere few months to graduation day. My parents had travelled from Nuneaton with an old friend and his wife, now the mayor and mayoress; and I entertained them to lunch in the refectory, no longer as a dishwasher or a cheque-writer, but a graduate. It was a sunny day, and we were all invited to a reception at the Botanical Gardens by the Lord Mayor of Birmingham. It was like something from a former life: people strolling in the gardens, a band playing in a white bandstand, a toastmaster announcing our names, a future as golden as the sunlight beckoning . . .

And now, arrived at last at Mecca, I was alone in anonymous crowds. Everybody seemed to know everybody else; nobody seemed to be as alone as I was; everyone was deep in conversation with a close friend. For one whole day this continued, and I returned to my tiny room in a very small private house in South Oxford, 'the unfashionable side', resolving that tomorrow I must be braver.

My courage consisted, the next day, in entering my college at Tom Gate, nodding to the porter, walking through Tom Quad into Peckwater, on into Canterbury Quad, and out through Canterbury Gate, speaking to no-one, looking neither to left nor right. I then decided that this was lily-livered, and so at one o'clock I steeled myself once more to enter the college, to go up that splendid staircase to the great hall, with the intention of

19

entering and eating. But once more my courage failed. At a smaller college I might have been bolder; but Christ Church, which I now love, is built on the grand scale and was then overawing. Apart from its sheer size, it has many unique features. Its chapel is Oxford's cathedral; it was once governed by Dean and Chapter – now by Dean, Canon and Students; its 'Students' are what are called in other colleges 'Fellows'; it is a college, but that word never appears in its title. It is called Christ Church, or The House, from the Latin *aedes Christi* – the house of Christ.

That first empty day dragged on, when suddenly I saw a familiar face, a boy from my old school. I at once hid my loneliness, but perhaps too readily accepted his invitation that evening to meet a few of his new-found friends. Among them, and indeed the only one that I remember, was Michael Croft, who has since become very well-known for his lifetime's work with the National Youth Theatre. The next day, which was Sunday, passed in almost equal loneliness; however, I had again accepted an invitation from one of the other undergraduates for coffee that evening, so for an hour or so I glimpsed something of the Oxford life I had come for.

Morning post on Monday brought with it a very official communication from my college. I was required to present myself to the junior censor, and to explain my absence from various formalities on the previous Friday. With less trepidation than relief, I hurried to the college and there met one of the kindest and shyest men I have ever known, M.B. Foster, a lecturer in philosophy. He listened stone-faced to my explanation, and then without apparent emotion extended a very warm hand of friendship – not personal friendship, but practical help.

'What are you doing at four o'clock?' he asked.

'Nothing,' I replied, blankly. 'I have no plans.'

'If you care to be here,' he said, 'I will ensure that you will meet some of your contemporaries in this college, who no doubt will accompany you afterwards into the hall for dinner.'

It was quite clear that he, too, had known my sort of shyness. It is sad to record that so gentle a man, with such a depth of human sympathy, should eventually take his own life. When I received an acknowledgement for the small donation I was able to make towards his memorial, the organizer commented that he could not possibly have suspected how many friends he had.

My loneliness was in fact entirely unnecessary and caused by my over-confidence. Having been for years the centre of a huge set of friends at Birmingham University, it never occurred to me to make prior arrangements with new friends in Oxford – and I did already have friends. For the previous two vacations I had been to Oxford, and had made contact with archaeologists in the university. Richard Atkinson, now a well-known television face and Professor of Archaeology at the University of Cardiff, had been recruiting young enthusiasts for a dig at Dorchester on Thames, and I had spent some time during the two previous vacations digging on a fascinating neolithic site there. Foolishly though, I had not taken either the addresses or even the colleges of those with whom I'd become friendly, and incredibly I failed to bump into any of them by chance.

It was not long, of course, before university life got into its swing, and I renewed those acquaintances at various meetings of the different societies – so much so that by the second term I was elected excavations secretary of the Archaeological Society, and by my third term I was its general secretary. I began my next year as president. By this time I felt as likely to be following a career in archaeology as any other.

In my first experience of digging on the sort of site where one is learning an exact technique of removing earth from earth (as opposed to clearing away earth or sand from brick and stone), I had been lucky enough to meet, however briefly, some of the great names in European archaeology: Professor Gordon Childe, Glyn Daniel (before he found fame in TV's *Animal, Vegetable, Mineral?*), Professor Christopher Hawkes, Professor Stuart Piggott, who was jointly running the dig with Richard Atkinson, and Sir Leonard Woolley. The Abbé Breuil visited the site at Dorchester, too, and I very nearly had the distinction of cutting off his foot as he stepped into the trench, which I was busily skimming with a rather sharp spade.

Richard Atkinson remains in my memory for his extraordinary kindness and encouragement. I must have seemed very raw and green in many ways, and when we met I had not yet graduated, so he could only guess at my intellectual ability. But what I responded to was his whole demeanour: he was neither a social nor an intellectual snob, and treated me as an equal; not an equal in knowledge or experience, but in potential and as a person.

He encouraged me when I expressed fears about giving my presidential address to the Oxford University Archaeological Society; and over a drink together after it he complimented me on it. 'You do realise', I remember him saying, 'that it was above the usual standard for this sort of thing?'

As I mentally began to preen myself, he added, 'But of course, it was far too long!'

He was right, of course; and I was grateful for his honesty. I was soon to learn that an honest opinion of one's work is the rarest of commodities.

Richard has recently told me that I was one of a group of undergraduates who made history in British archaeology by being paid to excavate. I remember him once explaining over sandwiches in a lunch break at the Dorchester dig, that he insisted on paying everybody, even if it were only two shillings (10p.) an hour. (We earned, I think, about 10 shillings (50p.) a day.)

'If I am paying you,' he explained, 'I can sack you!' Like many an archaeologist, he had suffered from the over-enthusiastic but under-qualified amateur.

My interests weren't confined to archaeology. I began my academic work preparing a thesis on Anglo-Saxon poetic imagery, and one of the minor regrets of my life is that I was persuaded to abandon that course. One day, shortly after I'd been lucky enough to be given a set of rooms in college, I received a visit from one of the great luminaries of Oxford at the time, Professor Nevill Coghill, who, hearing that I was researching into Anglo-Saxon, asked if I would take on some of his college's pupils in the subject. This I did, and for the next two years earned part of my living by acting as a tutor for Exeter College. Looking back, it's hard to believe that such a short time separated my life as an Oxford tutor and as an actor playing for the first time the part of Philip Archer.

In my first term my college, Christ Church, celebrated its 400th anniversary. The sovereign, from the time of Henry VIII, has always been given the title of Visitor of Christ Church and on 24 October we were honoured by a royal visit. His Majesty King George VI and Queen Elizabeth came to the college and, after a service in Christ Church Cathedral, joined us for dinner. At the end of a festive meal in which college champagne had flowed freely, vintage port was served, whereupon the Dean, John Lowe, in his pronounced Canadian accent proposed the toast: 'His Majesty the King, the Visitor of Christ Church.'

I shall never forget the look of delighted amazement on the face of His Majesty, when all 400 of us rose to our feet, grabbed our glasses, and following a short trumpet call played by the Honourable Francis Dashwood, burst into spontaneous, carefully rehearsed, singing of 'Here's a Health unto His Majesty'.

I have also a rather dimmer recollection of being urged by one of the Students of Christ Church (a Student at this college is roughly the equivalent of a Fellow at many others) to 'Come on Painting, give 'em a shove!' Which I did. Whereupon the two of us pushed the royal car, which was in no need of our help, through the gates under Tom Tower.

Another celebration at the college produced what I have now come to regard as perhaps one of the mistakes of my early life. A production of Shakespeare's *King Henry VIII* was arranged, and put on in Christ Church hall. I was offered a small part, which I accepted. However, as I shall describe in Chapter 4, my radio career was continuing alongside my academic career at this time. Indeed, the last year of my life at Birmingham had been largely subsidized by my earnings as a broadcaster. Now I was faced with an awkward decision: I had the choice of a good part in a new radio series, *Wot No Gloom*, or a small part in my college play. I chose the former. I cannot say that I was in any way criticized, let alone ostracized, in my college for crying off halfway through the rehearsals, but sometimes unspoken criticisms have greater force.

Soon, I became interested in the Oxford University Experimental Theatre Club, and found myself on the committee, with the opportunity of directing a production of a play by Jean Cocteau, *The Infernal Machine*. Cocteau has since become a great enthusiasm with me, especially his films and some of his critical writings.

I remember little about the weeks of rehearsal for my production of *The Infernal Machine*. Some of the auditions remain with me, though, because I then met for the first time people whom I, and later the world, was to know better: Nigel Davenport, John Bowen, William Gaskill, and John Schlesinger, with whom I was later to appear in several Oxford productions.

I do remember that we rehearsed in a room in the tower of Magdalen College, and I remember, too, that the production had a mixed reception. One professional from the local Playhouse wrote me a long letter which may explain matters: he felt that two of the acts were among the finest things he'd ever seen in Oxford drama, but the rest of the play fell so far below that standard he could scarcely believe it was from the same hand. However, a cartoon of me as, 'This term's producer', appeared in one of the Oxford magazines, and I was launched into the world of Oxford theatre.

In March 1948 the OUDS (The Oxford University Dramatic Society) put on at the Playhouse a spirited production by David Raeburn of Dekker's *The Shoemaker's Holiday*. Throughout the term I had been rehearsing the part of Firk, on the understanding that if an undergraduate who was preferred for the role was released from the army in time, he would play it. I had a small eight-line part as a consolation prize and standby.

The young man who was to play Firk *did* get there in time, and very politely, when introduced, said something of the order of: 'Pleased to meet you.' (We were very formal in those days.)

I remember saying jokily, 'I'm sorry I can't reciprocate the sentiment.'

The actor concerned went on to give a brilliant performance, and has clearly never resented my first remark to him. We all knew him as Tim, but today he's known and highly regarded as Robert Hardy. Local and national critics of the production quite rightly singled him out for special praise. Reading the reviews after so many years it is interesting to see how even then performers who were later to make their mark in the theatre were recognized and their names given special mention by the reviewers. Modesty does not forbid my mentioning that although I wasn't after all playing the long and showy part of Firk, I did receive very complimentary mentions in *The Times*, the *Spectator* and the local Oxford newspapers for my tiny cameo as Master Scott.

The *Oxford Times* for Friday 5 March contains, on the same page as a review of *The Shoemaker's Holiday*, an obituary of Sir Charles Grant Robertson. He was a great Oxford figure and then became a great Birmingham figure first as Principal and then Vice-Chancellor of Birmingham University. It was the scholarship which he had endowed that had made it possible for me to be studying at Oxford at all. I like to think that he would have been not displeased at the juxtaposition of those two items in the Oxford newspaper.

After my solitary start, I soon made many friends at Oxford. First of all, my small circle of acquaintances in the Archaeological Society quickly widened and my diary contains entries like: 'tea, Petronella, Woodstock Road'; 'Shelagh, coffee 2'; 'Sir Leonard Woolley at home, Ashmolean 4 p.m.'; 'Andrina, Norham Gardens'; and so on. I had, in addition, completely different sets of friends in the OUDS and the Experimental Theatre Club.

I quickly joined the college swimming team, and regular meetings at the Cowley Road swimming baths soon gave me another, and again quite different, circle of friends. This set were all six feet tall (1.83m), and most of them were colonials, Rhodes Scholars, who expected to be in Oxford for only two or three years at most, before returning to the ends of the earth. One of them, George Cawkwell, classicist and rugger blue did stay on as a don. But Arthur Motyer, a Bermudian, persuaded several of us that, as their time was limited, the thing would be to 'do' Oxford systematically.

This was an unusually good idea for me. Like most other English undergraduates, I was taking Oxford for granted: it would always be there, to be visited easily in the future. This so often means that Oxford men don't know Oxford at all. But thanks to Arthur, every Wednesday afternoon several of us went, Alden's *Oxford Guide* in hand, to visit a different college or district. In a mock schoolmasterly way, Arthur used to set us homework: we had to memorize passages from Alden or inscriptions on college monuments. I can still repeat passages about, for example, the Divinity Schools, without a crib:' . . . passing through the Proscholium, which derives its name the pig-market from the base use to which it descended in the reign of Henry the Eighth . . .' Whenever we passed from Tom Quad to Meadow Buildings, where Arthur had his rooms, I was always called upon to repeat the words of a monument in the cloister:

In memory of WILLIAM POUND
many years one of the Porters of this college
who by an exemplary Life and Behaviour
deserved and obtained
the approbation and esteem
of the whole Society.
1787

I had, by this time, moved into rooms in Peckwater Quad – the confusing Peck 9, 6. Confusing because, although the staircases were numbered 1 to 9, and still are, the sequence begins at 9 and finishes at 8. . .

Six of us decided to give ourselves a dinner-party – or rather five of us gave the party and we invited the president of the Junior Common Room as guest. This sort of thing was once a regular part of college life, but in those years of post-war austerity it had not come back fully into fashion. So it was something of an attempt to revive old customs.

Excellent champagne and port could be bought at reasonable cost from the college buttery, and although the food could have been prepared in the college kitchen, our experience of college catering did not inspire confidence. The kitchens were very much as they were when Wolsey and then Henry VIII had founded them, and the food was carried up long flights of stone steps by hand. We were inured to cold or luke-warm dishes. Towards the end of my time, things began to improve. There was a guest-table where the standard was considerably higher, although the food generally available was still limited. I recall one memorable, or rather infamous day, when we had kedgeree (fish) for breakfast, steamed fish for lunch, and fried fish for dinner!

Our little dinner-party worked well. The champagne flowed. One of my contributions had been a decoration to Arthur's rooms in Meadow Buildings, near those of Winston Churchill's mentor, Lord Cherwell: a brass jug full of mimosa. I recall trotting, staggering, weaving, or progressing in some unwonted way, through Tom Quad just as the clocks were striking two, clutching the jug of mimosa. There was a moon behind the clouds. Tom Tower stood outlined against the sky, and suddenly detached itself and glided sideways into the grey night. Later, my iron bed swung wildly from one side to another in undergraduate inebriation throughout the night.

The following day was the first Sunday in Lent, and we had all nobly agreed to attend chapel that morning. Painfully overhung, we tried to look bright and serious as we sat on the front row, at right angles to the altar in college chapel style. This meant, luckily, that it was difficult to catch each other's eye, so we merely gazed forward. There was a power cut, so the organ could not be used, and the choir sang unaccompanied, but wonderfully. Then, one of the hard-drinking cricket-playing members of the Chapter climbed into the pulpit and began his Lenten sermon: his theme was abstinence and mortification of the flesh. It was richly ironic coming from him, anyway: but to our group, in the state we were in, it was way over the top. Uncontrollable giggles combined with a serious hangover are, to say the least, extremely uncomfortable . . .

Although those who professed to know said that Christ Church choir was not at the very top of the Oxford league in those days, the standard of singing was extremely high, and certainly enough to coax me, if supported by friends, to attend college chapel most Sunday mornings. The old prayer-book words for the service, the quality of the singing, and the architecture of the chapel, which also happens to be the cathedral, made these visits an aesthetic experience of a high order even if, from a religious viewpoint, the actual service seemed to me lacking in point. I hope I can say that I have never been an intellectual exhibitionist, so I have avoided theological discussion and never flaunted my opinions. Like George Eliot, I went to church for my own reasons, on the understanding that I could believe what I liked. This did not, however, prevent many who saw me there from assuming that I was rather more than merely a Christian fellow-traveller. And the years have done little to change that. My religious views are even less orthodox now than then.

An Oxford generation covers about three years – the normal length of a course of study leading to a first degree. In any given year, there is usually at least one outstanding member of the university who dominates student life. Sometimes, it is a don or head of a college: Jowett, Spooner, John Henry Newman, come to mind. Sometimes, it is an undergraduate: John Wesley, Samuel Johnson, William Pitt, Oscar Wilde. Some would say that my years at Oxford were the Tynan years. Kenneth Tynan had arrived in Oxford determined to dominate it, and he did.

I had known him slightly at Birmingham, where I had seen his production of *Hamlet*, in which he also played the lead. In turn, he had seen my production of *King Lear*, in which I too had played the lead. In later years, Ken said some very nice things about my production and my performance. I seem to remember that one of us changed the subject when his production came up in conversation . . .

But that was his Birmingham *Hamlet*. Oxford was to be regaled with a further essay in the same field. Indeed, Tynan's Oxford *Hamlet*, in the First Quarto text and with Peter Parker as Hamlet, was, as he intended, talked about long before and long after it happened. Ken knew before he came up to university that the key to fame was to be talked about, and few places are more easily filled with outrageous and sensational whispers than a university town. Ken may not at first have had as much money as he purported to have; but he always had as much wit, nerve, verve, and talent, as he asserted. His methods were sometimes crude: his hench-men and -women would see to it that under every side-plate in every restaurant in Oxford would be found a slip of paper saying: 'This space reserved for Ken Tynan.' The following week, or day, a similar slip of paper would announce his next venture: 'Ken Tynan presents his version of *Samson Agonistes*, based on an obscure libretto by John Milton . . .'

Nothing he did was dull or predictable. Much of his activity, whether it was speaking at the union, appearing in revue, or acting and directing, was brilliant, unexpected, amusing, astonishing, unacceptable – but never nondescript.

I have only once in my life been 'cut' in the street, and that, I am glad to say, was by Ken. I thought at the time it was the end of our acquaintance; and in Oxford terms, it was. But in later years, whenever I met him in London (backstage at the Old Vic, for example, when we were both congratulating Jack May on his hauntingly brilliant performance as Henry VI), he was charm and affability itself.

The reason for this dramatic gesture on Ken's part sprang from his famous Oxford *Hamlet*. Ken had decided, without of course, any reference to me, that I would play Horatio, that I would immediately consent without question to playing Horatio, would feel it an honour to play Horatio. It would, I am sure, have been enormous fun, and it was something I wished then, and wish now, that it had been possible to do. But I had several other irons in the fire. Ken thought I was playing hard to get, so merely ignored my protestations that 'I'd love to, but I can't' and just assumed that I would do it. I've kept three of the letters he sent to my rooms in Christ Church, all written by Ken on his blue writing-paper which was merely headed 'Kenneth P. Tynan, Oxford' – his name written in facsimile of his signature.

The first says:

> Dear Norman
> To corroborate our conversation:
> Final *Hamlet* reading–&–meeting must be at 4 p.m. on Sunday May 30th here.
> Details then.
>
> Yrs
> Ken.

By this time, I was fully occupied with final rehearsals and performances of Frank Hauser's production of Ben Jonson's *Epicoene; or, The Silent Woman*. We were taking this production to France, after which I had planned a trip to Switzerland and Italy, which would keep me abroad until September, so I couldn't possibly take part in the Tynan *Hamlet*.

Ken tried not to take no for an answer. I received another letter, typewritten this time . . .

> Dear Norman
> Let's not beat about the bush. You must play Horatio, and your rose-red cities half as old as Victor Emmanuel can wait. Please.
> First full reading of Hamlet is at 4 p.m. on Thursday June 10th here.
> Do come.

And then in his own hand he added: 'Ever, Ken.'

28

The great man had ceased to command and had begun to sue. All to no avail. My only previous attempt to go abroad (to help a student team to rebuild the harbour and marshalling yards of Le Havre) had come to nothing, and I was determined to make the most of my forthcoming tour with the OUDS. So firmly but kindly (and I hope I said how much I would have loved to play the part) I declined.

I cannot precisely remember what happened next. But Jack May, who played Corambys, as the Polonius character is called in the Quarto, tells me that the production was given twice: once at the Cheltenham Festival and once in London. I was unable to appear in either; but after the first I must have met Ken at a party in Oxford – you were always meeting Ken at a party – and we must have talked. I can remember more than one such conversation, though oddly, not this one. Anyway, another letter came from 51 St John Street concerning the forthcoming London production . . .

Ref: *Hamlet*
Dear Norman
Dates: (1) Rehearsals from December 17th.. in London.
(2) Performances: January 3rd-7th with one matinée.
Horatio: rubicund German professor with no inhibitions: age 45: substitute father for Hamlet since death of Hamlet père: explosive, Frederick Valk type: water drinker: blows nose on *hand*: an eccentric, immensely fatherly and sympathetic don. A towah of strength.
How about Sunday at 12 noon in my rooms?

Ever
Ken.

He must have thought he was on pretty firm ground. His notion of Horatio was not only new, it was, as he knew, very tempting, especially as it was clearly the sort of interpretation which would fit me well. But, as I told him, I simply had not the free time.

Then it was that I was walking along the Turl, and saw Ken sailing towards me, hair, scarf, and jacket flying behind him. I smiled, and as he approached drew breath to say I hoped he'd got my letter and how sorry I was not to – Before I could speak, he did the complete Larry Grayson: he fixed me with a fishy eye, and then tossed back his head, and roared past me. It was a splendid performance, quite effective and impressive in its way. I was left dithering, mouth half-open, hand in the air: it was a sort of social *coitus interruptus*, and for a time just as fluster-making. I quickly

29

recovered, and went on my way, laughing to myself. I suppose I was secretly flattered that it meant so much to him.

The part was eventually played in London to acclaim and controversy by John Schlesinger, (Lindsay Anderson had played it in Cheltenham), whose career as a film-maker does not seem to have suffered because of it!

Returning to June 1948, I duly made my second OUDS appearance in Frank Hauser's production of *Epicoene*. I had now moved out of college to a village north of Oxford, but I was sharing rooms in Tom Quad with Frank for teaching purposes.

This production was given in the open air; not, as so often, in a college garden, but in the forecourt of Mansfield College. A stage was built up on scaffolding in front of the façade, which was used like a stage set. The great advantage was that steps, doors, and windows were the real thing. Several reviewers, whilst welcoming the production, feared that our exuberance might endanger the life of the scaffolding. In fact, it survived us without collapsing.

There were several people in the cast who have now become more widely known. Most famous of all, no doubt, is John Schlesinger, who played the sort of knock-about sendup at which he excelled. Robert Hardy also appeared, brilliant as ever, and this time I, too, had good notices for a much larger and more important part. The title role, it should be recorded, was played by Gillian Rowe-Dutton, who was later to become the wife of Peter Parker.

The whole production was taken on tour to France. We played in Tours, Poitiers, Avignon, and Paris. The most memorable of these places was no doubt Avignon, where we performed in the gardens of the palace of one of the popes, the Jardin d'Urban V. This tour of just under three weeks began my version of the Grand Tour of Europe. I stayed away for three months, and visited for the first time not only the places I have mentioned, but also the south coast of France (St Tropez, Ste Maxime and other Riviera resorts), Switzerland for a month, and Italy for three weeks, staying in Rome, Venice and Florence. All within the official currency controlled allowance of 50 pounds!

It was on the return journey I decided, sitting at a sidewalk café near the Arc de Triomphe in Paris, that an academic career was not for me. I had already changed the subject of my thesis from Anglo-Saxon poetic imagery to a study of Coleridge's tragedy, *Osorio; or, Remorse*, but it had become clear to me that I was not temperamentally fitted for the academic life. I therefore resolved to return to England and complete my thesis as quickly as possible, and with the agreement of my supervisor, Lord David Cecil, I would present it and continue with my career as a writer and broadcaster. This may have been one more mistake, but this is what I did.

Long before my thesis was typed and submitted, and some time before I had the examiners' verdict on it, I had begun my career with the BBC, as I describe in Chapter 4. My work as a writer was by now often being accepted for radio, and I was also taking part in many broadcasts. It was becoming increasingly clear that my future life lay much nearer to show business than to the academic world.

One of the most encouraging and stimulating people that I met in the BBC was the late Edward Livesey. He gave me my first audition as a poetry-reader and, on the strength of it, offered me not only work reading in radio anthologies, but also suggested that I might like to take part in radio plays and write radio scripts. He was actively helpful by giving me both work and advice, and soon had me earmarked for a project he had planned but which, alas, never came to fruition. His idea was simple: he was basically a writer, and, like all writers without private means, had the problem of paying the rent, without writing solely for money. His plan to solve it was by working for six months as a BBC features producer and for the other six months to write the novels he was so anxious to create.

He was a very enthusiastic and persuasive man, and for a time convinced the BBC authorities that his scheme was feasible. What was required was another person of like mind who would be prepared to work on this half-yearly system. It was quite clear that as someone just starting in the world, with ambitions both as writer and performer—director, I was the ideal candidate.

The project was discussed for some months. On one occasion, Denis Morris, Head of Programmes at Birmingham, who was later to become Controller of the Light Programme (now Radio 2), came to see me at Oxford. Over drinks at the Mitre Hotel he explained to me, off the record but in considerable detail, that this was not some wild plan of Ted Livesey's but a distinct possibility. He wanted my agreement in principle to be, as it were, the other half of the horse.

The scheme fell through for reasons which perhaps today would not operate. Ted, who had recently married, was naturally concerned about those sometimes boring questions of insurance and security, and it seemed the BBC system in those days was not flexible enough to allow for his working on a permanent contract for only six months of each year. I was disappointed, but was already being given commissions from different departments of the BBC, both in Birmingham and London, for scripts and interviews, pieces of research, and the occasional performance as reader or actor. Soon I was offered a contract as a writer–producer.

The word 'producer' has now been replaced by 'director'. I was a kind of general programmes assistant, turning my hand to whatever had to be done, whether as writer–producer, researcher, or performer. Thus, with a BBC contract in my pocket, my thesis completed and submitted, I began my career with the BBC, full-time. As the fifties dawned, I had to say my first reluctant farewell to Oxford. I have been saying farewell to Oxford ever since: if you lose your heart to Oxford it's for ever.

CHAPTER 3

America: impressions and illusions

I now spent a great deal of time travelling in order to find material for radio programmes. I still had my cottage near Oxford, I spent much time in London, and a certain amount in Birmingham. It was whilst working for BBC Midland Region that I received two phone calls from Oxford. One was from Lord David Cecil, telling me that my thesis had not been successful; and this was followed some months later by a totally unexpected call from my old Oxford friend, Jack May.

Jack was one of the few undergraduate friends that I personally encouraged to enter the acting profession, and for whom very early on I could see an assured future as an actor. The reason for this phone call was that a group of acting members of the university had formed themselves into a group called the Oxford University Players. A tour had been arranged to the United States of America, leaving in less than a month's time, taking Shakespeare's *King Lear* and Ben Jonson's *The Alchemist*, but there had been disagreements. The producer of one of the plays, Tony Richardson, later to make a name for himself as a theatre and film director, had walked out, and with him several of his acting friends had gone, too. The company was committed to its American tour and so a new director had been found – Alan Cooke, now well-known in television directing circles. But they were short of several acceptable Oxford actors, and the long vacation was already upon them. Within minutes I heard myself telling Jack that I was prepared to take on the part of Dapper in Alan Cooke's production of *The Alchemist* and Albany in the production by David William of *King Lear*. I had very few forward commitments with the BBC, and I would accept no more until we returned in September.

Once again, I found myself in Oxford acting circles. In the time that I had been away, a new generation of undergraduate actors had arrived. In particular, I remember an 18-year-old girl to

33

whom I was introduced. 'She is to play Cordelia to Peter Parker's Lear,' I was told, but she was presented to me as 'The first woman prime minister of this country!'

The prophecy was not fulfilled. She did not go on to become the first woman prime minister, but she has had and is having a most distinguished career in politics. Her name then was Shirley Catlin; she is now better known as Shirley Williams. We became great friends in the ensuing weeks, which were for both of us, in different ways, times of great personal difficulty.

I was recently very saddened to see rather snide remarks in certain magazines about the relationship between Shirley and Peter. As we rehearsed for the American tour, the truth was clear for us all to see: on Shirley's part, at least, this was a love affair, and an idealized undergraduate one at that. What became equally clear, during those gruelling weeks of travelling and performing in the heat of the American summer, was that Shirley was not to be the future Mrs Peter Parker. Peter was an enormously likeable person, and very gifted in a variety of fields. He seemed always to be living at twice the pace of the rest of us. Like Shirley, he had previously been in America, and like her, was clearly expected to make a great mark in the world, and to do it soon. His performance as Lear was very impressive. He had the physical strength for the part, as he was a considerable sportsman, and he was easily able to sustain that very long role. Having played the part myself only a few years before, I knew exactly how taxing it was. There was one other thing that I knew, too, and that was that for some of us love is never easy. For this reason perhaps, even though at the time we did not know it, Shirley and I grew close in a kind of brother and sister manner.

I remember one very hot American night, somewhere in the middle west. Everyone else had gone to bed, and Shirley and I sat in the quadrangle of the college where we were staying, and talked most of the hot night away, telling each other our secret feelings and merely by doing so, contriving to relieve them. Only a few days before, I had received a letter telling me of the end of a relationship which at the time meant a great deal to me; and I believe it was on that very evening Shirley had realized that, in spite of great affection and mutual respect between her and Peter, a more enduring and close relationship was not to be.

I hope she will forgive me for recalling these intimate personal matters from so long ago; but they had an innocence and poignancy that latter-day journalists seem to be either unaware of, or are unable to imagine.

At this time, Shirley was not yet 20; Peter 26. Both were brilliant intellectually, full of the drive and beauty of youth, both outstanding in their generation. In theory, they could have made a dazzling couple; in fact – and it was a fact that only emerged with any clarity during our time together in the USA – the basic chemistry was wrong. This was what Peter had recognized and Shirley had bravely faced up to that night in Ohio.

A foreign tour like ours inevitably threw everyone much closer together. It was a good test of any relationship; and halfway through the tour, it became clear from many small but significant signs that Shirley and Peter were not in the same harmony as when our journey began.

Then came that hot summer night in the middle west. The nervous strain and physical exhaustion were beginning to show in all of us, in a thousand little ways. Quite often, though, the almost electrical pressure which had been built up would be discharged by the rapturous applause we usually received at the end of each performance.

The night in question began gently. We were, unusually enough, not giving a performance that evening. Peter often looked up old friends he'd made when in the States before, and on this occasion he had invited not only Shirley, but also Ronald Eyre and me to tag along. This fact itself, one now realizes, might have been thought significant: they could have spent the evening *à deux*. The four of us, with Peter's American friend who was a professor at the university where we were staying, drove out into the country for dinner at 'Mrs Wagner's Colonial Kitchen'.

It was quite clear that Shirley was ill at ease and that tension had grown up between her and Peter. She ordered an enormous tomato juice and, as the meal began, launched into one of her enthusiastic discourses on some social or political matter which had arisen. The next instant an expansive, sudden gesture caught the tomato juice, and overturned it; and we sat at a table which seemed to be covered with a cloth of blood. It was not an auspicious start to a meal, and only served to intensify the feeling of unease with which the evening had begun. Hardly surprising that later, she and I should sit up all night, until the tension and the darkness disappeared with the dawn.

When we returned to England, Shirley and I kept in touch, meeting at intervals either in Oxford, or she would come out to my cottage some 15 miles from Oxford on her bicycle. She was then, as now, one of the most honest and unequivocal people I have ever met. She passionately believes in her political commitment and, unlike some people in the world of politics, is unwilling to compromise on basic principles for the sake of expediency. She is also a very warm and unfussy person. Were it not for her sense of humour and her humanity, the sharpness of her intellect would be very uncomfortable. She is entirely without cant or pomposity, and my great regret is that our separate lives have taken us so far from each other. It is, however, quite typical of her that when I wrote some years ago to congratulate her on her latest ministerial appointment, I received back not a formal note, nor even a fuller but obviously dictated reply, but instead, a long personal letter written, I'm sure, either late at night or very early in the morning when she might have been using her energies on more important matters.

What sort of showing did she make as Cordelia? Her performance had many virtues, some not commonly seen. Like Peter, she was sturdily built – anything but a will-o'-the-wisp – although her youth gave her a kind of ungainly beauty. They were quite credibly a father and daughter, once Peter had his make-up on: Shirley's Cordelia, in its strength and stubbornness, was clearly a chip off the old block. But this was not the only quality which made her performance so believable. As a person she was – and is – forthrightly honest, with a directness that brooks no argument. Shirley invested her Cordelia with that same uncompromising firmness. Goneril and Regan flattered Lear and gained more than their share: Cordelia, like Shirley, refused to say anything that she didn't mean. She said nothing; she got nothing. So her performance, and the resulting relationship between her and Lear, was a most compelling and effective piece of theatre, even though neither Shirley nor Peter had the sort of natural, or acquired, stage technique which gave such finesse to other performances in the production.

Playing to American audiences was a fascinating experience. They seemed much more earthy, more concerned with basics than a contemporary Oxford audience. In a way they seemed as one might imagine an audience of Shakespeare's own time to be. They responded noisily to the slap-stick humour of *The Alchemist*, with its antics of a couple of confidence tricksters and their moll. They related to Sir Epicure Mammon: he was a kind of aristocratic English Mr Big. More surprisingly still, they received *King Lear* not as one of the highest peaks in dramatic tragedy, but largely as a play of sexual intrigue: Goneril's two-timing of her worthy but dull husband, and Regan's relationship with hers, produced roars and flutters in the audience we'd never heard before.

As performers, it was an invaluable experience in other ways. There was, for example, an enormous diversity in the places where we played: vast auditoriums seating thousands some nights; small, inadequate halls seating only as many hundreds the next; and at Boston we played 'in the round'.

The least satisfactory performance was given in idyllic surroundings: the private theatre of an ex-silent-movie film star and her millionaire husband. We were given the freedom of the vast estate one sunny afternoon, and there was a lake where we could swim. Clearly the owners preferred the 'natural' look of dark water surrounded by trees, with the 'His' and 'Hers' changing cabins made of wood in a self-consciously rustic style. It certainly was a far cry from the huge, blue-watered, crystal clear, free-form pool one might have expected.

It was good to relax and let off steam; the tour had been hectic, with long performances in hot theatres and late nights after tedious car journeys.

It was inevitable that with a few hours of freedom and leisure a group of young people would start horsing around. As I remember it, there was something rather over-smug about the place that prompted rebellion. There were apple trees laden with rather tasteless apples around the pool. Someone picked up some of the countless fallen apples, and idly threw them at Dickie Evans and me, who'd found a row-boat and were lazily sculling around. This was the signal for a splendid game of Aunt Sally. Soon, half the company were scooping up windfalls and lobbing them in our direction. There were few direct hits, and the two of us in the boat rather enjoyed dodging the hail of apples. We half-heartedly pitched a few back, and it was all very silly, light-hearted, and enjoyable.

Then someone remembered that coffee and refreshments were going to be served before rehearsal; and, like urchins when the policeman appears, they all shot back across the sloping grass towards the mansion, with its chic little theatre in the grounds, leaving us in mid-pool.

Dickie and I looked at each other; and both, in one mind, said: 'Better tidy up.'

Suddenly the scene took on a bizarre air: a murky pool, in spacious parkland planted with fine trees, covered with bobbing apples. Like some three-dimensional game of joining up the dots, we rowed round and round, gathering up the apples, dozens of them, hundreds of them, till the little boat was laden with them, our legs lost beneath a mountain of wet fruit . . .

The performance that night was lifeless and flat; the audience was wealthy and pretentious. Unlike most of the audiences we played to, they were grim, undemonstrative, clearly bored and very boring. If we'd performed there at the beginning of the tour, our morale might well have been lower than the euphoric level it had maintained for most of the time.

Our simple scenery, props, and costumes travelled by lorry, with one member of the cast taking turns to travel with it, as our other transport, an ancient station-wagon and a 1936 convertible could not quite accommodate the whole company. On more than one occasion the highway police stopped us, unable to believe that such out-dated vehicles could still be on the road.

It was hard to say which was the more uncomfortable: the station-wagon or the convertible. So again, we took it in turns. When the weather permitted, the hood of the convertible was down. I shall never forget though that when, in torrential rain, it came to my turn to travel in it, the hood was up. This was the height of futility, as it had as many holes as a camouflage net. Sitting regally in the middle of the back seat, David William opened a large umbrella, which was surprisingly effective in providing us with shelter, if a little unorthodox. In a Lady Bracknell voice, David enlivened the journey: 'It reminds one of the worst excesses of the French Revolution!' he declared; adding confidentially, 'And I presume you know what that unfortunate movement led to?'

Early on in the tour, Dickie Evans and I had discovered a mutual interest in old music-hall songs, which we used to play as improvised piano duets: the result was a mixture of Rawicz and Landauer, Victor Sylvester and *Those Were the Days*. Whenever we were staying with private families, our first question was: 'Have they got a piano, and will they mind if we play it?' They never did.

Dickie Evans was, at one point, within millimetres of tragedy. When we had been dressing for the Oxford performance of *The Alchemist* at the union, I remarked on the most impressive operation scar I had ever seen. It was on Dickie's torso and seemed to make a half-circle round his body, from front to back and under one arm. Ever the leg-puller, Dicker said that during the war he'd been bayonetted while hiding in a basket of cabbages. I was, as he expected, tremendously impressed. Too nice a person to persist in untruth, he then came clean and said he'd had a kidney removed, and had never been bayonetted in his life. This conversation came back to my mind with horror a few weeks later in the wilds of Illinois.

Dickie was playing Edgar in *Lear* and the director, David William, had contrived a very athletic, dangerous, and exciting duel between him and Edmund, played by Michael Malnick. Just when Edgar seemed to be winning, he was un-sworded. Whereupon, Edmund gathered Edgar's sword, but instead of returning it hilt-first, suddenly and treacherously flung it at him point on. Dickie always ducked, and the sword flew harmlessly over his doubled-up figure.

On the fatal night, he either didn't duck sufficiently, or the sword was too low. It pierced his spine with great force. Bleeding profusely, he insisted on carrying on to the end of the play, by which time an ambulance was waiting to carry him to hospital. The audience, seeing his white shirt becoming slowly soaked with crimson, marvelled at the ingenuity of these young actors from Oxford. The rest of the company acted up splendidly, not knowing how serious or otherwise the injury was. Few were aware, as I was, that the sword, which was not too clean, might well have penetrated and damaged the other (and only remaining) kidney. I also knew, as the audience didn't, that for the scenes when Edgar is a mad wild spirit, 'poor Tom', Dickie's whole torso had had to be made up, first with dark skin colorant, and then with weals and sores added in grease-paint. For his appearance in the duel scene, Dickie merely cleaned up his face and put on a full-sleeved fencing shirt, not removing the filthy-looking body make-up until after the show. Now it was an astonished American hospital staff who had to do so, amazed that an undergraduate from Oxford, England, could be so filthy!

It was indeed only a flesh wound, though not exactly superficial; and Dickie was soon back with us. Oddly enough, he was the cause of some of us making contact again after 30 years. The tour over, we all went our separate ways, in the manner of undergraduates who have graduated. After many years my phone rang, and I heard the voice of Robert Robinson saying that Dick was very ill in a London Hospital, being cared for by Dr Jean Ginsberg, once a member of our Oxford acting set; and that all his old friends were being notified so that they could visit him.

I tried to do so, but Jean told me that he was about to have a critical operation. The next thing I knew he rang me up, having made a spectacular recovery. Long ago as they were, those American tour days came rushing back, hearing Dickie's voice sounding not a day older. Throughout our lives we've made a thing of ringing each other up, after a long gap, often of many years, and continuing our last conversation with: 'Oh, and another thing . . .!'

39

It was good to know we were going to be able to go on doing so.

Strenuous as the tour was, we did have time for some sight-seeing. The surprisingly beautiful Lakeside Boulevard at Chicago was as interesting, or more so, as Skid Row. The 'Englishy' atmosphere of Boston was to contrast sharply in the memory with the essential American-ness of New York. Why, I wonder, does no-one more often explain that the skyscrapers are not white, but every shade of stone, from rusty brown to the palest lavender? We enjoyed being billeted in Greenwich Village. We were playing 'just off' Broadway, but had plenty of time to see Manhattan with Central Park, Grand Central Station, the Subway, the Empire State Building, Radio City Music Hall with the Rockettes, Wall Street and the Statue of Liberty, and all the other standard sights that every tourist knows.

The last few days saw us stranded in New York. We never fully understood why, but there was some problem about our return flight. Our hosts were prevailed upon to go on giving us overnight accommodation; otherwise, we were on our own, with little cash, and that rapidly diminishing. Some of us learnt that a steak sandwich satisfied the pangs of hunger just as adequately as a grilled steak, at a third of the price; and we saw how tough New York could be, like all great cities, if you hadn't any funds.

The little money I had went mainly on Broadway shows. *Kiss me Kate* was still on. Menotti's *The Consul* impressed me in a Broadway theatre, and I was interested in his two operettas *The Medium* and *The Telephone*, performed in the round in a hotel. It was fun to see *Peter Pan*, with Jean Arthur as Peter and Boris Karloff as a very avuncular Captain Hook. These performances filled the days of waiting for our return flight to be arranged. If only we'd had money, it would have been enormous fun . . .

Then, suddenly, as Ronnie Eyre and I were on the point of entering the theatre to see Ethel Waters in her famous role in *Member of the Wedding*, Peter Dews appeared and said the plane was leaving in a couple of hours. The box office didn't want to know, when we asked if we could return the tickets, so we just threw them away, and rushed back to where we were staying. The next morning, after an extremely bumpy flight through a stormy night, we were back in England.

I personally found the tour of America, whilst interesting and at times highly enjoyable, extremely exhausting. When I returned home, I found myself for some weeks afterwards perpetually tired, falling asleep at the theatre, for example; and the whole

experience seemed a blur of names, images, rehearsals, and performances . . .

Then, in Oxford one day, Shirley suggested that I might care to
meet her godmother, Sybil Thorndike, who was playing that
week at the New Theatre. We went to the stage door between performances, and Shirley asked if she could see Dame Sybil. Perhaps
we weren't the most impressive of couples: neither of us is known
for sartorial elegance. The doorkeeper was not prepared to admit
two unknowns, who were clearly little more than autograph-hun-
ters. He was less than polite. Shirley tried again to explain that
Dame Sybil was indeed her godmother. This was received with a
look of outraged disbelief. Jumping on to my white horse, I
became Sir Galahad, and with unwonted vehemence suggested
that the best course the doorkeeper could follow, would be to go
at once and give the name of Shirley Catlin to Dame Sybil. My
tone was gratifyingly effective, and grudgingly he disappeared in
the direction of the dressing-rooms.

There was a pause and a silence and then, suddenly, all hell was
let loose. Screaming shouts of welcome from the depths of the
theatre, Dame Sybil advanced upon us like a human dynamo, as
the shamefaced doorkeeper scuttled back into his box. Anyone
who met Dame Sybil will agree that a conversation with her was
not unlike communing with a windmill in a high gale. What I
found so astonishing was that this old lady, having already given
one performance and waiting to go on and give another, seemed
to have more energy than most of my undergraduate friends put
together. Even more astonishing was her complete recollection of
the names of the theatres, and in some cases small halls, at which
she had performed on her American tours years before, and
which we had just revisited. 'Did you go to Champagne, Illinois,
dears?' And, 'What about the Eliza Fowler Hall!' A memorable
meeting of two very memorable ladies.

For the greater part of the American tour, I had shared a room
with John Schlesinger. Although we were good friends, I was at
the time being rather pompous on the question of the over-crow-
dedness of the theatrical profession. I felt very strongly that John
had gifts as a film director, having seen a film which he and Alan
Cooke had made some years before, and which had been quite
rightly praised by Dilys Powell, the noted film critic.

I remember on one occasion in a not-very-bright hotel in the
middle west, when John lay in a cool bath and I was resting in the
adjacent bedroom, hearing his voice drift out saying, 'But, surely,

41

after my performance in *The Alchemist*, you can't go on saying you don't think I should go into the theatre?'

I remember replying that it was precisely because of his performance in *The Alchemist* that I was quite sure he would not have a very happy life in the theatre. I said perhaps as a comedian in intimate review he might have a small chance. I recall still his bemused disbelief that I was so obstinate in my view. After all, we could both remember occasions at Oxford, in France, and here in America where his antics had produced shrieks of laughter from a delighted audience, and there is no doubt he could be very amusing. What I felt was, however, that his range was not wide enough to ensure regular employment. I was therefore delighted to hear, years later, no less a performer than Glenda Jackson saying after the success of *Sunday, Bloody Sunday*, she, too, felt that highly as she rated him as a director, John Schlesinger was not the world's greatest actor. Indeed, when directing actors and occasionally performing scenes, he was often unintentionally amusing, she said. 'But', she continued, 'you knew exactly what he wanted as director.' I felt that was some sort of vindication.

In addition to Peter Parker, Shirley Catlin, Jack May, and John Schlesinger, there were other members of the cast who have gone on to make considerable names for themselves. David William, and Peter Dews, for example, are now experienced and highly respected theatre directors: Robert Robinson is a household name; Alan Cooke is an esteemed television director, and Ronald Eyre, who has appeared on television as a presenter, is also well-known in the theatre as a director.

In a footnote, I may say that the girl who crossed the Atlantic in my arms on the way out came home in the arms of Robert Robinson, whom she eventually married. Her name was Josée Richard. When we were stranded in New York, I remember meeting her and Bob on Broadway and being told beamingly, 'We have just spent our last dollar.'

'What on?' I asked them.

'We bought a gin and shared it', said Bob.

We had all been extremely careful with our limited cash – we were restricted to a very small amount – but I had several dollars left, so I lent them a dollar. Several years later, I received a letter from Robert Robinson saying something like, 'I suddenly remembered the other day that I had never repaid you the dollar you kindly gave us on Broadway all those years ago.' An there was a cheque for seven and sixpence (37½p.).

Our tour had lasted for some six weeks, and we had covered

many thousands of miles, often doing one-night stands, and on some occasions travelling a couple of hundred miles and then performing that same evening. At the end, most of us immediately came home again. Peter Parker, however, stayed on, in order to take up a Commonwealth Fellowship, which would enable him to study at Cornell and Yale. Nearly everybody else in the company was still up at university.

Robert Robinson wrote a brilliant article about the tour which was called, typically, 'Hygienic Barbary'. I wrote for *The Oxford Magazine* my account of the visit, which was called less brilliantly, 'Bridge of Words'. I also recorded a talk, giving my impressions of America, in the New York studios of the BBC. Once the great adventure was over, for most of the company it was a case of completing or continuing their courses of study at Oxford. But for me it was yet one more farewell to Oxford, and one more return to the BBC.

CHAPTER 4

Broadcasting House: studio work

It's odd how the sun seems to shine on the other side of the valley. All my life I'd been not so much stage-struck, or even film-struck but, in my earlier years, radio-struck. I've got photographs to prove it. But when I actually entered the world of broadcasting, and was soon making an enjoyable living out of it, I never realized that I was living through some of the golden days of radio. The sun was shining on the other side of the valley.

Not that I haven't always been passionately keen on theatre and film and now television, but radio had the edge at first. My parents couldn't afford to give me expensive film projectors, though I did have a primitive slide projector. I had, at one stage, my own theatre – not a model, but the real thing in a basement room, with curtains that opened and closed. But my favourite plaything was a microphone, with which I used to broadcast from one room to another, talking, acting, singing, and playing the piano. The only snag in those pre-cassette recorder days, was that I couldn't hear what I sounded like.

Then, one day, many years later, I did.

It happened like this. Having made something of a name at university as an actor, I quickly became accustomed to playing the lead in any given production. I readily agreed to play the principal male role in Masefield's *Tragedy of Nan* when the chance came. It was not a happy production, and it was pulverized by the *Birmingham Post* critic, T.C. Kemp. His review began ominously by reviewing the history of the Birmingham University Dramatic Society and recounting the names of previous students who had made good, notably the film star Madeleine Carroll and, if I remember rightly, the actresses Dorothy Green and Dorothy Reynolds (who at the time had yet to make her mark in partnership with Julian Slade).

'But in this production,' Mr Kemp went on unequivocally, 'the society touches rock bottom . . . One might exclude Nancy

Lavender as Nan, and Norman Painting as Gaffer Pearce for being aware of some of the beauties of the play, but for the rest, silence is kinder.'

This was the sort of comment that could not be accepted unchallenged, even though some of us felt that the severity of the criticism was justified. Quite clearly, our next production would be make or break. Against some opposition, I argued that if we did something simple and still got it wrong, we should be even more severely criticized; if, on the other hand, we tackled something virtually impossible and made a good stab at it, we might redeem ourselves.

'Nobody'll blame us if we don't quite climb Everest', I said, 'But they'll trounce us if we don't reach the top of Lickey Hills.'

I had my way, and so was born my production of Shakespeare's *King Lear*, with my over-weening notion of playing the lead myself. But it worked. The Birmingham and Coventry papers gave us excellent notices; *Guild News*, the university newspaper, printed comments from dons and students alike, speaking of 'the greatest achievement the university has known', and 'the best production I've ever seen'. Sir Barry Jackson and Donald Wolfit, CBE, as he then was, both agreed to be patrons; I was stopped and congratulated personally by the vice-chancellor; and John Waterhouse glossed over a lecture he was due to give by saying that if he lectured till doomsday he could not give students as much insight into the play 'as one visit to Mr Painting's excellent production could do'. It was all very gratifying and bad for one, but I don't think my hat size increased too grotesquely. At least I hope not. It is a source of satisfaction to know that even today it is still possible to meet graduates who have vivid memories of it after so long.

As luck would have it, the actor and writer Robert Speaight was in Birmingham, compiling a sound picture of the city for the Overseas Service of the BBC, aimed at France. Unfortunately for him, but luckily for us, the only stage presentations available were either pantomimes or a Molière play in translation at the Birmingham Rep., and to send Molière back to France seemed rather unadventurous. He was anxious to include a short extract of live English theatre to show the people of France that Birmingham had some culture, and what better than an extract from a student performance of Shakespeare's *King Lear*? So four of us went along to the BBC studios in Broad Street, which I was soon to know so well, and there we made a four-minute recording of Goneril's refusal to house Lear.

45

After that, my fate was sealed. I hated my own voice; but was mesmerized by the whole business of broadcasting. I began at once preparing audition pieces, and giving auditions, in Birmingham and in London.

I very quickly learned that there were some doors that were closed, quite rightly, to someone who was not yet a full-time actor. The Drama Department of the BBC in London made it clear that I could not be considered for work in radio drama, where only fully professional actors could be employed. But as a poetry-reader, and as someone with specialized knowledge, the field of documentary and features was open to me.

I gave an audition in Birmingham to Edward Livesey, shortly after he had been appointed Features Producer, Midland Region. Although I was given ample time to read through the script provided – it was a selection of very tricky pieces of verse, including a short poem by Thomas Hardy, and a long extract from Masefield's 'Dauber' – I failed to notice that one letter in one word had not been printed clearly by the duplicator.

With the confidence born of reading all sorts of poetry aloud to critical student audiences over the past few years I sailed into the Masefield with gusto:

Slowly the sea went down as the wind fell.
Clear rang the songs, 'Hurrah! Cape Horn is bet!
The co –

– and then I stopped short. I was faced with this:

The com less seas were lumping into swell.

The what seas? the com less seas. . . What on earth could it be? 'Cape Horn is bet!' was mystifying enough. But com less! I tried to panic my mind into thinking of a word. None came.

I stopped, hesitated, and then candour took over: 'I'm terribly sorry,' I said. 'I didn't spot this when I read the script through. I can't imagine what the word can possibly be!'

'Not to worry, nor can I', said the cheery voice of Edward Livesey over the talk-back. 'We'll check it.'

I felt less than adequate. Why hadn't I spotted it before attempting to read it? I was certain I would be written off as over-confident. Not a bit of it. Ted's voice came back, with a laugh in it, over the loudspeaker.

'The missing letter is 'b'. The word is "combless"– without a comb.' Few people could be expected either to know, or guess, such a word; but I think my honesty had saved me. If I'd tried to fudge it, I might have put myself out of court. The incident, as such things often do, relaxed the inevitable tension of the audition atmosphere. I went on to read with my accustomed aplomb, and far from hearing a voice say: 'Thank you. We will get in touch', I heard the studio door open and there was Ted Livesey. He was clearly pleased.

He wasn't to know that speaking poetry has been one of the delights (and torments) of my life. It is something I have done, usually in public, from childhood days. I have recited to school inspectors, prospective headmasters, in school poetry competitions (as a fourth-former competing with boys in the sixth) at many a university gathering including, towards the end of my time at Birmingham, reading the illustrations to formal lectures.

I suppose my most memorable recital of verse up to this time had been on VE night, in Nuneaton. My father was a town councillor, and I found myself in the mayor's parlour with the aldermen and councillors and their wives, the local MP, Frank Bowles, and the Newdegates of Arbury Hall, Commander the Hon. J.M. Fitzroy and his always radiant wife, the Hon. Lucia, who had, as chairman of the Library Committee, appointed me to my first post some years before.

I don't know whose idea it was, or why I was foolish enough to agree to it, but I was going to read verse. At a given moment, the mayor and corporation and distinguished guests went out on to the balcony in front of the Council House, as Nuneaton's town hall is called. It seemed as if the whole town were jammed into the space in front of it. The mayor made a speech, everyone cheered, over-excited irresponsibles let off fireworks among the crowd, and then it was my turn. I stepped to the front of the balcony, and to the largest but by no means the most receptive audience I had up till that time played to, I spoke the whole of Kipling's 'Recessional'. The roar of applause from the crowd at the end was, I'm sure, relief that their ordeal was over. It was as much an ordeal for me, too. I heard Mrs Newdegate murmur words of appreciation and congratulation to my mother, and then we retreated once more to the mayor's parlour for real, and if I remember, not entirely sedate celebration, which my parents left early, taking me with them.

No doubt, these years of poetry-reading (which I still find one of the most rewarding but excruciatingly difficult activities) stood me in good stead. I hate the poetry voice, the reader who acts instead of reads, and above all the reader who neutralizes, usually by over-dramatizing, the rhythm carefully created by the poet; I can only assume that my reading during that first radio audition avoided at least these most common blemishes.

Edward Livesey was direct and uncompromising. 'I like your work. I can and will use you as a poetry-reader. But we don't do many poetry programmes. Would you like to take part in other programmes as well?'

Speechless with delight, I mumbled that I was keen to learn the whole business of broadcasting. I still had over a year to go before my finals, but I was beginning to think about my future. I knew that I had no wish to be a schoolteacher, and so declined a most tempting grant which would have come my way in return for committing myself to the teaching profession. Thoughts of an academic life at university level, though, were beginning to stir, both in English literature and in archaeology. I had ambitions, too, as a performer, acting and reading. Above all this, my conviction that writing (whether poetry, drama or academic works) would have to be a major part of my life grew steadier. Broadcasting attracted me, not only for itself, but also because I could learn the technique of radio writing and performing while continuing with my studies.

Good as his word, Edward Livesey gave me a succession of opportunities. Sometimes he would cast me in tiny supporting parts so that I could work with, and study, some of the great practitioners of radio. My third broadcast, which happened to be the first of my dear old friend Mary Wimbush, was, believe it or not, a radio feature about modern art, called, 'It Isn't Like Her!' Playing the lead, in a way that I found brilliant and electrifying, was Howard Marion Crawford, whom in time Mary was to marry. He was known to us all as 'Boney' – a nickname of the type that calls short people Lofty and tall people Shorty. His ample tweeded figure and dimpled face, framed, then, in crinkly hair, assorted oddly with the light and delicate voice of great beauty which he produced at very low volume close to the microphone. His first reading was a revelation. At the end of it, he held his script at arm's length, and, as it fell to the floor, said: 'What in hell does it all mean?'

How this brilliance was then carefully cut and manipulated and polished into something even more dazzling was an object lesson I have never forgotten.

I sometimes used to joke that I first appeared on the air in the title role of Shakespeare's *King Lear*. But my first professional engagement, in September 1945, was in a feature programme (what today would be called a documentary) on Coventry. I had four small parts. One, in verse, was as one of the Shepherds in the Coventry Nativity Play. The first lines I ever spoke professionally were in Latin, as a mediaeval herald. Rehearsals began on Saturday evening, and continued through until Sunday evening, when the programme was recorded. This was unusual at the time. Most programmes were broadcast live – in fact, during the next few years I was to take part in some hundreds of live broadcasts. This, my first show, however, was pre-recorded.

The cast repaired to the BBC Club bar just before the final run-through and, although I did not then, as now, drink before a broadcast, I naturally went with the crowd. The Narrator, Alan Howland, newsreader and actor, was the possessor of a very famous BBC voice at that time, and he engaged me in conversation, which as a newcomer I found very encouraging. But, almost as a throw-away, he said: 'By the way old boy, shouldn't you be using the mediaeval pronunciation of Latin, not your modern one?'

I was devastated and panic-stricken. I had practised my four-line speech incessantly and now had it fixed in my mind. He was, though, clearly right; and so, with his help, I wrote out the speech phonetically, fully expecting to make a hash of it. I had, for example, to pronounce, *dei graciae* not as 'day-ee grahkee-ai', but 'dee-ai grayshay' – and that was only a small part of it! It was a diabolical tonsil-twister; but, when I heard the transmission two days later, I was relieved to hear all the vowels in the right sequence.

The Broad Street studios were only a few hundred yards from the old, now demolished, Edmund Street buildings of the university, so broadcasting was not only convenient but became the greatest possible delight. Financially, too, it was more than welcome. For my final year I had applied to the Charles Henry Foyle Trust for help, and was required to fill in forms giving the trustees details of my total resources. It was then I found that for the previous three years I had been living well below the recommended subsistence figure. A yearly sum of £220 were then regarded as rock-bottom minimum: in no year had I had more than £180. I received very generous help from the trust, for which I shall always be grateful. With it, and the welcome grant from the local authority, plus what I could earn from fire-watching and broadcasting, I was able – just – to keep my head above water.

Edward Livesey was only one of the producers at BBC Midland Region. Robin Whitworth was his co-features producer, Philip Garston Jones produced variety and comedy series, Godfrey Baseley did agricultural and country programmes and Peggy Bacon had just been appointed to look after children's programmes. For Robin I was to work only a little, as performer and as writer. Philip and Godfrey heard my work on the air, and employed me increasingly. Philip gave me amusing work in revue, comedy serials, whodunnits and musicals, most of it highly enjoyable, and very good for widening one's range.

Philip was a writer, actor and musician, who had worked with, and much admired, Martyn C. Webster, one of the BBC's most gifted producers of lighter drama, revue and musical comedy. After many years at Midland Region, he moved on to, and largely dominated, for a time, the London scene of Light Entertainment. Martyn's methods, and methodicalness, had greatly influenced Philip, who presented some extremely polished and sophisticated programmes. (It was also part of his brief to produce variety shows of a broader nature, but I was never involved in these.)

He was particularly good at light comedy-thrillers with music, and there was at hand a writing and composing team to provide them – Edward J. Mason and Basil Hempseed. They were enormous fun to do, if extremely hard and concentrated work, involving quite a large cast and a live orchestra. Philip never wasted a minute, and worked to a very tight schedule. So one day when, as a comparative newcomer, I arrived 25 minutes late, it is not surprising that I heard the acid side of Philip's tongue. The absurdity of it was that I had thought I was five minutes early, and had walked up and down Broad Street outside killing time.

'Ah! The late Mr Painting', said Philip ominously, as, thinking this was my last broadcast for him, I stammered out my explanation, which seemed extremely lame. And so of course it was, for everyone else had read both script and contract carefully, and had duly arrived at 2 o'clock, not 2.30. I silently resolved never to be late again.

Most of my colleagues in those days are no longer household names. But there are two that stand out.

One is Janet Brown, now at last justly famous for her devastating impersonations of Mrs Thatcher, Esther Rantzen and Barbara Woodhouse. She was extremely easy-going, vivacious and friendly, a good comedienne, but equally capable of turning in a first-class characterization as a straight actress. She also sang delightfully. She was – and I'm sure still is – in a word, fun.

We were chatting in Studio Two in Broad Street, Birmingham, waiting for one of Philip's rehearsals to start (I was on time that day) when a Jeep (JPE – Junior Programme Engineer, now called studio manager) began to prepare the studio.

He moved a large boom microphone to the end of the studio where Janet and I were chatting and, not satisfied with its position, swung the boom. Over her shoulder, I saw the mike swing backwards and then relentlessly forward. I yelled: 'Look out!' Too late. The heavy microphone caught Janet such a blow on the back of the head that she shot across the studio and fell against a row of chairs. The engineer was horrified and repentant; and we rushed to her aid. Smiling broadly, she insisted that it was: 'All right . . . No, really!' But she must have had one hell of a headache. I silently admired the game way she carried on, re-hearsing both dialogue and songs with gusto. The clichés about 'being a trouper' and 'the show must go on' may be corny; but when you see them in operation, they take on a new significance. To have played it for drama, lying down in a darkened room, etc., might have been more comfortable for Janet, but she wouldn't have won the lasting admiration of at least one of her colleagues. She may have forgotten the incident completely; I remember it vividly and can still recall the sickening *clonk* of the heavy metal against her skull, and the click of her jaw as her teeth clenched.

The other memorable colleague from these times was Edward J. Mason. With Basil Hempseed, he had written programmes that I had enjoyed in *Children's Hour* as a young teenager; and later the partnership was to write a long series of musical fantasies for children called *Through the Garden Gate*, in which I regularly appeared, along with my old friends Fred Yule, Bob Arnold, June Spencer and Hugh Morton, amongst others. Looking back, it now seems providential and far from accidental that in those five years of broadcasting before *The Archers* began, I was not only learning the business, but was also regularly performing, and making friends, with colleagues who would later be so much in-volved in the series. The technical supervision of many of these programmes directed by Philip Garston Jones was often in the hands of Tony Shryane, later to produce *The Archers*. But most significantly, it was by playing a wide variety of parts written by Edward J. Mason at this time, in revue and comedy series, that my work became well-known to him. When, with Geoffrey Webb, he began to write the character of Philip, he was writing for a per-former whose work had been familiar to him for a number of years.

Godfrey Baseley, himself a superb and frequently under-valued poetry-reader, employed me in programmes where I was required to read both verse and sometimes rather complicated prose. He was among the most sensitive and helpful directors I ever worked with; and it was in these early days I realized that his bluff and gusty manner, and his occasional apparent megalomania, were the mask on the face of a deep-feeling and imaginative man.

Godfrey, for his part, grew to know me as both person and performer, so that when some four or five years later he was preparing the trial run of his brainchild *The Archers,* I was his first choice for the part I have played for so long, Philip.

My friendship and frequent collaboration with Peggy Bacon had a very unpromising beginning. She received one of my usual letters asking for an audition and, having called me into her office for a brief chat, agreed to listen to me. The material I chose was way off target. She was very new to the business of directing programmes and artists, but she had very clear ideas of the sort of items she proposed to use. I offered her precisely the type of material she had no intention of broadcasting. She came into the studio at the end of my audition and said quite frankly, she didn't think she would be able to employ me.

I was very bouncy in those days, and took this rejection in my stride, with a resilient sort of 'can't win them all' attitude. It so happened that I went straight from her audition to a rehearsal for a remarkable programme written by Edward Livesey in collaboration with Ludwig Koch. Ludwig was a great favourite in those days: he spoke highly idiosyncratic English with a jaw-breaking accent. He was a wizard at sound-recording, working wonders with the limited equipment of the time. He is, of course, especially remembered for his natural-history recordings.

He had made a series of brilliant recordings of a great number of industrial machines, and introduced them in Ted's programme which was called, 'The Song of the Machines'. The title is taken from Kipling's poem on the subject, which I was required to speak in its entirety halfway through the live 45-minute broadcast. As a finale, using every gramophone turntable in Broadcasting House, Ludwig built up a sound montage of increasing intensity and complexity up to the highest possible volume. Then it ceased. There was a silence. In the silence, I repeated the final stanza of the poem. It was a highly unusual and fascinating programme; and my part in it, though small, was very showy.

The next day I heard from Peggy Bacon. Both she and her assistant, Dorothy English, had heard the programme and had rung Ted, asking for the name of that marvellous young man with the good voice who had spoken the verse so superbly! To her eternal credit, Peggy didn't persist in saying that (having only the day before turned me down) she couldn't employ me. In fact, she offered me the first of a very long line of parts in *Children's Hour.* As well as becoming good friends, sharing an interest in good food, and red wine and religion, she commissioned my first full-length radio play, which, as will be told in Chapter 6, was also the first of many.

The name Reggie Smith is a golden one in the history of British broadcasting in the fifties and sixties. He was one of that incredibly talented group of writer–directors that Laurence Gilliam gathered round him in his famous London Features Department: Louis MacNeice, Joe Burrows, Terence Tiller, David Thomson, Alan Burgess, Francis (Jack) Dillon, Douglas Cleverdon and so many others. Reggie Smith was a graduate of Birmingham University, and kept in regular touch with his old haunts when, as he did so regularly and faithfully, he visited his mother. Reggie, under the form of his name which he always used in public, R.D. Smith, is yet one more of the 'beneficiaries' in Auden and MacNeice's 'Last will and testament'.

It must have been through Edward Livesey that I met Reggie, who employed me for I think my second broadcast ever: a sad little piece marking the anniversary of the Coventry blitz. We at once took to each other, and with the greatest generosity of spirit, Reggie gave me first-rate advice and help over the next few years. The experience I gained from working for him in the London studios was invaluable. Broadcasting for Reggie, though, was always an adventure. His casts had a habit of growing as rehearsals progressed: some out-of-work actor would call to see him, and be given a part on the spot. You would often start with four or five small parts such as newsboy, professor, Indian, worried old man, cultured voice, etc., and end up with only two or three. And if Dylan Thomas happened to arrive, he was sure to be given one of your parts; but nobody minded. The converse was often true: you could sometimes end up playing a far more important part than you started off with.

On one occasion I arrived in the studio for a programme in the series, *Professional Portrait*. This one was written by Michael Barsley, and was called 'Cricket Pro'.

The cast met and sat in a circle with Reggie, who said, 'Take pages four to eleven, pull them out of the script like this, screw them tightly into a ball, and then throw them over your shoulder like this.' And he did so.

Then he said: 'Norman, I want you to read in the part of Jimmy. I'm auditioning some boy actors at 12 o'clock, but you may have to do it.'

I took a peep. It was an enormous part. I crossed my fingers.

After the reading, Reggie looked at his watch.

'Right, it's now 11.45. Be back at 6.30. That should be plenty of time. We're on the air at 10.5.'

And so we were – with me playing the lead, not helped by some unrehearsed background chatter provided by Jack Dillon and a few friends who had 'happened to pop in'. The script was still being cut as the red light winked to say we were on the air. This brinkmanship of Reggie's was not entirely accidental. It had the extraordinary effect of 'hyping up' a cast. You really were on your mettle. When it worked, when the performers didn't fall victim to the nervous strain, it was often brilliant. We were quite used to Reggie creeping into the studio during a live transmission, putting his arm around you as you spoke into the microphone, and following with his pencil the line you were saying. Then the pencil would drop, dragging your eye to a line at the bottom of the page. In this way, cuts were made during the actual transmission. We hadn't thought of the word 'hairy' then, but that's what it was.

Towards the end of transmission, who should walk into the studio but the great Stuart Hibberd himself, the chief announcer? I had left home that morning to play a couple of tiny parts (known in the business as coughs and spits). Imagine my surprise, therefore, at hearing the most famous voice in broadcasting announcing: 'You have been listening to Norman Painting as Jimmy in "Professional Portrait of a Cricket Pro" by Michael Barsley.' The next time you worked for Reggie it was back to third soldier, cultured voice, worried old man, etc.

The most extreme example of having my part changed was in a script called, 'Shadows of the Great: Jean-Jacques Rousseau'. I had received a contract for this a few days ahead of the broadcast, something that did not always happen. Then came a telegram from Reggie: 'Rehearsal 9.30. Imperative make early start.'

When I reached the Maida Vale studios and was given a copy of the script, I understood why. It had been written for two narrators and a boy actor. Once Reggie had begun to work on the script he realized that it would be more effective if the two narrators were to become not only one, but if that one were to be Rousseau himself, looking back to dramatized incidents. I was not playing third student after all, but the now enormous part of Rousseau. Live. At 4.30 that very afternoon, with page after solid page of narration, interspersed with dramatized scenes.

Reggie confidently steered me through it, occasionally making helpful remarks over the talk-back like, 'Try not to sound so chatty, chum. You do realize you're in bed with her, don't you?'

I hadn't, especially as Rousseau was in his teens and the lady in question, Madame de Warens, was in her forties. That part, by the way, was played, most helpfully by June Spencer, with whom I was later to play so many scenes. She became Peggy Archer!

After the broadcast, the question of fee came up. In due course I received exactly twice my normal fee of six guineas (£6.30p.). But the value of the experience was inestimable. Needless to say, there were headlines in the local papers that week.

Reggie also employed me as a researcher and scriptwriter for a series, *This Correspondence Must Cease*, which he was doing for Radio 3 – it was called the Third Programme in those days; and he advised me whom to write to for further work.

Some time before the two broadcasts I have just mentioned, I had been told that Features Department were starting a mass auditioning programme, as so many people had applied during the previous few years following the war, and there was a huge backlog.

I took my place on the list, even though I continued to broadcast regularly in London and Birmingham. Then at last I was called to the Aeolian Hall in Bond Street for my first Features audition. It was held by Douglas Cleverdon, whom I merely heard over a loudspeaker and didn't meet. He made very encouraging noises, and said I'd probably be hearing from him again.

In time, I did. I received a telegram, the day after I'd played the lead in 'Cricket Pro'. It was inviting me to a 'seeded' audition for Features Department.

As I sat in the waiting-room at the Langham Hotel where the auditions were being held, I exchanged the odd word with waiting actors. One said he'd been in the BBC Drama Repertory Company for a couple of years, but was doing these auditions to bring his work to the notice of Features producers. I noted the point, and consoled myself with the thought that if I officially failed this final audition, as I'd 'failed' my *Children's Hour* one for Peggy Bacon, there might be one of the other producers who'd still employ me.

In the event, I didn't fail. I don't know how usual it is for audition pieces to be received with applause and encored: but this is what happened.

Douglas Cleverdon was this time visible, sitting at the drama control desk behind a glass panel. Behind him were rows of Features producers and other interested people. The script provided was far from easy. One had to choose three or four pieces from a possible eight or so; but not one piece was for a single voice. The only piece I remember performing was from a book by Gerald Kersh. It concerned a quarter-master sergeant and two privates, one cocky, one nervous – at least that's how I played them. I modelled the sergeant on QM Sgt Kelly who'd issued me with my kit and uniform for the Training Corps.

As I finished, Douglas Cleverdon put the key down so that he could thank me over the loudspeaker and I heard gales of laughter, with Douglas making shushing sounds. He thanked me, and asked me to do my own choice of piece. I did from memory, in dialect, the part I'd played in my first broadcast, the Shepherd from the Coventry Nativity Play.

As the key went down and Douglas's voice came over the talk-back I heard a voice say:

'Oh yes, please, Douglas. It was so amusing.'

Whereupon I was asked to repeat the Gerald Kersh piece. I did so, using all the microphone technique I'd learned to make the three characters different, one close to the mike, the others at varying distances, in different accents, with different voice-qualities. At the end of it, I looked up into the cubicle. They were not only laughing, but applauding. A tall wispy man got up and left as Douglas thanked me and said that I would no doubt be hearing more.

Outside, in one of those wide Langham corridors the tall wispy man was waiting. 'Congratulations. I did enjoy that. Most amusing. My name's Stephen Potter.'

He had especially responded to the humour that I'd managed to find in a not noticeably amusing piece of script. And knowing his reputation as a humorist from his, *How* programmes with Joyce Grenfell, and his *Gamesmanship* and *Lifemanship* books and programmes, I was considerably flattered.

I would like to say that as a result of this highly successful audition, I received countless invitations of work for all the great names in the Features Department. I would like to say that. But it didn't happen. Just as I was becoming regularly employed, I joined the cast of *The Archers*. And that was the end of my career as a radio actor. And, in another sense, the beginning.

Before this, however, I did several memorable broadcasts for Douglas Cleverdon, and Alan Burgess, David Thomson and Terence Tiller. Sadly, I never met Stephen Potter again.

The broadcasts with Douglas Cleverdon were memorable on several counts; two of them stand out because in both of them the leading part was played by that incredible, outrageous, endearing man, Robert Farquharson.

The name by which he was universally known, Robin, seemed inappropriate to many of us. For 'Robin' suggests delicacy and the innocence of youth, whereas he cultivated the notion of being extremely old, heavy jawed, occasionally lame in a built-up surgical boot, and always mysterious. Many people feared him; some hated him. Others, including dear Carleton Hobbs, acutely disliked him.

He encouraged dark rumours that he was a diabolist. He had, years before, certainly known some colourful characters: Aubrey Beardsley, Oscar Wilde, Max Beerbohm, Aleister Crowley. His mind was stocked with a wealth of recondite and sometimes startling information, with which he would frequently regale unwilling and squeamish audiences.

I, too, was in awe of him, until, quite quickly, I realized that he was really a naughty schoolboy, taking the greatest delight in shocking. If one was not shocked, and even managed to answer back, he softened at once.

He could be very cruel, especially to some women – though others he adored, and clung to. On one occasion, as the red light was winking, indicating that the studio would be on the air in a matter of seconds, he faced an actress across the microphone and mumbled into his script, 'Let me see now. Oh yes, this is the young lady who smells.'

But he could be wonderfully amusing. Before we had met formally he once stood behind me at the reception desk of the hotel where we were staying, and I asked if Courtney Hope had yet arrived. On being told she hadn't, I asked if Mrs Dorothy Cooke had checked in – Courtney's real name. Again the answer was negative. I was then aware that this well-dressed heavily jowled man, wearing a touch of rouge on his cheeks, was beginning to breathe with heavy impatience behind me.

I stammered to the receptionist by way of explanation that Courtney Hope and Dorothy Cooke were the same person.

'Then what's the matter?' stormed Robin, 'Do you want her examined by a Board of Matrons?'

Later he said to Courtney: 'There was a d-dreadful little man enquiring after you . . . like a g-g-goose!'

We were assembling for four one-hour programmes broadcast live on four consecutive Sunday evenings, on the French Revolution. Robin, as Narrator, remained in one studio, in a specially constructed 'tent'.

'It's so lonely here in the breeding-box!' he complained.

The rest of us had to move about to three other studios – multi-studio productions were greatly in vogue then.

For the third time in succession I shot into the studio where

Robin's 'breeding-box' was, said a line or two, and then went out. The next time I came in he remarked: 'You are a busy little man. Every time you come in here you have a different voice. How DO you do it?'

Here was my chance. 'Well you see,' I said cheekily, 'I find it simpler to change my head, so that's why I keep going outside, to do that!'

'Splendid!' he said. He never picked on me again. Indeed, we passed many hours of bejewelled conversation – Robin talking, I being the straight man – in succeeding years. The stories about him, and quotations from his studio talk, are legion. He it is who, when staying at the Queen's Hotel, Birmingham, which was in fact part of the New Street Station complex, is alleged to have rung down to reception in the middle of the night and asked: 'What time does this hotel get to Paddington?'

Like most wits, his comments were rarely spontaneous. Some indeed one heard repeated, at different stages, as they became neater and more polished. In spite of the face of blank wonderment that anyone should laugh at his words, the mock-innocence, the stammer which was purely for effect or to give thinking time, it is quite clear that Robin knew he was being funny, was expecting to be found funny, if not downright outrageous; and many of his quips were meant to shock, such as:

'I often regret that I have had no experience of incest: but I did not have a sister, and my brother was terribly unattractive . . .'

'I went to a P-P-Public School: you know, where Freeman and Hardy were terribly unkind to W-Willis; and Marks was much too fond of S-S-S-Spencer.'

'Oxford . . . where nowadays the undergraduates look like errand-boys . . . And the errand-boys look like undergraduates.'

After a long gap in which we didn't meet, because most of my working life had all been concentrated into *The Archers,* he professed somewhat surprisingly to be a devotee of the programme.

'N-N-Norman dear, I ADORE *The Archers*. They're so HORRID. Everybody's so BEASTLY to everybody! Lovely!'

Once, in the studio at the beginning of the day's rehearsals, I asked if he'd slept well.

'Not badly, until dawn. Then a well-built woman in the room above shattered my sleep by doing her exercises, jumping up and down on the spot, picking up p-p-peas in her breasts, and Heaven knows what!'

He once said to me, breaking off a conversation with Jill Balcon in mid-flight: 'Ah, Norman dear, are you still attached by an umbilical cord to Oxford, or are you now out in the world?'

'I find your imagery a little confusing, Robin', I replied, before answering the question.

Years later, we met in the Birmingham BBC restaurant. I had Timus, my corgi, on a lead.

'Norman, dear, I haven't seen you for so long! Oh, and you've had a little dog! And it's so LIKE you!'

He was a showman, and he knew he was being the little boy who had to have attention. Once, in a serial play of mine, *Tomorrow is a Stranger*, one of his colleagues was Mary O'Farrell. By this time, he was walking with a stick, which he genuinely needed. Mary accidentally dropped her script, and all the young men, myself included, bent to pick it up. Robin merely said, very dramatically: 'Ah Mary!' and then added . . . 'You see, everyone dives to your rescue, but I just sit helplessly here and say "Ah . . . Mary"!'

I never met him socially, though I knew he had countless stories of many figures that interested me, especially from the early part of the century. Gradually I lost touch with him.

There had been persistent rumours that he had died. Then one day, when I was living in London, a mutual friend said that Robin had expressed a wish to see me again. He was living in the house of Mrs Helen Stirling Winslow, whom I telephoned and invited me to tea. On the day in question, I was called to the studio for a 'topical insert' into *The Archers*, and so had to ring and postpone my visit for some three weeks.

Shortly after this, I was leaving the Old Vic, when I saw Douglas Cleverdon and his wife. We hadn't met for some years. I rushed up to him, quickly exchanged pleasantries, and then mentioned that I was hoping to see Robin very shortly.

'I'd thought that he was dead', I said, 'but he isn't, you know.'

'Oh yes, he is', said Douglas. 'He died this morning.'

So Fate had deprived me of what might have been both amusing and revelatory conversations with one of the great eccentrics, one of the most colourful and amusing people I ever met, who ought not to be forgotten.

His handwriting was superb; his jewels, I now realize, must have been of enormous interest. I once worked with him every day for ten consecutive days, and he never appeared twice in any garment of clothing, and everything he wore was exquisite. For that same production he used to arrive at the studios in Maida Vale on a magnificent green and gold bicycle with every possible extra attachment. At lunchtimes he could be seen polishing it with a silk handkerchief. On one occasion I found him struggling with the dynamo.

'Having difficulties, Robin?'

'I don't think so. I'm just trying to ensure that this stays permanently in the "on" position, so that when I ride through the Park, people will say: "Light's on", and I can bow, and say, "Yes . . . I KNOW"!'

This was during rehearsals for Douglas Cleverdon's own adaptation of Max Beerbohm's *Zuleika Dobson*. Robin was brilliantly cast as The Warden of Judas and, in that first broadcast, I played the unspeakable Noakes. Douglas asked me to concoct a nonexistent Midlands-type accent for the part, and this I had done. We rehearsed in those vast old HMV studios in Maida Vale for two weeks, and the day of the first live transmission arrived. The broadcast was in two parts of nearly two hours each, and we spent the morning doing our final rehearsals for part one. After lunch Douglas met me with a baleful half-apologetic look on his face.

'I wrote to Max about your accent,' he said, 'and he's replied: "I think a cockney accent for Noakes"!' The Master had spoken. I had to adopt a cockney accent at once, and went on the air that night live, in a major Third Programme production, never having rehearsed part one in cockney.

In those spacious days, the whole production was repeated, live, after a well-known critic had given his impression of it. The critic in our case was Tyrone Guthrie who was not unkind. Douglas Cleverdon was, at this time, building up his fine reputation as one of the most distinguished radio producers, after coming late into broadcasting. He had been a bookseller, and publisher of fine printing, and had invented book tokens before turning to radio, first as a free-lance actor and writer, and then later on the staff. He was the most genial of men, with a wide cultivation that sat lightly on him; and working for him was pure delight. He had the highest standards, but coaxed and beguiled his actors into reaching them. He was responsible for several milestones in radio, mainly on Radio Three; among them, Dylan Thomas's *Under Milk Wood* is probably the best remembered.

I have said elsewhere in this book that one of my regrets (and there are few in my life) is that I never set out to cultivate the friendship of so many of the remarkable people I've been privileged to know. They no doubt misread my shyness for standoffishness. But of all the people I met in the early years of my career, the one I regret not knowing better was Dylan Thomas. I worked with him on countless occasions, often drank and swapped stories with him; even saw him when he was not doing his public performance as Roaring Boy. But I cannot remember any occasion when I was alone with him, when I might have tried to get behind his defences.

When we first met, he was still to create the materials for the cult that has grown up around him. Few of us who knew him in those last five or six years of his life ever guessed that he had, in fact, already completed the bulk of his life's work. He was to write little of the sort of verse for which he is remembered after the publication of his *Collected Poems* in 1952. But for a young man like me, who had serious, if occult, aspirations to write poetry, merely to be in the same studio or bar with Dylan was to breathe the air of Parnassus.

My first encounter with Dylan came through Reggie Smith. I had been asked to take part in a programme about Oxford, written by Dylan and produced by Reggie, who had asked me to call in to see him in his office as soon as I reached London. It was a dead time, the Saturday after Christmas. I found Reggie alone in his office in Rothwell House, New Cavendish Street, his head in his hands.

When I asked if everything was all right, he raised his hands above his head, and said: 'No bloody cast! No bloody script! No bloody Dylan!'

He held up a schoolboy's exercise book, and let it drop on to his desk. Then he had a sudden inspiration: 'You can type, can't you?'

'With one finger, that's all!'

'That'll do!'

The next thing I knew, I was typing on to one top copy and no less than five flimsies, the only scene which Dylan had written in that penny exercise book, in his clear, precise, usually upright handwriting. A very grateful Reggie sat by encouragingly; and, when it was finished, said he'd see me at rehearsal the next day, Sunday, at St Hilda's Convent, where the BBC Transcription Service studios were.

In spite of my resolve about punctuality, I was a few minutes late. This I managed to do by the simple expedient of getting on a tube train going in the wrong direction. I eventually arrived in something of a steamy state. But I need not have worried. Reggie had assembled a large cast, but the only script he could show them was that one scene, hamfistedly typed, and largely illegible, apart from the top two copies. Gallantly, the cast rehearsed the scene: it was an Oxford party. We went through it again. And again. It lasted barely four minutes. Then came a message: Dylan was being driven in from Oxford. (He was at the time the drawing-room 'lion' of the wife of a well-known don.)

The cast were told to break for coffee. Like the rehearsal, the coffee-break was extended and unhurried. Dylan arrived in the middle of it, wearing a pork-pie hat and a coat made from an army blanket. He had not, as we all hoped, brought the completed script with him; but it was, he said, in his head. He seemed not in the least repentant or apologetic. He strode happily round the tiny St Hilda's canteen, amiably smiling, and chatting to all and sundry. What seemed to matter most to him at that moment was that the driver of the hire-car who'd brought him, had been delighted when Dylan sat in the front with him, and not in the back, even though he'd been told his passenger was a famous poet. What pleased Dylan even more, though, was that the driver had said in conversation that a certain customer whom he'd recently driven was very grand and stuck-up: 'Not an ordinary working chap like you and me.'

Poor Dylan! He did so want to be thought an ordinary working-class chap, in spite of his solid middle-class background. I heard him tell the story repeatedly round the room; and when my turn came and he told me, I could not but be aware of the irony, remembering his background and mine, and feel amazed that such an apparently small incident should mean so much to him.

Suddenly this whole production began to take on a surreal atmosphere. Reggie, having been called to the phone, came back and proceeded to ask all the men in the cast if they were free the following day. Several of us said we were, and asked why. Reggie then said that his colleague David Thomson had to produce a live feature the next afternoon called 'Under the Dome', a portrait of the British Museum reading-room. He had understood from the writer that the script called for 4 men and some 16 women, and had booked them. Now, rather late, the script had arrived and called for 4 women and some 16 men. No secretarial staff were on duty to book him other actors, as it was the Sunday after Christmas.

Reggie, realizing that the cast he had with him at St Hilda's were without a script to rehearse, agreed to release us for the afternoon. So, feeling bemused, several of us got back into the tube and went to Broadcasting House. David Thomson was almost absurdly grateful to the group, several of whom were total strangers to him; but the atmosphere was soon made agreeable by Carleton Hobbs, who circulated, announced his name and, in the most welcoming way, shook hands with everyone. Hobbo, the

most urbane and gentlemanly of performers was not only a per-
fectionist in his craft, but a congenial and often witty companion.

Our afternoon's rehearsal passed swiftly; and soon we were
back on the tube, wondering what would meet us at St Hilda's.
Half the cast were wandering about as if they couldn't quite
believe what was happening. By now, an orchestra had arrived to
play the specially composed 'Oxford' music by Elizabeth
Lutyens; and when we asked about the script, we were told that
Dylan had been pacing up and down all afternoon dictating to
one of the actresses in the cast, Joan Geary.

Seeing me, Reggie cried out: 'Norman! You play the piano,
don't you?'

Suspiciously I said that I did, sort-of. But when I realized that
Reggie's idea was that I should play at sight, from manuscript, the
exacting twelve-tone score of Liz Lutyens's music, I cried off. In
the end, a member of the orchestra conducted, releasing the conductor, Edward Clarke, to play the piano part.

By now it was early evening, and some members of the cast had
done virtually nothing all day, whilst others had had a surprisingly busy time.

So we recorded the party scene, stretching and elaborating it
wherever we could with improvised party talk and party action. I
still have a transcript of the recording, which has frequent gaps in
the text, with the note, 'transcription impossible owing to bang-
ing and shouting etc.'

It still only played for just over four minutes: Dylan had been
commissioned to write a half-hour script.

Then, with all the confidence in the world, and clutching a few
tattered pages of script, Dylan came into the studio, and in what
he called his cut-glass voice, spoke an Oxford nocturne which he
had written . . .

> Even Oxford goes to sleep
> the tired eyes of the mind go blind
> they pull the blinds down over the witty eyes . . .
> towers are tall funerals . . .

The orchestra played the Lutyens music. It fitted. It was magic.
After the briefest of rehearsals they recorded it. Then the
orchestra recorded the rest of the music, and went home. Dylan
recorded a funny Oxford poem . . .

> and the don's wife chaste as an icicle
> bicycling away like mad!

With head philosophically on one side, Reggie ruefully thanked
us all, and said that some of us might be called again to complete

the programme one day. Far from 30 minutes, there could not have been more than 10 or 12 in the can.

The following day, I played my small parts in 'Under the Dome' and then went home to Oxford. Not very long after I received a note from Reggie saying that he urgently wanted from me 350 words describing the centre of Oxford from the top of a high building. I duly obliged.

Then one day came a telegram asking if I could be in London the next day 'for re-make of Oxford programme'. I could, and was. I expected to find half the cast there. But there was only Reggie and an actor called André, who read a long poem by Dylan called, as the programme too was called, 'Packet for Princeton'.

There was still no script! We improvised it: I never heard the finished programme, and indeed never asked if it got finished. It seemed one of those delicate matters not mentioned unless they arose naturally in conversation. This one never did.

I had another encounter with Dylan of a very different order. I went for an audition with a man who was producing programmes of a high academic standard for Overseas. In the studios at 200 Oxford Street, he listened patiently to my choice of verse, Wordsworth and Edith Sitwell amongst it. Then he emerged and said that it was 'all right'. He would give me a job when he could, and did I realize I had a habit of introducing an intrusive 'T' into my diction occasionally? I was quietly horrified at this, but in the kindest possible way he drew my attention to phrases in my chosen poems where the fault had occurred. I'd been saying ontce for once, and making no distinction between, for example, presents and presence. I set about curing the fault immediately, so that there would be no trace of it if I were given a job. It seems there wasn't. For I was employed by that kindliest but most forthright of producers. His name was John Arlott.

I have since worked with John over a 20-year period in a series of programmes called *Guilty Party*; but it won't be until he reads these words, which I hope he will, that he will know how grateful I am to him for one of the most memorable days of my life.

It was spent at 200 Oxford Street, recording under John's direction, a half-hour programme on the poetry of Sidney Keyes and Alun Lewis, written by R.N. Currey. The Alun Lewis was read by Dylan Thomas; the Sidney Keyes by Norman Painting.

We met in the splendid restaurant, reputedly the best in the whole of the BBC. John had just come back from a week in France. Ever the gourmet, he was suffering from the effects of the unwontedly rich food and wine. With a sideways look, he said that in desperation he'd had to send his secretary out for some kaolin. Dylan was curious to know what that was for. Without circumlocution John explained that it was a desperate remedy for violent diarrhoea.

The secretary met us in the basement studio with the kaolin, and John poured some into a BBC regulation tumbler, adding water and stirring it with a pencil. Then he drained the cream-coloured stodge, and we began our rehearsal. R.N. Currey sat at one microphone in the corner of the studio; Dylan and I faced each other across a mike at a centre table. His teeth were broken and stained; stained too, with nicotine, were his tiny fingers, smaller even than mine ('What a little hand for a farmer!' a blind listener said to me, years later). But as Dylan spoke the poetry, that splen-did organ voice rumbled up from somewhere under the rumpled sports coat, and beating time he conducted himself like an orchestra, to keep the rhythm, with his stubby yellow fingers clutching a cigarette. John had very few production points to give him. I received and deserved, and greedily gobbled up, all the pro-duction points necessary. For John was a poet, too, and I knew a professional when I saw one. Eventually, though, I seemed to be reading the poems satisfactorily, and we recorded the programme without difficulty.

I'm sure there was a convivial lunchtime – there was venison I remember, as it was the first time I ate it, though many other details have gone from my memory. I'm now almost equally cer-tain that there would be a convivial evening after the recording, though that too has evaporated in the mists of time. What I do remember, and shall never forget, is something that happened half an hour or so after the day's rehearsals began.

In a pause, Dylan looked down and saw on the studio table below the microphone, the red pencil with which John had stirred his kaolin mixture. The kaolin had set like a thick encrustation of plaster around the pencil.

'My God!' cried Dylan. 'Is that what it's doing to your insides? I must try it!'

And he did. A generous quantity of the powder was mixed with water in another studio tumbler, and with those wide eyes even wider Dylan drank off the brew like a marvelling schoolboy savouring newfound wonders. I remembered the story of Keats peppering his tongue so that the claret could soothe it.

The kaolin appeared to have no discernible effect upon Dylan, and the incident took place without emphasis or exhibitionism.

But I saw in it a glimpse of the true poet following his nature, enquiring and experiencing, in spite of the heavy masquerade of the beer-swilling, rabble-rousing roisterer in which he so often indulged; and which after that day seemed to me more and more to be a spectacular and defensive shell that was too often mistaken for the real man, and the real poet, underneath it.

CHAPTER 5

Out and about: local colour

I was by now broadcasting frequently, mainly from London, and it soon seemed that as earning my living as a don slowly lost its appeal, so my career as a free-lance writer and broadcaster burgeoned of its own accord.

It was at this time that Denis Morris, the Head of Programmes at BBC Midland Region, and his Assistant Head, David Gretton (another beneficiary under the Auden–MacNeice 'Will'!) began to woo me with offers of a job on the staff at Birmingham as a writer–producer. I was not at all sure that this was what I wanted. I was enjoying my taste of a free-lance's life; I liked living close to Oxford; and I felt that I had several major plays inside me that I was anxious to get written.

I still have a copy of the letter in which I declined the offer of a permanent post on the established staff of the BBC in Birmingham. Rather cockily, I said that the security which it offered me was not something I then needed, and that no doubt it would be felt at Midland Region that I was 'young enough or foolish enough' to decline the offer of it. I think I was right. Just as I had grown to realize that I was temperamentally unsuited to the life of a don, so too would I not have blossomed at a desk job in the BBC.

Confirmation of this came with the Corporation's next gambit. I was offered a series of three-monthly contracts as writer–director and general programmes assistant, based in Birmingham. I could scarcely refuse: I would be tied for only a very limited time, and the experience of seeing how the BBC worked from the inside would be invaluable.

Perhaps it would help if at this point I recapped 'the story so far', as so many of the events in the last three chapters overlap each other:

My first professional broadcast was during my last year at Birmingham University, as were my first archaeological digs.

The auditions and the broadcasts with Douglas Cleverdon and Dylan Thomas and Robert Farquharson came during my Oxford years and immediately after.

The American tour took place in the summer of 1950, after my first departure from Oxford, and after various offers of work on the staff at BBC Birmingham.

The first year of the fifties was a decisive one for me. In May I played Philip for the first time in the trial run of *The Archers*. July to September were spent in the States. September to November saw me completing my first individual series of broadcast talks called *Night Shift*.

On 15 November I narrated a programme on colonial rule called, 'Through the Gates of Zanzibar', produced live by Peter Hardiman Scott before he went on to grander things in London. I left the next day for Marseilles, where I went on board the tiny merchant ship, *Le Cérons* (954 tons), and visited Sidi-bou-Said, Carthage, Sousse, Sfax and Tunis. I flew to Palermo, went by ship to Naples, and eventually arrived back in Birmingham (via Capri, Sorrento, Rapallo, San Remo, Marseilles and Paris) on Friday 15 December to record six programmes: one called 'Announcing the Archers', and then the first five episodes of the series.

I was beginning to enjoy the life of a free-lance writer and performer. I could afford the upkeep of my cottage near Oxford, and life was divided between travelling to London or Birmingham (sometimes farther afield, too) and being back at my home, writing. I was satisfied by this pattern, as I was not only writing BBC programmes to order, and often presenting them on the air or acting in them myself, but I had ample time in between to 'write your masterpieces' as Jack May put it. (I certainly completed a long verse play called *The Man in Red*, of which the only two existing copies have disappeared.)

Free-lances take whatever work comes along, if they feel it is within their scope, and is sufficiently rewarding (financially and otherwise). At this point I was offered the part of Philip in *The Archers* for three months, and as it seemed new and interesting and would take only two and a half days a week, I readily accepted. The reluctance came later: it was a reluctance not of beginning, but of continuing, once the noose began to tighten. . .

In the year or so since I had come down from Oxford, my life had been full of variety.

The three-month contracts as general programmes assistant had given me a chance to write and produce talks and dramatic features. I had then spent an enjoyable spell with David Martin and Peter Cairns in Recorded Programmes, where I learnt the technique of interviewing and editing – sometimes I would produce and introduce reports of a topical or documentary nature for news programmes.

Much of what I did was by its nature ephemeral, though I was startled not long ago to hear on my car radio Steve Race mention my name and then play an interview I had recorded many years before. It was with the Misses Dodgson of Leamington Spa, who were, I think, great-nieces of Charles Ludwig Dodgson, a some-time don at my own college, Christ Church, Oxford, who is known to the world as Lewis Carroll. I little thought that so apparently slight a conversation would find its way into the BBC sound archives.

I have an uneasy feeling that a report I did over the 1949–50 Christmas season may also be preserved for posterity. It was an account of an Oxfordshire village mummers' play, and my uneasiness comes from the fact that, although I concealed my nervousness in my speech, it betrayed itself in a mispronunciation: I said tungs for tongs, if I remember.

My first attempt at a recorded report is not, I am glad to say, preserved for posterity. Mobile recording, in those days before tape (or even wire) recorders, was done on four-minute discs. Incidentally, the engineer in charge on many occasions was S. Unwin, or Stan, now known as the cult figure 'Professor' Stanley Unwin. As he drove the recording car, there would often be a flow of his 'double-talk', which was as hilarious then as it is now. He was a master of the dead-pan face. He once stopped the huge Humber, as we crawled through market-day crowds in Lichfield, and asked solemnly of an astonished housewife: 'Excuse me: is this the way to Aberdeen?'

One of the skills I had to learn was to shape an interview or report so that it would last about three and a half minutes; and it was only practice that gave one this facility.

The first report I recorded for news (as opposed to a straight talk) was the crowning of the May Queen at Flore in North-amptonshire, on May Day, 1951.

The village schoolchildren had gathered thousands of wild and cottage-garden flowers with which they had made garlands and had decorated carts, a throne, and in fact nearly everything in sight. The crown itself was made of flowers. I found a position on the wall of the school playground, standing above the crowds, and cut one disc setting the scene, and chatting to one or two bystanders. I then gave Stan the chance to set up a new disc, while we waited for the 'royal' procession of the May Queen and her attendants to arrive on the dais where the crown sat waiting almost ominously. As the procession neared the dais, I gave a 10-second cue, and began to describe the scene in my best Wynford Vaughan Thomas manner . . .

'And now, in their white dresses and carrying posies of spring flowers, the procession of children reaches the dais where the May Queen's throne awaits . . .'

All the mums and big brothers and sisters were standing by for the moment of truth with their box Brownie cameras. I'm sure we all expected the Queen to stand for a few seconds before sitting on the throne, awaiting the actual moment of crowning. So, as she approached and turned, I began to describe in detail her dress and those of her attendants.

Meanwhile, in a flash, the village schoolteacher who had trained the children and arranged the whole event, shoved her onto the throne, jammed the crown on her head, and turned with the melon-like grin of One Who Has Done Well towards the crowd.

My training had always been to tell the truth, whatever it was. So, not thinking as quickly as I hope I would now do, I finished my descriptions without hurrying, gave a small pause (thinking that would help the editor) and then said in a Richard Dimbleby voice: 'And now the Queen has been crowned, and all her attendants are doing homage.'

It was quite useless. I had set the scene, built up to the Moment – and then there was no Moment! I should have stretched the truth slightly and, although the organizer had jumped the gun, gone on to say, 'And now, with great ceremony, the headmaster takes the crown of spring flowers, and holds it above the May Queen's head. Slowly . . . slowly, he lowers it . . . and the crowd applauds!'

Of course, the crowd wouldn't have applauded. Like me, they'd scarcely seen the moment of crowning. But I could quite easily have persuaded them to do a little clapping, and even a touch of cheering, which could have been superimposed later.

The News Editor, Ted Parkinson, the kindest of men, didn't exactly bawl me out; but he made it clear that I had plenty to learn.

For many years those four-minute discs provided a great part of broadcast output. The Ludwig Koch programme, 'Song of the Machines', already mentioned in Chapter 4, was such a case. So, too, were the early Charles Parker programmes. Not only did the technique require the sort of instant quick-thinking I have described, it made enormous demands on the skill of the programme editors. They could drop a needle on to a record in just the right place to pick up a given word or sound, and equally accurately fade out when the required extract had been made. In this way, sentences or paragraphs from a given interview or report could be lifted and assembled to make a continuous item, just as tape editing is done today, but far more cumbersome.

One of the most mystifying operations was called 'recording atmos'. This meant recording one full disc of nothing . . . an interior, say a church or someone's living-room, or an exterior, a field, a path near a river, and so on. The reason for this was that if two pieces of speech on disc were lifted as I've described, there was inevitably a gap between them, as if momentarily, the world had stopped, the birds ceased singing, the wind stopped blowing, the river ceased to flow. But with the disc of 'atmos', of 'nothing', of 'atmosphere', playing throughout in the background the joins of editing were inaudible.

The brilliance of the editor, though, was not very often allowed to over-ride the need for economy. (Charles Parker, on the other hand, would sometimes cut hundreds of discs for a one-hour programme. David Gretton once found him prostrated in the recording channel with something like 18 hours of recorded material, the day before a live first broadcast of one hour's duration! But Charles was the exception to most of the rules: many thought him, and still think him, a genius.)

Most of us were taught not to be prodigal with materials, not to rely too much on the editing. The first of a number of items I submitted, as a reporter, writer and producer, to that excellent series, *In Britain Now*, was a sound portrait of an itinerant lead-caster in East Anglia. His name was Gibson, and he would travel round from church to church, set up his crucible and his sand-bed, strip the lead from the church roof, melt it down, skim off impurities and then recast it in shining flat sheets on his sand-bed. Mr Gibson sounded exactly as he looked, and as he was: an East Anglian craftsman. I knew the item had possibilities, and so I thoroughly enjoyed myself, interviewing him as he worked, and describing each process as it happened.

Peter Cairns my mentor stood by, saying nothing, until duty forced him to break silence. He drew me to one side: 'How long is this item to last, chum?' he enquired, kindly.

'Six or seven minutes, I imagine,' I replied.

71

'Well, I just thought you ought to know: you've already recorded twenty-four and you're barely half-way through!'

It was also in East Anglia (Midland Region used to have a transmission area in Norfolk and Suffolk) that I recorded a highly successful item, and got reprimanded for it.

In Britain Now was produced from Bristol, and each of the regions contributed an item. For one edition it was decided to have 'islands' as a theme. This presented few problems to most of the regions, except London, which had no coastline, and the Midlands. London solved the problem by putting a commentator, Stewart MacPherson, on a traffic island; and the Midlands sent me to East Anglia to visit an island that wasn't always visible: the sand-bank, Scroby Sands.

Peter Cairns and I were also recording items for the weekly magazine, *Around and About*, and so we persuaded the Lowestoft lifeboat to let us go with them on an exercise – and the persuasion went so far as to include a trip very close to Scroby Sands. I interviewed lifeboat personnel, talked about the dangers of this treacherous sand-bank, and recorded the bell-buoy which warned navigation to keep clear. Any suggestion that I should land and record even a few seconds of commentary was deemed unthinkable, as far too dangerous.

The item was broadcast, and the following day it was much praised on the inter-regional hook-up (a kind of inquest where producers of the items in the previous night's edition would sit in studios in their own region and be linked by radio).

After the hook-up, though, I was called to the office of David Gretton, and told: 'Now this isn't a rocket. But you do have a tendency to promise more than you deliver. You didn't actually *land* on the island, nor did you fly over it, did you?'

I stammered that it was impossible for *anyone* to land, and that all my attempts to persuade the RAF to fly me as a passenger had failed. I learned to be very cautious after this; so much so, that I sometimes had difficulty in interesting producers in ideas I was putting forward, since I undersold them for fear of being accused of promising too much.

It should perhaps be recorded that from the same source came criticisms of *The Archers*, a few months after the programme began and became such an immediate success. Those who were responsible were told they had given the impression that they intended to produce a serious agricultural programme; but what was being transmitted was full of rustic comedy, from people like Walter Gabriel!

David Gretton was, in fact, extremely helpful to me in many ways. Over coffee in the canteen, we spoke very much the same language. It was only when he was behind his desk that he revealed himself as a direct descendant (in BBC terms) of Lord Reith. I never forgot one thing he told me, when I was discussing a contract with him. He said that his family solicitor had in fact vetted his own contract of employment with the BBC years before, and had said: 'This is a monstrous document. And you have no alternative but to sign it!'

There have been many occasions when those words have come to my mind, but I still love Auntie dearly.

David was a severe critic, but also a very generous appraiser. I once had to put an item together and get it on the air very quickly. The actuality recordings had been made some time before; but I had to edit them and write a script in a very short time. As David's office was only a few paces down the corridor, I popped in and asked if he could spare five minutes to listen to the item. Without hesitation he agreed; listened; approved, and to my utter amazement said: 'The actualities are good, and there's some distinguished writing in the commentary!'

Distinguished writing? To me it seemed routine and run of the mill. I could see nothing 'distinguished' about it. It seemed unbelievable; but he clearly meant it.

He often referred to my bounciness, 'Talking to you is like having a conversation with a galvanometer!' he once said. It took me some time to realize that my energy and garrulousness were often mistaken – not only by him – for over-confidence, when in fact they were blatant signs of unsureness and lack of confidence.

Another of the things I learned about myself in these prentice years was that I was fascinated by a difficult technique; but having learned it, I was all too eager to pass on to something else . . . trying to find out what I really wanted to do, I suppose. I shall return to this in Chapter 6 when talking about writing scripts for *Country Magazine*.

As I said to Edward Livesey at my first audition, I was keen to learn the whole business. I did just that, as a general programmes assistant. I gained an insight into such routine matters as programme budgets; booking artists; preparing copy for the 'billing' in *Radio Times*, often weeks before the transmission day; BBC office routine and practice; meetings; policy; protocol (much stricter 30-odd years ago than now); contracts and copyright; the use of quotations; the timing and duration of rehearsals, and their concomitant problems of fares for artists and overnight subsistence allowances; the booking of studios – and a thousand and one other things to which the ordinary listener, quite rightly, never gives a thought. I was meeting people at every level of society and travelling all over the country by public transport – when I didn't have the comparative luxury of going in the BBC recording car.

I met, and also worked with, several people of above average interest. I much enjoyed a series of programmes produced by Godfrey Baseley called *Midland Roads and Rivers*. We recorded them on location, and my part was to read the quotations, often ranging from the fourteenth century onwards. I especially remember programmes on the Avon, the Severn, the Teme and the Yare. They were written, and introduced at the microphone, by the novelist John Moore. His comparatively early death probably robbed the world of more books like his 'Brensham' novels, lively pictures of Cotswold life, and also more substantial works like *The Waters over the Earth*, a great novel dedicated to another colleague of the time, Paul Humphreys. For Paul, over a period of more than 20 years, I took part in a series of programmes of original verse, when one of my fellow-readers was, as often as possible, Mary Wimbush.

Whilst working in Recorded Programmes, I met someone who has remained a friend and colleague ever since: Phil Drabble. Oddly enough, the first – and very memorable – programme I recorded with him was deemed in parts unsuitable for broadcasting! We were doing a feature on ratting, and Phil with some of his Black Country friends, had earmarked several ricks and hen-runs on a farm where his marvellous old Staffordshire bull-terrier bitch, Rebel, and a little Jack Russell, could catch and kill the rats. As Phil Drabble has amusingly recorded elsewhere, it was on that occasion that I learnt to tuck my trouser turn-ups into my socks – rats will take any way out when threatened, and it's better that their escape-route is not up one's trouser leg! Although this was a genuine wild-life recording, the sound of the dogs' teeth crunching the bodies of the squealing rats was felt to be too gruesome to be broadcast in its entirety. It was curiously horrific.

Phil, in spite of his carefully cultivated country directness, was the highly respectable son of a doctor. He has, surprisingly enough, two things in common with Dylan Thomas: one is an ear for a telling phrase; and the other is a dislike for the middle-class milieu into which he was born. He likes to keep fairly quiet about the fact that he went to Oxford, to Keble College; although he's quite happy to say that he got sent down for spending more time at his glasses than at his classes. In fact, when I first met him, Phil was trying hard to convince the world that he wasn't at all intellectual: that the only knowledge he really valued was that of the poacher, or gypsy or anyone not quite respectable.

He always used to say that his pet hates were The Three P's – Parsons, Politicians and Policemen! Time has mellowed him, however, and he now regards the police in a more favourable light. I'm glad to say that there is one 'P' that has never been on his 'hate' list: P for Painting. Phil also has a very strong feeling for place; and that place is Staffordshire, on which he once wrote the standard book.

For some reason, he took to me the first time we met; and soon he and his wife Jess were among my friends. Once I had admitted, when staying with them (having only just realized it myself), that both my parents had been born in Staffordshire, then I just had to be All Right. (Phil believes you need a passport to go out of Staffordshire, though the fame he has found in recent years through his wonderfully authentic country books and his television appearances in *One Man and his Dog*, have made what he calls 'foreign travel' – i.e., travel outside Staffordshire – more and more essential.)

I remember how, on the phone, he was telling me of his doubts about the very first programmes in the *One Man and his Dog* series. Several programmes have, perforce, to be recorded and filmed in one day, and before the first day's filming, he was apprehensive. Having just begun to do television myself at the time, I understood his apprehension. But I knew one other thing, too – perhaps Phil himself did, which is why he was so apprehensive – and that was that a TV series is the surest way to becoming well-known. For a man committed as he now was to supporting himself and his wife and his marvellous wild-life sanctuary, his 'Beloved Wilderness', by his writing, a series of successful programmes was something he couldn't refuse. So it turned out. I've known Phil as a friend and colleague for over 30 years: it's only been since his telly series he's become, so very deservedly, a household name.

After those early broadcasts together in *Around and About*, we've worked in other radio series. One was produced by Paul Humphreys and was called *Sunday Out*. This was in the sixties, by which time I had become so well-known as Phil Archer that I was given chances of appearing in other radio programmes all too rarely. But Paul Humphreys, after an interval when *The Archers* started, having begun to engage me once more as a poetry-reader, had the idea of teaming me with Phil for one programme. It dealt with Quorn in Leicestershire. Two people – Phil and I – spent a day in and around the village; and then, partly scripted, partly in conversation with each other and with local characters, attempted to paint a sound-picture of the place. We hoped that we would make the place so attractive that listeners would choose it for their next 'Sunday out'.

I, as always, thoroughly enjoyed working with Phil; and at the end of the recording, he very kindly said to Paul: 'I like working with this fella. Why don't you ask us again?'

Paul said he would when he could.

When I thanked Phil for his kind words, he replied in his direct way: 'I meant 'em, mate. You don't pinch my material. Half the folk you work with pick your brains, listen to what you're saying, and then when it comes to the broadcast they steal all your best lines!'

Of course, part of the reason for our working well together was that not only did we have two genuinely different viewpoints, but two quite different voice qualities.

Paul eventually used us as a team in another series later in the sixties, called *A Grant of Land*, where Phil and I visited stately homes which had been in the same family for 400 years or so, in most cases without the owners being ennobled. These programmes were a delight to do: Paul was calm, urbane and genial; Phil was laconic, dry and never easily deceived; and although I was gradually learning when to chatter and get a laugh, I was also learning – more importantly – when to shut up!

It was while preparing the programme at Blithfield Hall in Staffordshire that I first stayed with Phil and Jess at Goat Lodge, which Phil had showed me so long before when it was, as its name suggests, nothing more than a goatkeeper's tiny cottage. The herd of Bagot goats on the Blithfield Estate had been famous for centuries, and Goat Lodge, as converted and extended by Phil and Jess, is one of the most delightful homes I know.

The great thing about Phil is his Staffordshire genuineness. He doesn't suffer fools at all, let alone gladly; but if he accepts you, then you have a loyal friend for life. When, many years hence, the time comes to add up all the good things that my broadcasting years have brought me, high on the list will be knowing Phil Drabble, and his good wife, Jess.

This year, the first of the fifties, saw me striking out as a freelance. I had satisfactorily worked through the series of three-month contracts, and had decided to risk going it alone – without a safety-net, as it were.

One of the reasons why it worked, and why, when the time came to devote most of my time to *The Archers*, I was so reluctant, was that I had several strings to my bow. As an ex-academic I could research and do off-beat interviews and reports – relatives of famous writers, discoveries of paintings by old masters, or manuscripts or sculptures, that sort of thing. I was a trained interviewer and reporter. I was, above all, a writer. Now that I was working full-time in broadcasting, I could appear in any radio production, dramatic or otherwise. And I did.

Quite consciously, I looked on this time as my apprenticeship. I was learning my craft. Most actors will tell you that, no matter how good their formal training, they learnt most from working with other actors, especially the masters of the craft. So it was with me. I seized every chance to work with, and study the work of, those who had found success at the microphone.

Gladys Young, for example, had become, during the war years and the years that followed, the undisputed First Lady of Radio; and from the late forties I regularly worked with her, until being in *The Archers* made my voice too well-known to be used for any other drama character but Phil. I then wrote parts for her in my radio plays. The splendid thing about her was a kind of deceptive ordinariness. Always neatly dressed, often beautifully tailored, in fact, she was small and neat and trim and totally unspectacular. As a person she was anything but flamboyant or showy. But as an actress! She understood the microphone perfectly, and used it, without apparent effort, to convince the listener that she was a waif-like girl of 15, or Catherine of Russia with all her foibles. Like Paul Scofield or Peter Sellers, she merely seemed to think the part and she became it.

She was one of the first performers to be invited to take part in Edward J. Mason and Tony Shryane's programmes called *Guilty Party*. A small cast would record a 'whodunnit'; and then (occasionally, months later) would be cross-examined by a panel of experts. It was all rather nerve-racking, although we were very well briefed by Ted Mason, who always stood behind the panel, nodding or shaking his head or helping with some expressive gesture or other. It really was very difficult, as one had to re-assume the character one had played and answer the team's questions accordingly.

The panel consisted of John Arlott, the journalist F.R. Buckley, and Bob Fabian (the real-life 'Fabian of the Yard'). After her first experience, Gladys roundly declared that she would never again accept an engagement in *Guilty Party*. It was much too frightening. But she did, and she reduced the somewhat fearsome panel of interrogators to helpless silence when, in reply to some such question as: 'Do you enjoy making nasty remarks about people?' She replied like a shot-gun, in character, 'No . . . Do YOU?'

As the series progressed, we all got to know the panel quite well. Indeed, I'd known John Arlott and F.R. Buckley for some time. But Bob Fabian, entertaining though he was in the bar, could still be fearsome when cross-examining. All those years of dealing with hardened criminals were certainly not wasted. Even he was reduced to helpless laughter, though, by a piece of repartee from Wilfrid Babbage, an actor with whom I must have appeared hundreds of times. He was playing a meek solicitor's clerk, and Bob Fabian, trying to throw him off his guard, suddenly shot at him a question, the answer to which not even Ted Mason had prepared, as it wasn't in fact material to the plot. The exchange went something like this:

> BOB   You say you're a solicitor's clerk?
> WILFRID   I am. Yes.
> BOB   You've worked with the firm for some years?
> WILFRID   Yes. I have.
> BOB   What's the name of the firm of solicitors?
> (*Gasp from Ted Mason.*)
> WILFRID   (*without a second's hesitation*) Wet, Hand and Tilt!

Collapse of panel, and temporary end of recording session! (For those not used to the liquid-soap dispensers, fitted in most BBC cloakrooms, 'Wet hand, and tilt' is the legend engraved on them!)

Wilfrid's voice was once known to millions of children as The Observer in *How Things Began* in Schools Programmes, as Piglet to Norman Shelley's Winnie-the-Pooh, and in Toy-town and countless other shows. I always look for him whenever I see a re-run of Noel Coward's film, *Brief Encounter*. In that moment when Celia Johnson panics, runs into a park, and sits on a bench, a friendly policeman comes along and asks, 'Is everything all right, ma'am?' That tiny part was played – most sensitively – by Wilfrid.

It would be tedious to list the names of all the actors with whom one spent so many hours in studios; but looking back, so many of them were 'characters'. Ernest Jay, who seemed such a *good* man without ever seeming 'pi'; Deryck Guyler, so very studious and serious and quiet – and so hilarious when the part called for comedy. And Stidders, Charles E. Stidwell, whose eye I tried not to catch if there were the least suspicion of a *double entendre*. He was a wonderful storyteller, too.

I still laugh when I recall his account of a broadcast which he and Wyndham Milligan had to do, live, for schools. They were supposed to be in a spaceship describing the various astral sights and sounds, and Stidders had to say, without a flicker, 'So if you hear a roar, you'll know I've passed an asteroid!' I can believe him when he says that Windy Milligan got through most of that live broadcast with a hanky stuffed into his mouth.

What can I say of dear old Norman Shelley, with whom I worked so often, and for whom I wrote on several occasions, long before he joined the cast of *The Archers*? I first wrote him in as Canon Meridew, before he created the part of Colonel Danby. He enjoyed singing; I liked playing; so we both had fun one day when the script called for him to sing 'Won't you Buy my Pretty Flowers?', accompanied by me at the piano.

Betty Hardy and Mary O'Farrell were not only unrivalled in their brilliance and versatility, they were such amusing and interesting people to be with. Can I be wrong in thinking that conversation in the BBC canteen then was wittier and livelier and less concerned with agents and overtime and contracts than it seems to be now?

In those heady pre-Ambridge days there were three exciting moments for me in any radio production. The first was receiving the contract (which often came out of the blue, not preceded by a phone call). Then came the script, which one would scan to see who else was in it. Then the broadcast itself, often live, usually after a mere day or two's rehearsal. It was an event, partly filled with adrenalin-stimulating fear, but mainly enriched by the delight of good company, enlivening talk and the deployment of professional skill of a very high order.

I was always delighted to see in any cast-list the name of Harry Lockwood West. He was so calm, so assured, so re-assuring. He seemed unrufflable; and, when rehearsals were over, he was the most beautiful listener I think I've ever known. I'm a talker. I know. It's often a fault. I've even learned to say: 'Am I boring you?' But I never asked Harry that. His face always seemed to reflect interestedness and encouragement. Of course, he is such an accomplished actor, I may have been wrong. I hope not.

An actor I worked with a great deal was James McKechnie. I admired his work enormously. He was the complete radio actor. His stage and film work never seemed to have the same impact, though he gave notable performances in films like *Scott of the Antarctic* and *The Life and Death of Colonel Blimp*. I more than once wrote leading parts for him, and he was never less than extremely good. When, in the early fifties, *The Archers* won a *Daily Mail* best programme award, it was a great pleasure to see that the award for best actor went to Jimmy.

I have already recounted my first meeting with Carleton Hobbs – known to us all as Hobbo. Even when I had changed roles from radio actor (apart from Phil Archer) to radio writer, I went on meeting Hobbo, and my only regret is that a projected meeting after a long interval towards the end of his life was not to be. He had written me a typically warm and generous letter when I was appointed OBE, very much a kind of 'Welcome to the club', suggesting that as he was spending some time in Pebble Mill, recording episodes of the TV series *The Brothers*, we might meet. I wrote back eagerly agreeing, and suggested a date which I knew would coincide with his schedule.

In due course, having finished my *Archers* recording session for the day, I went along to Studio A, only to find that far from having finished, they had only just begun, as they were running very late. Leaving a message saying that I had called, and would make another date as there would be dozens of future opportunities, I went happily on to my next appointment. Sadly, Hobbo died before we could meet.

I remember him as he was: always perfectly prepared, with every nuance of the script discovered, examined, considered, evaluated; doubtful pronunciations carefully checked beforehand. I can hear him now saying: 'It is pomm-granit, I think, not pommy-granit!'

His high standards always seemed to affect the rest of the cast: it was impossible to be slipshod or careless in his presence. He had a splendid sense of humour, too. For years, his greeting to me – to the mystification of strangers – was, 'Knocked up any good puddings recently?', referring to two unintentionally Rabelaisian recipes in the Ministry of Food's advice to busy housewives which I'd spotted in *Radio Times* years before.

Hobbo was among the best speakers of verse in his generation. He clearly understood every word in every line or, if not, he managed to convey the essential ambiguity of so much poetry; he never came between the poet and the listener; he respected but was never a slave to the rhythm of the verse; and he never put on a fancy-dress poetry voice.

I was present when the scriptwriters, planning a new character for *The Archers*, agreed that it would be superbly played by Hobbo. I, from long experience, knew what a joy to us all it would be to have him in the cast. But his failing health meant that it was not to be . . .

In the early days, I worked many times with Arthur Young. I felt that he was a stage and television actor by temperament more than a radio peformer, though he was in the top flight of all these media. We shared a sense of humour, and he played the lead in a radio biography I wrote about Sir Josiah Mason, founder of Mason College which eventually became Birmingham University. But I remember him most amusingly when we were playing together in a *Children's Hour* play called 'Pedro and the Donkey'. He played one of the leading parts; I played the other. I was Pedro!

Arthur was busy rehearsing for a television performance as Henry VIII in *Rose Without a Thorn*, and arrived in the studio complete with beard and a beret. At times, he would put on the beret, straddle his legs, and strut, trying to get the Henry VIII walk. All this, in between rehearsals, was amusing enough. But five o'clock came, and the red light winked, then became steady, and we were on the air. We both had a great deal to do. I had an opening scene without the donkey, and then went straight into a long scene with it. I half looked up to see where Arthur was, and saw him gently advancing towards the microphone, beard jutting, one eye squinnying, beret tilted rakishly, legs apart – the complete Henry VIII, visually, but uttering the first line in his lovable, friendly, donkey voice, 'Hello, little Master . . . Hello Pedro!'

It was not easy to continue, but we had to! Seeing the agonies I was suffering, to avoid outright guffaws, he whipped off the beret, resumed a more asinine posture, and the play continued. It had been a near thing. His widow, Beatrice Kane, later appeared in *The Archers*, as that fierce Mrs Travers Macy, Jennifer's first mother-in-law.

There were a number of leading radio performers of the period that I was not lucky enough to work with, or else I only encountered them briefly, people such as Laidman Browne, David Kossoff, Rita Vale or Lydia Sherwood – though Lydia later played in one of my scripts.

But I remember having lots of laughs working with Rupert Davies, long before he became Maigret, and Toke Townley, who usually seemed bewildered, many years before Emmerdale Farm; and I often acted with or wrote for Andrew Faulds, before he entered Parliament.

Someone I look back to with particular affection was Philip Wade. I'd known his work as actor and dramatist all my life, and for some reason expected him to be tall, boisterous and well-built. He was just the opposite: short, dry, with a twinkling eye and a wonderful way with an anecdote. I once travelled from Glasgow to London with him, Dorothy Reynolds and Stephen Jack. I was sitting with Dorothy some seats away from Philip, and I was soaking up her store of theatre stories and experiences – and, incidentally, her sound commonsense advice about the theatre as a career. For coffee, lunch and tea we joined Philip and Stephen, who were quite clearly getting more and more on each other's nerves as the journey progressed. As only actors, I think, can, they needled each other with sharper and sharper barbs until there was open, but highly comic, warfare. It was a fitting end to another incredible Reggie Smith extravaganza.

Reggie had produced for overseas a feature programme called 'Middle East' for which he had commissioned special incidental music. When the time came to broadcast it, the only staff orchestra available was in Scotland, so the whole cast were transported to Glasgow. I was researching at the British Museum Newspaper Library (as it then was) at Colindale, for a Third Programme feature on Disraeli, and so could not travel up with the main cast, but had to make the journey later.

'Book a sleeper', said Reggie, airily.

There were no sleepers. I sat up all night, wedged into a full carriage. When I reached the Beresford Hotel, Glasgow, and asked for my room – there was time for two hours, rest before rehearsal – the receptionist looked embarrassed. Apparently Mr Michael Bazalgette had been assumed to be Miss Michele Bazalgette, and had been assigned to share a room with Dorothy Reynolds. Even when that was sorted out, the complications weren't over. Philip Wade had moved out of the room he was asked to share because his room-mate snored so loudly. Philip could still hear the snores three floors down in the public lounge! Eventually, after much shuffling, I shared with Philip, who, producing a terrifying-looking atomiser as we prepared for bed, said, 'It's all right, lad. Don't worry. I've trouble with me lungs.'

The programme itself was far from easy. At one point it was found that there were no suitable records available for night-club music. I found myself playing 'Two Sleepy People', one of the few swingy tunes I could play from memory. It only occurred to me later how appropriate it was, as, owing to the confusion over rooms, there had been no chance for me to rest before the day's rehearsal and recording.

Working in this way with a wide variety of performers in every sort of production from verse-reading to revue, from documentary to drama, in many different studios in London and elsewhere, was the most valuable apprenticeship a would-be broadcaster could possibly have. And more than that, it was highly enjoyable.

CHAPTER 6

The desk: pen and ink sketches

There is one hat that I have worn most of my life – my writer's hat. All children make up plays, and act them out, and I was no exception. But unlike most, I began at a very early age to write them down. Having done that, I then set about acting in them, and directing them, thus setting a pattern that I have followed all my life. In other words, besides my writer's hat, I also wear an actor's hat, and a director's hat. Also, I have always made up tunes, so there is another, slightly smaller hat that I wear, my musical hat.

Very early in my career I accordingly joined the Society of Authors (still my favourite professional body) and then British Actors' Equity. I was at the inaugural meeting of the Writers' Guild and have been a member of that from then on; and finally, mainly in order to play piano and organ legally, as Phil in *The Archers*, I eventually joined the Musicians' Union.

I am, therefore, and have always been, that uncomfortable thing, a hybrid. Our highly organized computerized society is uneasy when faced with something or someone that does not fit into a neat, pre-calculated slot. For what it is worth, I have always paid my tax as 'Writer and broadcaster' or 'Author, actor, etc.' – which indicates the difficulties of classifying me and often surprises those who know me only for my performance as Phil Archer.

In the previous chapter I gave some account of my early experiences as a radio actor. Overlapping and interlocking with these, were my first scripts as a professional writer.

As I have said, though, I have been writing all my life. I have photographs of playacting with my Leamington neighbours, the Guests, in which there were witches, dwarfs and giants. I have kept since the late thirties the programme of a school concert in which my first play, *The Deception*, was put on. It owed a great deal to a radio play I had heard some time before.

At Nuneaton I wrote and produced, and played the piano

accompaniments for, pantomimes put on by the local church. An embarrassing headline in the local paper proudly declares; 'Boy showman writes panto – and plays the lead himself.'

It was scarcely surprising that, as already mentioned in Chapter 1, I should write, in collaboration, an original play, *Housewarming*, at university, not to mention a version of *The Women of Troy* in rather bleak, Eliotian blank verse. (Incidentally, I chose that style in an attempt to reflect the directness of Euripides, as opposed to the lyricism of Sophocles – some famous translations seemed to suggest that all Greek drama had the same style of verse. How I managed to find time to write the translation at all during the year when I was preparing for Finals is today a mystery to me.)

I wrote several scripts during my last months at Oxford; in particular, an account, mainly in contemporary verse and prose, of the death of King Charles the First, which was broadcast for the 300th anniversary of the event in January 1949.

In December of that year, two other programmes of mine were broadcast. One, called 'Summer Solstice', was a celebration of summer, narrated by me with my old friend Bernadette Hodgson, together with two other figures often seen in Broadcasting House, Birmingham, in those days: the angling writer, Alf Waterhouse, and the famous cricketer, Arthur Gilligan.

The other programme was called 'A Red Rose for the Washingtons'. I had been asked, as part of my duties as writer–producer, to write a programme about Sulgrave Manor, the ancestral home of George Washington. I took the title from a deed which specified that the rent should be a red rose each year. I took part myself, along with a small cast: the star part was the Narrator, and this I had written with James McKechnie in mind. As I was a staff member, I received no fee for my performance, merely my weekly wage-packet of something like nine pounds.

Because of its subject, the programme was taken by the North American Service of the BBC, and broadcast all over the USA. It was also repeated several times in the domestic service here in Britain. Some months later, when I was a free-lance, I met Jimmie McKechnie, who said he thought I must have made a fortune out of the programme if, like him, I kept getting repeat-performance cheques. When I explained that it represented one week's work for which I got one week's pay, he could scarcely believe it. The incident confirmed me in my view that, with all its risks, I preferred the free-lance life.

It was during 1949 that I began to write two series of documentary programmes. One was a radio equivalent of those small extracts one sees in some newspapers under the heading 'A hundred years ago today'. For this, I used to go to the public library of any town I happened to be visiting (my work tended to take me all round the Midlands at this time, preparing news-reports, documentaries, or researching programmes) and look up the old newspaper files. Then, with long extracts and a commentary, I could often compile a quite interesting programme. This series was called, *What They Thought*.

The other was called *Opposite Numbers*. It was a series of six, half-hour live programmes based on an idea of Edward Livesey, who produced them. The writer spent some time in a selected town, finding three pairs of people typical of the area, whose life and work was sharply contrasted: a refrigerator worker and a furnace-man, for example, or a miner and a steeplejack. At first another writer and I were given two programmes each: Ted had decided that whichever writer proved the better would then be given the other two. I am glad to say that I wrote four out of the six: on Derby, Wolverhampton, Norwich and Leicester.

The format of the programmes was very similar to that of the highly successful Sunday lunchtime series called *Country Magazine*. This was produced by Francis Dillon, introduced by Ralph Wightman, with folk-songs arranged by Francis Collinson. I had worked on several of these, trying to discover a way of writing a script which a real person, not an actor, could read with the greatest possible conviction – for the whole point of the series was that genuine, often unlettered, countryfolk had to appear as themselves, and somehow manage a script. It was undoubtedly a gimmick; and undoubtedly it worked. Many of the speakers were poor readers, hesitant, mis-pronouncing, awkward – sometimes, indeed, reduced to panic-stricken silence, in which case the fruity avuncular voice of Ralph Wightman would come to their rescue. But that, apparently, was part of the programme's appeal to listeners.

I was fascinated by the problems of writing such a script. Having found the people you felt would sound interesting, both vocally and from the point of view of character and what they had to say, the next step was to write something which would convey as much of that as possible. Tape recorders were not portable in those days and never used, and most people were inhibited if they saw you taking notes. One would therefore engage them in conversation, often in the village pub, and try to remember as much as possible of the exact words and phrases they used. What baffled me was that, even if I remembered whole passages of conversation (as I often did) and reproduced them word for word, the speakers would often stumble and splutter and, especially when reproducing their most telling phrase or proverb, sound stilted and unnatural. It is odd that many people cannot read their own words with the same conviction as when they first say them.

I soon discovered several tricks that worked, however. Above all, sentences had to be short, preferably without dependent clauses: plain simple statements. Attempts at vivid language were doomed, so had to be avoided. Yet, there was available a very rich and descriptive vocabulary, which nearly every country person I scripted used without the least hesitation: the language of the prayer-book and the Authorised Version of the Bible.

Having learnt the tricks, I quickly became used to the technique, and writing *Country Magazine* became proportionately less challenging. But its town equivalent, *Opposite Numbers*, was just as challenging. The prayer-book and the Authorised Version could not be so heavily relied on. The other elements still applied, though, especially the short simple sentence; for, as with *Country Magazine*, most of those taking part were completely new to the microphone. The idea worked surprisingly well; and a large share of the credit for that must go to the actor Ivan Samson, dear old Sammy, another much-loved colleague from those golden days of radio, who introduced the series.

Not quite all those taking part in *Opposite Numbers*, though, were strangers to radio. When I was in Leicester, looking for pairs of people, I noticed that there was a play on at one of the local theatres, starring a local boy called Richard Attenborough. Now this was too good a piece of luck to pass over, for his father, F.L. Attenborough, was Principal of Leicester University College. They would make an excellent pair of 'opposite numbers' if it could be arranged.

Mr Attenborough and his wife received me with great kindness at their home and, though not in the least anxious to appear on the wireless, he said that of course he would do so if I thought it would help his son's career. I could scarcely pretend that this was the case, as it was a modest little local series. But Mrs Attenborough said she felt he ought to take part, if Richard was happy about it.

I arranged to see Richard after one of the performances of the play. It was then, I think, called *Home of the Brave*, but was eventually retitled *The Way Back*. He agreed to have lunch with me on Friday 17 December 1948 at the Grand Hotel where I was staying. He asked me what I thought of the play; and, as my friends in

the theatre will confirm, I cannot do the 'darling, you were marvellous' thing. With the big-headedness of youth, I said what I
thought. Richard listened very attentively. He knew that the production wasn't yet right; but, on the tour before opening in
London, they were hoping to iron out its more obvious faults. I
don't know whether my comments were helpful or absurd; but I
hope that he took them for what they were: the frank and direct
comments of a non-hostile member of the audience.

We discussed the script of *Opposite Numbers* and what he'd
like to say in it, and up I went to my hotel room to write it. I also
had to write a script for his father. The theme I chose was photography, since Frederick Attenborough listed music and photography as his recreations in *Who's Who* and Richard was known
as a star on film.

The next day I went back to the Attenboroughs' delightful and
comfortable home – I remember pale green walls and long windows opening onto lawns, with Mrs Attenborough dispensing
tea. When I produced my first draft script for Mr Attenborough,
he quite fiercely said: 'Oh, I can't say that!'

My heart sank, and querulously I asked why. He replied that it
was too fancy.

I'd written a script which carefully paraphrased the things he'd
told me on my previous visit, and had written something like: 'I
have been keen on photography all my life, and I have photographed Richard from a baby. This no doubt is why he is so naturally photogenic.'

Tentatively, I asked what he would suggest.

Without hesitation he replied: 'Oh, something like this . . .
"I've been an amateur photographer all my life, and Richard grew
up seeing me with a camera in my hands. That's why he's always
ready at the drop of a hat to pose and posture in front of any camera you hold in front of him!" '

I replied that I wouldn't have dared to write anything so . . . I
nearly said 'defamatory'.

But Frederick Attenborough said: 'Ah, but then you're not his
father!' His wife laughed, the atmosphere relaxed; and we spent a
merry hour, in which all my careful, guarded words were translated into the sort of language a devoted but honest father would
say about his son. Needless to say, the script was very well received.

Richard's part in the programme had to be pre-recorded, as he
was playing elsewhere on the day of the live transmission. The following day, Sunday 20 December at four o'clock, when we recorded it, he and I fell into a conversation about Gilbert and

Left *Ken Tynan never understood why I allowed such an 'unflattering cartoon' of myself to be published. – I thought it quite amusing. 22 Oct. 1946*

Below *Among the several hundreds of congratulations on receiving the OBE, this cartoon with its Rolls Royce tractor by my cousin, Punch cartoonist Noel Ford, gave me greatest pleasure. Jan. 1976*

Left *The joys of my own family life have so far escaped me but I grew very close to my niece Diana and nephew Roy. About 1950*

Right *Reluctant even at 4 to be photographed with my sister*

Left *Checking my script minutes before my presidential address to the O.U. Archaeological Society. 1 Dec. 1947*

Right *A proud moment for me when Spot won first prize at a local dog show*

Below *Me as* The Speaker *in 'that Greek tunic with all those girls', as Larry Grayson put it in 1941*

Bottom *Looking every inch the man with the mike. 22 Aug. 1951*

An avid listener even at the age of 2. 28 May 1926

Cycling in the Cotswolds. 16 April 1947

My sister (front row, second left) and me (far left) aged 17, with the cast of one of my early pantomimes. Nuneaton, 1941

...neaton Councillor's Son to ...ct in London

Before Lord Mayor and City Corporation

("Tribune" Special)

Son of Councillor and Mrs. H. G. Painting, of "Avalon," Trinity Walk, Nuneaton, Mr. Norman G. Painting is, this week, appearing with considerable success in the Oxford University Dramatic Society's presentation of Thomas Dekker's "The Shoemaker's Holiday" at the Playhouse, Oxford. His mother journeyed to Oxford to see the play, yesterday (Thursday).

For amateur actors, even those with the tradition of the Oxford University Dramatic Society behind them "The Shoemaker's Holiday" is about as difficult a piece as they could choose, for the play has characters on which to res_ flagging invention and few me_ when the inexperienced ac_ feel, at any rate, his au_ carry him along.

Shoemaker as Lord M_

The production de_ full of matters for _ing, with a shoemaker_ then Lord Mayor_ downing tools _ masters an_ out trade u_ the world _ of all _ with re_ dr_ g_

John Schlesinger, who plays with some authority; Mis Couper, whose performa_ wife who cannot believe _ killed touches those _ which saves the pla_ only a romp; and _

For a student to "work his way" through a University is a common enough feature of young American life. The youth raises the money for his fees by working during the vacation as, say, a book-salesman and supports himself while at the University as a waiter in the dining-rooms.

One-time Library Assistant.

"I have heard, however, of only one person doing that sort of thing at a university in this country," says a writer in "The Sunday Mercury.—Norman George N. G. Painting—the chairman of the Dramatic Society of the University of Birmingham." "He is Mr. to almost everybody, _man Painting is the only son of Councillor and Mrs. H. G. Painting, of 2, Trinity Walk, Nuneaton.

"Leaving borough, at the age of 15, he managed to save enough money to pay school _ his fees by working for three years Library, and h_ contrives to get assistant at Nuneaton just sufficient cash to live on by doing general chores, including washing-up in the University's refectory and by acting as steward at the Overseas Club, a job which involves occasionally some coal-heaving."

Outstanding Personality.

"For pocket money as distinct from maintenance money," the writer adds, "he does a little broadcasting and lecturing. Blonde, slight and volatile, Mr. Painting is undoubtedly one of the outstanding personalities of Birmingham University."

Working Way T_ University

Nuneaton Young Man Making Good

("Tribune" Special.)

he who was respo _Dramatic Society's r_ _tion of Shakespea_ _Lear,'—a particularly_ _venture for amateurs; a_ _ing in the name-part wa_

Mr. N. G. Painting.

_with unusual enthusiasm by the critics. He is co-author of 'House Warning,' a satirical comedy of university hostel life, and at the moment is occupying his spare time with the writing of a victory pageant and preparations for the Dramatic Society's next production, Jonson's 'Alchemist.'

"An idiosyncrasy of his is a daily early morning swim. He boasts that during the whole of the time he has been at Birmingham University he has not missed a swim on any morning."

Making the front pages in the forties

V

Above left *The cast of David Raeburn's production of Dekker's* The Shoemaker's Holiday *at the Playhouse, Oxford in 1948. Including Professor Nevill Coghill, Geoffrey Johnson Smith, John Schlesinger, Jack May, Peter Hayworth, Robert Hardy and me (*front row, third left*)*

Left *University of Birmingham Guild of Undergraduates Council 1943– including Edward Downes (*front row, first left*)*

Above *Prof. R.J.C. Atkinson as I knew him at the Ashmolean Museum, Oxford*

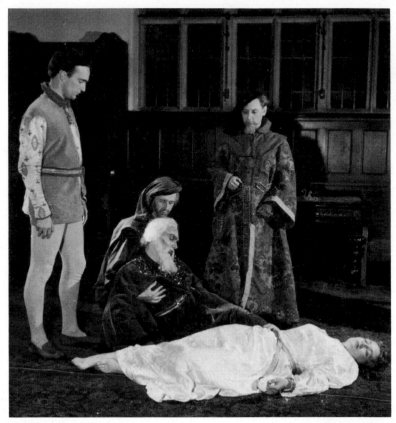

Sir Peter Parker (Lear) is comforted by Jack May (Kent) following the death of Shirley Williams, M.P. (Cordelia). Watched by Dickie Evans (left) and myself. O.U. Players, 1950

With Dame Vera Lynn (Don't Know Where, don't know when)

e Robert Hardy **Below** *Peter Parker*   **Above** *William Gaskill* **Below** *John Schlesinger*

THE BRITISH BROADCASTING CORPORATION

Head Office : Broadcasting House, London, W.1

Broadcasting House, 282 Broad Street, Birmingham 1

TELEPHONE & TELEGRAMS : MIDLAND 3761

RP/1/GB.

24th May, 1950.

Dear Norman,

    I would like to thank you for all the work you did to make the first recording of "The Archers" a success. The team spirit was excellent, I only hope the powers that be will be pleased, so that we shall all meet again on the job before long.

        Yours sincerely,

        (Godfrey Baseley)

Norman Painting Esq.,
The Old Library,
Fitwell,
Bicester,
OXFORD.

MV.

RELUCTANT ARCHER

Rec. No.: DOA.79302   BOOK OF VERSE 114
Duration:
(without anncts.)   SIDNEY KEYES AND ALUN LEWIS

Script by R. N. Currey

Produced by John Arlott

Transmission:
        EASTERN SERVICE: SATURDAY, 14th DECEMBER 1946: 1450-1520 GMT

Recording: Sunday, 1st December: 3.00-4.00 p.m.
Rehearsal: "   "   "   10.30 a.m.-3.00 p.m.
Studio: O.S.3.

ANNOUNCER: This is London Calling in the Eastern Service of the
'Live'   B.B.C.   We present this evening BOOK OF VERSE -
             Number 114.   These programmes. based in general on poems
             being studied at Universities in India, are produced by
             John Arlott.

             BOOK OF VERSE - Sidney Keyes and Alun Lewis -
             by R. N. Currey.

             MUSIC

READER: Young men, walking the open streets
             Of death's republic, remember your lovers.

             When you foresaw with vision prescient
             The planet pain rising across your sky
             We fused your sight in our soft burning beauty:
             We laid you down in meadows drunk with cowslips
             And led you in the ways of our bright city.
             Young men who wander death's vague meadows
             Remember your lovers who gave you more than flowers.

             When truth came prying like a surgeon's knife
             Among the delicate movements of the brain
             We called your spirit from its narrow den
             And kissed your courage back to meet the blade -
             Our anaesthetic beauty saved you then.
             Young men whose sickness death has cured at last
             Remember your lovers and covet their disease.

*Front page of my most treasured script for a poetry programme produced
by John Arlott in which the readers were Dylan Thomas and me*

Norman Painting, Gwen Berryman, Pamela Mant and Harry Oakes who play the parts of 'The Archers' in the popular B.B.C. Serial.

'The Archers' choose

Spire and White Queen shoes

The 'Archer' family all find shoes to suit them in the Spire and White Queen ranges. The men appreciate the sturdy build and fine leathers of the many Spire styles, whilst the ladies like White Queen for their clever combination of fashion and comfort. For the children there are 'Junior' shoes in each range.

See the wide range of

Shoes for the whole family

at your local stockists at prices to suit all

Spire	White Queen	Juniors
47/6 to 75/-	39/11 to 55/-	15/- to 42/-

G. T. WHITE SHOE CO. LTD. LEICESTER

This page *Despite the Charter, we were eventually allowed to promote various products*

"Here are "The Archers" with feeding stuffs packed in MEDWAY MULTI-WALLS

Above right *Oxford, Ohio. August 1950. (left to right) me, Anne Lever, Shirley Catlin, Jo Page and Bob Robinson*

Right *Merton College, Commemoration Ball, 1951. Our party included Bob Robinson, and Josee (his wife to be), Peggy Bacon and Ralph Hallett. I am with Pamela Mant, the original* Christine Archer

AUTHOR

Edward J. Mason

PRODUCER

Tony Shryane

AUTHOR

Geoffrey Webb

PHILIP ARCHER

Norman Painting

GRACE FAIRBROTHER

Ysanne Churchman

SIMON

Eddie Robinson

TOM FORREST

Bob Arnold

MR. FAIRBROTHER

Leslie Bowmar

The cast of The Archers, *early 1950s*

THE ARCHERS"

DAN ARCHER

Harry Oakes

DORIS ARCHER

Gwen Berryman

CHRISTINE ARCHER

Pamela Mant

WALTER GABRIEL

Robert Mawdesley

MRS. PERKINS

Pauline Seville

JACK ARCHER

Denis Folwell

PEGGY ARCHER

Thelma Rogers

LEN THOMAS

Arnold Peters

Above *Studio groups like these were fairly common: R.D. Smith's wife
Olivia Manning's version of George Eliot's* Mill on the Floss.
*(back row, left to right) Anne Johnson (Kezia), Norman Painting (Mr Moss),
Georgie Henschell (Narator), Nan Marriott-Watson (Mrs Clegg – the
original trial-run* Doris Archer), *Geoffrey Lewis (Mr Clegg), Mary
Wimbush (Mrs Moss), Chris Gittins (Mr Pullet), Courtney Hope (Mrs
Pullet), Dorothy Summers (Mrs Deane – more famous as ITMA's Mrs
Mopp), Denis Folwell (Mr Deane – later Jack Archer), Christina Wilson
(Effects), Mr. B. Boughton (Junior Programme Engineer), Mr T. Shryane
(Programme Engineer – later producer of* The Archers), *and Mr Lewis R.
Jennings (Secretary of the George Eliot Fellowship).*
*(centre row) Susan Richards (Mrs Tulliver), Felix Felton (Mr Tulliver, better
known as the Mayor of Toytown), Theo Bryan (Tom Jakin), and Mr William
Hughes (Producer).*
*(front row) Ann Chatterley (Maggie), Brian Roper (Tom), Esma Wilson
(Lucy Deane)*

Right *A memorable visit at which thousands of people lined the streets of
Shanklin, Isle of Wight, was made by Norman Painting (Phil) and Ysanne
Churchman (Grace) on 21 July 1955*

SHANKLIN WELCOMES the ARCHERS BY SHANKLIN Y.F.C.

PHIL & GRACE ARCHER

19 B.G. PARSON Cliff Farm, Shan

Above *Away from the microphone, we open garden fêtes; but Ambridge Fête has to be opened too. In June 1962 the opener was film star Richard Todd, here seen with* Jill Archer (Patricia Greene) *and* Phil Archer (Norman Painting). *The fête coincided with the 3,000th episode of the programme*

Right *With me, welcoming Princess Anne at the opening of Pebble Mill, are my old friends Jill Spencer and Tony Shryane*

Above *June Spencer (Peggy) and me with Gwen Berrymen at the gala evening to honour her as 'Midlander of the Year'. Behind us is John Dunkerley Controller, BBC's Midland Region, through many years of* The Archers

Right *A sentimental journey to the cloisters, Oxford. July 1982*

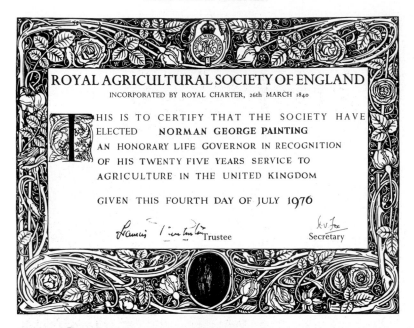

ROYAL AGRICULTURAL SOCIETY OF ENGLAND

INCORPORATED BY ROYAL CHARTER, 26th MARCH 1840

THIS IS TO CERTIFY THAT THE SOCIETY HAVE ELECTED **NORMAN GEORGE PAINTING** AN HONORARY LIFE GOVERNOR IN RECOGNITION OF HIS TWENTY FIVE YEARS SERVICE TO AGRICULTURE IN THE UNITED KINGDOM

GIVEN THIS FOURTH DAY OF JULY 1976

Trustee

Secretary

Popular Gardening

every Thursday
edited by
FRED WHITSEY

December 4, 1976

12p

PHIL ARCHER
(Norman Painting)
IN HIS
GARDEN

EVERGREEN
SHRUBS

COLD SPELLS AND
YOUR GREENHOUSE

WEEPING TREES

MORE VEGETABLES
FOR LESS WORK

Above left *A unique honour for a writer! . . .* **left** *and more than once I did get muck on my boots*

Above *Unlike* Philip, *Norman is keen on gardens, as was featured in* Popular Gardening *(reproduced by kind permission of* Popular Gardening *and IPC* Magazines, *photograph by Peter Salkeld)*

Overleaf *Few moments in life compete with this. Here I'm proudly showing the insignia of officer of the OBE, flanked on my right by John Milner Painting and on my left by my dearest friend, the artist, Joan Hassall*

Sullivan. *The Mikado* came up, and we disagreed about a line of one of the songs. Each was sure he was right: Richard said that he had in fact sung the part in a school production. A couple of weeks later I checked with a score. I was wrong. Richard was right, and I had to write a humble-pie letter. Our paths have never crossed again: I can't help feeling he must have found me no end of a big head, for more reasons than one.

I have one other recollection of that Leicester programme. It was broadcast live from the splendid Guildhall; and one of the contributors was blind. I had agreed that if he didn't mind waiting after the broadcast until our equipment had all been de-rigged, and the place put back in order, I would accompany him home. He readily agreed. We had struck up a friendship, for I had spent a certain amount of time with him and his wife improvising a script, as we had no facilities at the time for providing one in Braille. As an old soldier, St Dunstan trained, he had many good stories to tell, and he told them well.

Eventually everyone left the Guildhall, and the caretaker appeared to see the last two of us out, and to lock up.

'It's a pea-souper out there,' he said. 'You can't see your hand in front of your face.'

I was horrified. Then I heard my blind friend chuckling.

'Makes no difference to me, Norman,' he said. 'Don't you worry. I'll see you back to your hotel!'

So the roles were reversed. Outside, the fog was as thick as we had been told, but my companion, grabbing my arm, set off at a fast military pace. I was terrified. It seemed to me as if every minute we should bump into something. But on we went regardless, my companion giving a commentary. 'There's a passageway on the right. Feel it?'

'What do you mean, feel it?' I asked.

'Can't you feel the cooler air?'

I couldn't, but he could. He described every feature on the way back. Luckily his home was not far from where I was staying for I felt it my responsibility to see him home. It was only when I came to retrace my steps alone for the few hundred yards back to my hotel that I realized what courage my friend had shown, and was showing – every day of his life.

About this time, William Hughes, a genial man with whom I'd broadcast from the Birmingham studios regularly since my very first transmission, was appointed radio drama producer, and he offered me work, not only as actor, but as writer and researcher. Thanks to him, I spent many hours back in the Bodleian

Library in Oxford transcribing plays with a possible view to adapting them for radio. The only title I remember was a play with music called *The Coffee House*; but it never got put on.

A not very good play of mine, *The Man who Murdered Himself*, originally a three-act who-dunnit for the stage, was given an airing by Bill Hughes, adapted for radio and reduced to one hour's duration by me. I never heard it: the day it was broadcast I was halfway between Marseilles and Tunis being rather sea-sick, for this was between the American tour and the beginning of *The Archers*. That summer in the middle west had proved so exhausting, I adapted my stage play for radio, sold it to Bill, and with the proceeds went on my North African holiday, knowing that the first *Archer* recordings were on 15 December and the programme might last for as long as three months!

The beginning of *The Archers* on 2 January 1951 did not at first have any appreciable effect upon my writing career. In those early months before the programme became popular, it was very much just another job on a three-month contract, so I continued as actor, writer and researcher. When not writing on commission, I would begin one of my own plays – usually large-scale ambitious works for the theatre. The usual number of bookings as a radio performer continued to flow in, as my voice was not yet instantly recognized.

The Archers began its regular run in January: and in February I introduced and wrote the commentary for a programme called 'Willenhall Wakes', that was based on the Black Country reminiscences of Joseph Wilkes, a great character with whom I'd spent many hours during preceding months trying to elicit from him as many anecdotes and dialect phrases as possible. On the fourth of June that year, I wrote and introduced a programme celebrating the Jubilee of the Harper Adams Agricultural College, produced by Godfrey Baseley. I had had a fairly fierce disagreement with him over fees and conditions for *The Archers*, and his asking me to write this programme was, I am sure, a kind of olive branch.

When, in March 1951 I agreed to continue in *The Archers*, I knew that I would have to concentrate working more and more as a writer, and if possible a producer (in today's parlance a director), the more my voice became better known. I was still being cast for occasional performances in *Children's Hour*, but the new problem of being recognized quickly became a drawback. Acting in a period piece, I would say lines like: 'My name is Percy Bysshe

Shelley' and an unheard chorus of listeners would cry, 'Oh, no, it isn't, it's Philip Archer!'

Peggy Bacon, Midland Region's *Children's Hour* organizer, had commissioned a couple of talks about my American impressions, which I was able to give as myself; but she was also enormously encouraging by commissioning me to work for her as a writer.

My first effort for her was a 50-minute play in a series on stately homes and their history, called *The Walls Remember*. The play was 'Holdenby House', broadcast on 15 May 1951, and it was the longest and most ambitious piece that I had so far written specifically for radio.

Some 10 days later, on the night of Saturday/Sunday 26/27 May, I experienced one of those occasions which happen by accident and which one remembers for the rest of one's life.

Although I had yet to pass my driving test, I had acquired my first car, an ancient Ford Tudor. As I was unable to drive it, my friend Jack May frequently obliged. We collected David William from Oxford for a weekend at my cottage in Fritwell, and on the Sunday evening went over to Welford-on-Avon, where a mutual friend, Ralph Hallett, rented a tiny but exquisite thatched cottage. He was one of the two members of our American tour whom I did *not* try to dissuade from an acting career in the theatre. (David had thoughts of an academic career at the time, I think; or at least had greater leanings towards direction rather than acting.) The other was Jack. Ralph had given a performance as Cornwall in *Lear* which had grown in stature as the tour progressed; and now, after some radio and stage work, he was in the company at Stratford-on-Avon. His parties were already becoming famous, not because they were noisy or orgiastic or in any way outrageous; but rather because of the quality of the food, the wine and the interesting people who attended them. The stars of the company had all been present, even though Ralph was a junior member, playing small parts.

Of the first half of the evening I recall nothing: all I remember is that from midnight until an hour or so before dawn, Jack, David and I were locked in passionate argument with Richard Burton, who was that season playing Prince Hal. We were so absorbed in our talk that the hours fled like minutes. I had up till then not been in any sense an admirer of the young Richard Burton. At Oxford, his student performances were still talked about in my time (he left Oxford three years before I went up), especially his Angelo in *Measure for Measure*. I had, early in 1951, seen *The Lady's not for Burning* twice, carefully studying his performance; and quite frankly could not see what all the fuss was about. Although he had that mysterious thing 'stage presence', he seemed to be just standing there and doing nothing.

I had felt the same about his performance as Prince Hal later the same year. But talking to the actor was a revelation. We argued the night away, discussing almost every line he had to say; and though we ended by agreeing to differ, what emerged was that his performance was deeply felt and deeply thought out. It appeared casual, almost off-hand, to some of us: my impression was that he was so afraid of being too 'hammy' that he underplayed. Most actors agree that judging how much to give is far from easy: only a narrow line divides over-acting from under-acting, and experience is usually the best teacher. Richard himself tells the story of his first encounter on the film set with Elizabeth Taylor. She appeared to be doing nothing. When they viewed the 'rushes' together, her performance was telling, delicate and eloquent: his struck him as too big, broad and exaggerated. He has since given many great performances in the theatre, as well as in films; but sometimes, when seeing film performances of his which the critics have not enjoyed, I sometimes fancy I see that same problem of fine judgment as to how much to give that we discussed that night in 1951.

Richard and his family were living at Ettington, a village near Stratford, then; and as Jack, David and I rattled home in my ancient car, Richard and other friends whose names and faces I forget, overtook us. In a voice that could have been heard at the back of the Albert Hall, he bellowed, cupping his hands, 'No rear light!', as the car he was in roared ahead of us.

That wasn't the only thing wrong with that old car of mine. Much of it was held together with wire; the battery-charger frequently failed; and few of the dials on the dash gave a true picture of speed or fuel or even mileage. I needn't say that this was long before MOT tests were introduced.

It had been a fascinating evening; and indeed we continued the discussion in the car, as the May dawn lightened the misty Warwickshire countryside. (There may even have been a fourth member present: if so, and if he or she reads these words, I apologize for the omission.) We were still in full flood as we approached Sun Rising Hill: one of us didn't agree with Burton's basic reading of the character; one of us defended it; my view was that his performance in the theatre was so controlled and at times statuesque that I'd been amazed to discover how much thought and research he had in fact put into it, and how little came over . . . Then, suddenly, the car died; the engine stopped; and, miles from anywhere, we slid to a halt. We had run out of petrol. Jack had managed to steer into the side of the road. I can remember groaning drowsily, and declaring that I was going to sleep, and that, I think, is what I did. But we must have got home somehow.

I remember Jack driving me to London not long after that – I didn't pass my driving test until 22 September. As we struggled up the hills near High Wycombe, the car engine began to make odd noises. We crawled into town, Jack dropped me at Culross Street where I was staying, and drove slowly but very noisily away to wherever it was he was staying, saying he 'feared the car needed attention'. I telephoned him next day, and in those Baroque tones of his, in what I call his Demise of the Monarch voice, he said: 'Painting, I have grave news!'

Somebody I thought, somebody near and dear has suddenly died. But no.

'It is what are called "big ends",' Jack continued, in the same retreat-from-Moscow tones. 'And they have gone.'

I asked where they had gone, and what were they, and what was he talking about? And how much?

'It will cost about fifty pounds, I fear!'

This was about a quarter of what I'd paid for the car not long before; but, as I was to learn with later second-hand cars, there are some repairs – most in fact – which are not optional but essential. So of course I paid up.

Living as I did in the country between Oxford and Banbury, working alternately in London and Birmingham, I knew that once I had learnt to drive, a car would be very convenient. Yet in those pre-Beeching times, the train service was still very useful, even though one did sometimes feel that there was a framework round one's life made of train departures. It was also essential to have regular places to stay both in Birmingham and London. I was always glad to get back to the country, though; and it was there that I did most of my writing.

We were now in 'Festival of Britain' year, the year which it was hoped would set pulses racing a little faster, and lift up spirits that had been flagging in the immediate post-war years. As a young man, with everything before me, my spirits were in need of no such boost. I wanted to write, and here I was writing: indeed, I was being paid to write. I loved acting, and I was being paid to act. I was even, occasionally, being paid to direct as well. My first three-month contract to play Phil in *The Archers* had been extended indefinitely (but with one month's notice of termination) and the programme seemed to be on its way. I was not yet so fully taken up with all the additional activities that were soon to go with being in a highly popular daily serial (photo calls, charity work, appearing at official functions and so on) that there wasn't time to write non-commercial pieces that I felt important. I was working steadily on the verse-play *The Man in Red,* which I have already mentioned in Chapter 5, on Cardinal Wolsey, the original founder of my college at Oxford. The final manuscript, now lost, would have played I calculated before I could set about slimming it down, for some four hours. But the great thing was, unlike so many subsequent projects, it really did get written and was not squeezed out of my life by other commitments.

And other commitments did begin to arrive: I was delighted to be asked to research, write and produce a programme which was broadcast on 25 September 1951. It was called 'Show a Leg', a light-hearted enquiry into the history of the stocking, and what went into it, written and produced by Norman Painting.

Then Peggy Bacon commissioned the first of a series of plays on the lives of the saints. They were 50 or 55 minuters, and the series began to be broadcast early in 1952. Over the next few years, at irregular intervals, they became an accepted part of occasional Sunday broadcasting. I wrote some 13 of them, and 4 were repeated in the sixties.

Peggy's early training had not been in drama, and she never claimed to be a great creative radio drama director. But she made no secret of the fact that she engaged the best professionals she could afford, used the best qualified technical staff, and then largely left them to get on with it.

So many of these early scripts of mine had first-class casts, with people like James McKechnie, Marjorie Westbury, Mary Wimbush, Peter Coke, Deryck Guyler, Kenneth Connor, Alan Wheatley, Jack May, Mary O'Farrell and many others. Eventually two volumes of the plays appeared in book form, edited by Father Michael Day of the Birmingham Oratory, with whom I also wrote a novelized life of St Antony of Padua called *The Man who Found Himself.* This was translated into German and French, was sold in America, as were the first two volumes of *Stories of the Saints,* and eventually appeared in a second German edition on the other side of the Iron Curtain.

As *The Archers* continued, I had less and less time, or indeed energy, for writing; and I was, as I had expected, employed less and less as an actor. When Douglas Cleverdon revived his version of *Zuleika Dobson*, it was unthinkable that I should again play Noakes: the voice of Philip Archer would have robbed the part of all credibility.

Towards the end of 1952 a new studio manager joined the Corporation and was set to provide both recorded and 'spot' effects for *The Archers*. ('Spot' effects are noises such as cups and saucers, doors closing and so on, which are actually done on cue in the studio and not from recordings.)

Not all those who are, even today, called upon to provide these effects in the studio, with the actors, seem to be aware of their importance. A mistimed clatter of knife and fork on plate, for example, can be very irritating, even distracting, to a radio actor; and some young engineers, though gifted in other ways, never seem to learn the art. Usually their stay with *The Archers* is for a limited period; and the cast as a whole usually sees the departure of such individuals as a benefit. But the young man who joined us in 1952 quickly endeared himself to the team by his quiet conscientiousness and, even more important, by his dramatic sense. Like all good studio managers, the actors felt that he was acting along with us, too. He is now, hardly surprisingly, among the most distinguished of sound radio directors. His name is Graham Gauld.

Gwen Berryman (Doris Archer) and I quickly became friends with Graham: we three shared both a sense of humour and, although it can only seem pompous to say so, an unspoken sense of dedication to *The Archers*.

Inevitably, Graham's abilities were recognized, and he was soon promoted to be Peggy Bacon's assistant in *Children's Hour*. There were, it was said, mumblings and grumblings among other young engineers when they heard of his rapid promotion. But as Harold Casey, one of the pillars of the Midlands administrational staff was heard to say: 'Gauld is fully certificated'. By this he meant that Graham had trained at the Royal Academy of Dramatic Art, and so was fitted, after his experience of studio work, for promotion to director.

Whilst Peggy, though an extremely convivial person, tended towards the more serious themes in music and drama for older children, Graham's interests at the time were of a lighter nature for younger listeners. His later work has moved towards more serious drama, and he has been especially associated with Dames Sybil Thorndike and Flora Robson, and most recently has won acclaim for his direction of the series of adaptations of Anthony Powell's *Dance to the Music of Time*.

Graham began by producing magazine programmes, and then graduated to light entertainment programmes with music. Then, in response to a comment that was looking out for new ideas in this field, I suggested a series of programmes called *The Incredible Adventures of Simple Simon*. The idea was well received when he offered it to his superiors, and so I began to write yet another series of programmes. Each one involved Simple Simon, played by the veteran of Savoy Hill days, the comedian and writer, Leonard Henry, in a series of complicated encounters with a wide range of comic characters from nursery rhyme, fairy tale and the imagination of Philip Bentinck. And who, it may be asked, was Philip Bentinck? He was a pen-name for Norman Painting: as *Simple Simon* and *Stories of the Saints* were running at the same time, however irregularly, it was felt advisable that one series should be under a pseudonym.

Leonard Henry became a great friend of mine, and many hilarious sessions were enjoyed at The Savage Club, working on the scripts. The programmes were live, with an orchestra, and contained several songs – not to mention a signature tune composed by guess who? Norman Painting.

The *Simple Simon* programmes were so popular that eventually (from Christmas 1956) a full-length Simple Simon pantomime was put on each Christmas for some years. The Boy Showman was growing up, but had returned to his original form as panto-librettist.

Life was becoming extremely busy; and then, one day in 1953, I received a letter from another old friend, who had been with me on the American tour, Peter Dews. 'You won't believe this,' he wrote, 'but the BBC have taken leave of their senses and appointed me as a kind of side-kick to Bill Hughes.'

So began the brilliant career of director Peter Dews. He was writing to me asking for advice as to where to stay in Birmingham. I introduced him to the famous Mrs Tooth in Augustus Road, where he lived for many a merry month. Peter's letter had ended with the sentiment that he looked forward to seeing me again and to working with me.

I remember writing back and saying that he would find there was now opposition in Birmingham to employing members of the cast of *The Archers* in other radio drama or features, unless they normally used an assumed voice (like Walter Gabriel, for example). We were just too easily recognizable. But I hoped to work for him as a writer.

Good as his word, Peter – once he had found his feet in radio drama – commissioned me to write some scripts for him. I especially enjoyed contributing to a series on the history of old inns called *At the Sign of. . .* The scripts I wrote about The Whittington Inn near Stourbridge, which I made a ghost story, and The Three Crowns Lichfield, where every line spoken by Dr Samuel Johnson, the leading part, was from Boswell's *Life*, were among the best things I had done up to this time.

I had by now moved to a single-storey cottage on a farm at Wormleighton, and while Peter was staying with me on one occasion, I happened to mention that I had written a three-act comedy for the stage, *Rest you Merry*, as well as my four-hour verse-drama on Wolsey. Peter read them both. He later telephoned me and said he'd 'been a bit naughty' in showing the comedy to David Gretton, even though I'd firmly said that I did not want it to be considered for broadcasting. I was beginning to feel that the time was long overdue for my first stage play to appear.

Peter was very flattering and persuasive; and I finally agreed to let him put on *Rest you Merry*, so long as the *Radio Times* billing, and the closing and opening announcements could say, 'adapted for radio by the author from his stage play'. Peter readily agreed; the result was I was paid at a lower rate than I would have been if I'd kept quiet about it being a stage play in origin! One lives and learns. Gladys Young and Mary Wimbush headed a good cast, which also included Ivan Samson, Ronald Baddiley, Hugh Manning and Rosalind Boxall; and it was found to be satisfactorily amusing.

It is not always easy to assess the success or otherwise of a radio play, unlike one in the theatre. If the management asks for more, then one must assume that the work is successful. The cast and director can be enthusiastic, of course; the Programme Heads can send pleasant memos; there can even be appreciative letters from listeners; but there is no radio equivalent of the 'long run'. At least, not for the play, unless it happens to be a serial. But even if the play doesn't have a long run, the writer can! I suppose I may claim to have had, in fact to be still having, a long run.

I did have one failure, and this was for someone whose talent, especially latterly in television, I have much admired: Philip Donnellan. I first knew him as an announcer at Birmingham, and had both written and acted for him on occasion. Then he sent me a script which had already been attempted and partially researched by someone else. I, not entirely happily, took it over, and never managed to get it off the ground. To my shame it was rewritten by the producer in a couple of days. This had never happened to me before, and has never happened since, apart from one occasion where, by mutual agreement, Ted Mason reworked a story in *The Archers* concerning the famous Nelson Gabriel mail-van robbery: Ted was a far more expert crime-writer than I was.

These small hiccups apart, I have been writing to BBC commissions for the whole of my working life.

William Hughes continued to ask for several adaptations for radio from me: among them *Mountain Air* and *My Lady of Cleves* both in the mid-fifties, when all the time I was pursuing my other life as actor in *The Archers*. Grace could die and Tom Forrest could be arrested for manslaughter; but once the episodes were recorded, I was back at the typewriter, or in the library, writing or researching my next script, or reading some novel or other for possible adaptation.

Graham Gauld had suggested that a series of programmes about the seven wonders of the ancient world might be of interest to *Children's Hour*, and I was asked to look into the possibilities. I came back with an idea for a serial play of seven episodes, in which a little Egyptian boy travelled the ancient world, trying to visit the famous wonders, ending up at Bethlehem in time for the Nativity. The proposal was accepted, I was commissioned, and a highly popular serial play was the result. With *Children's Hour* programmes one did have some notion of what the listeners thought, as there was an opportunity for them to ask to hear their favourites again. The serial was not only voted into Request Week, it was repeated in its entirety, once called 'The travels of Toto' and again under the title 'The Boy and the Wonders'.

Some years later, I followed this up with another seven-part serial set in modern times, but dealing with the seven wonders of the mediaeval world. It was called 'Tomorrow is a Stranger', and it, too, seemed to go down well. Both of these serials had excellent casts and production.

By the end of the fifties, television was taking all the limelight, and Peter Dews enhanced his reputation as radio producer by becoming a brilliant television director. Feeling that the market for radio scripts might well dwindle, I attended a three-month course in London on writing for television, given by the British Screenwriters' Association. Most of my efforts now went into writing television scripts. (I also found myself an agent, who spoke highly of my work; but not one of my scripts was accepted.)

Not that this was one of my most productive spells as a writer. My work both in, and connected indirectly with, *The Archers* was now at its most demanding. There were photo calls and public appearances; books and records; and increasing requests for interviews and charity work. I had by now moved to London, where, it must be admitted, I found it more difficult to write than I did in the country—at least, it was more difficult to concoct the more imaginative and original pieces. I found I was able to settle more easily to more routine technical matters such as adaptations, though.

It was in connexion with radio adaptations that I first encountered one of the most stimulating, brilliant and completely professional people I have ever worked with: Anthony Cornish. Many actors and writers agree that he is, quite simply, the greatest. Working with him is both highly enjoyable, and enormously taxing. One's abilities are tested to the full, but the results are almost always satisfying. I have yet to meet an actor or a writer whose eyes do not sparkle with delight at the thought of working for Tony.

He is now known the world over as an outstanding director for radio, television and stage. I first met him when he asked me into his office and offered me the chance of adapting for radio in seven parts a novel by John Buchan called *Midwinter*. My scripts seemed to be satisfactory, and soon Tony was directing my seven-part adaptation of another novel by Buchan called *The Blanket of the Dark*, in which the leading part was played by an excellent actor, then much under-rated – but not by Tony – called Alan Devereux, better known to millions as Sid Perks in *The Archers*.

Then my old friend Ysanne Churchman suggested that I should do an adaptation of one of her favourite novels, *The Little Girls*, by Elizabeth Bowen. Tony Cornish was consulted and was at once enthusiastic. (One of Tony's qualities is that by asking one to do rather difficult things he indicates his belief in your ability to do them.)

In his usual encouraging way, Tony accepted the first draft of my adaptation with barely an alteration, and we recorded it in London with a first-rate cast: Mary O'Farrell, Mary Wimbush and Ysanne Churchman, with Ralph Truman, Grizelda Hervey and others, and it promised to be a memorable production. Sadly, though, Mary O'Farrell, consummate artist as she still was, was closer than any of us thought to the end of her days. She had been plagued for many years with bronchitis. I remember how, during *To-morrow is a Stranger*, for which I'd written her a leading part, she had been confined to bed in her Birmingham hotel, and how the doctor sent by the BBC was overwhelmed at meeting her: he'd been a fan of hers since he was a youth. He'd seen her, a young Irish rose, in her first star part as Peg in *Peg o' my Heart* at the Globe Theatre with A.E. Matthews. Mary wryly described the scene later: a tired old actress ill in bed and an adoring ageing doctor meeting at last a heart-throb from his past. Mary had worked less and less in the theatre and, although she starred in television plays in the immediate post-war years, had made radio her life.

She was enormously versatile: she was hilarious as the somewhat macho Dame Hilda Tablet in Henry Reed's incomparable radio plays, and she could play with equal conviction an ethereal nymph. Indeed, for this production she was required to play the same character as a formidable and mature woman, and as a little girl. Alas, the bronchitis asserted itself. The mature woman was acceptable: but the normally clear limpid little bell of a voice was fogged and clouded. Tony completed the recordings; but they were never used. Mary died shortly after. The play might in theory have been a memorial to her; the sad fact was, though, that vocally she could not do herself justice.

I had the enormous fun of working with her, writing for her, and talking to her, for 20 years or so. I remember how I signalled to her during rehearsals for *Zuleika Dobson* that I had saved a chair for her next to mine. She sadly shook her head and sat elsewhere. I was mystified, and began to think things about best friends not telling me. At the first opportunity she explained, in a very few very precise words: if she'd come over and sat with me, on her other side would have been her worst enemy. This was the first I had heard of the famous feud between Mary and Vivienne Chatterton, which lasted for years; but, unbelievably, ended in friendship.

Out of many conversations and much wisdom from Mary, I remember her views about reading verse – at which she was unrivalled. She said that in the few moments before she actually spoke the first word of any poem she suffered agonies of nervous apprehension, even after a lifetime of doing it. (That in itself was something to remember: performing does not become easier as one becomes more experienced.) Mary was not speaking merely of pre-performance nerves, but of something far more rudimentary. Unlike singing, where the key is set by the accompaniment, the pitch of the words is vital. It is not merely the vocal pitch, though, that is important: but the tone, the volume, the pace, the speed (which is not the same thing) and the rhythm. Start off right, and you can hang the rest of the poem on it: put your first foot wrong, and the whole reading falls away. Years later I know that that is wisdom.

Tony Cornish was not the man to allow what he knew was a good script to remain unperformed. And so, some years later, he re-recorded it with a different cast, and it was broadcast on Radio

Three. It was very well received. *The Times* gave it a long appraising review; and in *The Listener* for 1 May 1969, Donald
McWhinnie devoted half his 'Radio' review to it:

> Adaptations of novels in any medium are liable to disap-
> point if you know the original. So much has to be left out: all
> those digressions and parentheses which seem so irrelevant
> yet give form and substance to the whole; the masses of
> descriptive prose; and, most vital, the author's own reflec-
> tions and comments. Radio is probably the ideal medium in
> which to do some justice to the literary novel, but even in
> radio it is by no means easy to deal with a work as tenuous
> and delicate as Elizabeth Bowen's *The Little Girls*. I'm glad
> to say that Norman Painting's version was almost wholly
> pleasing . . . The whole thing could have been quite ruin-
> ously cheapened by a less imaginative and understanding
> adapter. But Mr Painting and his highly sympathetic pro-
> ducer, Anthony Cornish, saw how easily it could come
> apart in their hands and made sure that it wouldn't. Apart
> from occasional overemphasis of echoing voices and under-
> emphasis of time and place, I couldn't fault it . . .

Mr McWhinnie then went on to praise the thing in detail mentioning in particular the performances from the new cast, especially Ruth Dunning, Joan Matheson, Penelope Shaw, Ralph
Truman, Douglas Storm and Liane Aukin.

Here, at last, I had found a director who was not blinded by my
appearances as a soap-opera actor or writer of pieces for children
to the fact that I was more at home in Radio Three than anywhere
else. Tony urged me to offer more scripts. So, too, did the new
programme Head at Birmingham, Alan Rees, who quite specifically invited me to submit more ideas. *The Little Girls* was very
highly thought of, he said, 'whereas, these scripts you're doing for
The Archers, good as they are, won't advance your career as a
writer'.

This, too, was wisdom. And I was foolish enough not to heed it.
I had been writing scripts for *The Archers* since 1966. I shall
return to this question in a later chapter (9). All I want to say here
is that I had never wanted to write for *The Archers* until I actually
did so – even in this I was a reluctant Archer! Then I found that
the technical difficulties were so fascinating, and the restraints on
the writer's expressions of deeply-held convictions so few, that it
was, in those days, an extremely satisfying art form to work in. I
remember trying to explain this to Tony, who replied that what I
said might be true, but it was a kind of self-indulgence that would

not get me taken seriously as a writer – or as he put it, won't get your name in the reference books.

At the party for *The Archers'* 21st year, Alan Rees again begged me to write more literary material. He knew that it was where my real interests lay; and predicted that the day would come when people would say: 'Painting? Norman Painting? Yes, I think I know the name. Didn't he write a few good scripts for *The Archers* once?' 'And you've got a lot more inside you than that, chum.'

So why did I continue? In two words, money and loyalty. The money in itself was not at a high rate; but as then there were only two or three scriptwriters, there was a good income to be earned, because of the sheer number of scripts one wrote. It is difficult to talk about loyalty; but the fact remains that by now, having, in spite of myself, devoted so much time to *The Archers*, and gained so much from it, I knew it would be churlish and indeed ungrateful not to write when the health of my fellow-scriptwriter was causing serious concern. Today when it has become possible for anyone who can persuade the Editor that they can write five episodes, to be commissioned to do so, it is hard to imagine the conditions that applied in the first 25 years of the programme.

There was then an aura of mystery around the programme, and the writing and editing were hermetic and occult. Only the few initiates were permitted to the sacred mysteries. This produced continuity and homogeneity, but it did seem to wear out scriptwriters. Geoffrey Webb and John Keir Cross had died, and Edward J. Mason was in rapidly failing health. The Keepers of the Seal, as it were, were Godfrey Baseley, the prime mover, Tony Shryane, the producer, and myself. The new BBC policy for radio, as outlined in *Broadcasting in the Seventies*, predictably, changed all that.

I had been a busy and productive writer throughout my whole working life. For a greater part of that time I had been an acting member of *The Archers*. There was no real reason why I should not continue to be a busy and productive writer, in other fields.

So, encouraged by Tony Cornish, I continued to write radio adaptations whenever I could fit them into an increasingly busy schedule. There is an enormous amount of work involved in adapting a novel into five hours of radio, which I did, for example, with John Masters's *Far, far the Mountain Peak*. In those days I seemed to spend most of my life sitting at the typewriter. That particular novel was far from easy to adapt, as a great part of the final episode takes place on the face of a high mountain. I wrote that episode first, to convince myself that the mixture of realism and abstract radio which I had in my mind, could work. Directed by Tony Cornish, with a brilliant performance from Robin Ellis, backed by Elgar's 'Crown of India' suite, it succeeded memorably.

My adaptation of the same author's *Venus of Konpara* – a lesser novel in my view – was less successful as a Saturday Night Theatre presentation.

It was a sad day for me when Tony Cornish left the BBC for wider fields in theatre and television here and abroad. I, rightly or wrongly, allowed all my writing effort to go into scripts for *The Archers*, writing around the time of Ted Mason's final illness, as many as 170 in a year, and on occasion, 30 scripts in 30 days, without, I must insist, any lowering of standards, as the listening figures indicated. There may seem little of the reluctant Archer about this if it is not remembered that my reluctance came from the continuous and relentless recording schedule and accompanying personal appearances as Phil Archer. This I found draining and exhausting; my writing, even my writing as Bruno Milna was satisfying and rewarding in a quite different way.

Soon, by the mid-seventies, I was writing almost nothing but scripts for *The Archers*, though, as the next chapter records, I was beginning to write for and appear on television in a modest way, and I was increasingly writing articles for magazines.

Then, in January 1975, my old friend Phil Drabble rang me up and said that his new publishers were looking for someone to write the history of *The Archers* ' . . .and I told 'em, mate, "there's only one bugger who's literate and that's Norman Painting"!' However unjust that may have been to my colleagues, it was in fact a typical act of generosity on Phil's part.

I have in my possession a letter from a BBC spokesman in Birmingham saying categorically that the BBC could not allow me to write such a book – even though my agent had negotiated a contract between the BBC and the publisher. But the contract was re-negotiated, and so, having lost a valuable month, I set about writing *Forever Ambridge*. Within a few weeks of its appearance, it was in the bestseller lists; and five years later, in time for our 30th birthday, I brought out a revised enlarged edition. Since then, having written some 1200 scripts for *The Archers*, I have been resting from the task I performed over fifteen years as 'Bruno Milna'.

One of the pleasures of recent years has been to write once more for Tony Cornish on Capital Radio, which has broadcast two series of mine. One was on London saints; and the other, called *Bowen's Blitz*, was a linked dramatization of seven of Elizabeth Bowen's short stories set during the London blitz.

I have had more than one motive in writing this long survey of my work to date as a writer. It is by no means complete, and does not pretend to mention every script, article, play or prose work I have written. It must surely demonstrate, though, that when close friends in critical mood try to stir me to write what they call 'better things', they are at fault when they say that I've only done one thing for most of my professional life: *The Archers*.

My life, so far – and I like to think that I am barely at the middle of the professional part of it – has been extremely busy and enjoyable. Two whole areas of activity have so far been untouched: music and television. Perhaps they should be painted into this portrait next . . .

CHAPTER 7

The keyboard: tones and undertones

There has always been music in my life. My whole family and relatives on both sides have all been musical. My only and much-loved niece is a graduate in music and is married to the composer Peter Anthony Monk. I really ought to have been born, like Gwen Berryman and Benjamin Britten, on St Cecilia's day.

One of my earliest recollections is of playing with a toy gramophone: it was silver and had green and red elves and goblins chasing each other round it. The records were tiny, three or four inches across; and one of the tunes I remember was 'I waander, I wander, I waaaaaander . . . I waaander how I look when I'm asleep', which of course I learnt parrot-fashion.

There were other gramophones, too. Wind-up ones. Before I could read I astonished the family by being able to say what each record was by the colour of the label, the shape of the printed title and other signs. There was 'Yes, we have no Bananas!', 'All by Yourself in the Moonlight', 'He Played his Ukelele as the Ship went Down', 'Casey's Court', 'Bells across the Meadows – with bell effects', and 'Songs my Mother Taught me'. There was also a record of Caruso singing 'Vesti la giubba' from *Pagliacci*. An enterprising, but ignorant schoolboy, I swapped that nasty old scratchy thing during a 'special offer' at our local record shop for a nice new record of some Scottish tenor singing 'My ain Folk' which none of us ever liked.

When my father announced that he was going to buy our first loudspeaker-type wireless, I remember producing all sorts of schoolboy arguments as to why a gramophone was better – 'you can hear what you like, when you like!' It had to be one or the other, not both, in those difficult years of the thirties.

There were, in any case, the headphones and crystal set, which I'd been listening to since I was born. When a babe in arms, I'd been taken to visit a sick aunt, who died in her early twenties, in a London hospital, and delighted her, I'm told, by my unrestrained chuckles of delight when her bedside headphones were put on my head. I have photographs taken a little later when the look of concentration on my face suggests that I was listening to the news in Hindustani or the fat stock report.

Another aunt, Margaret, always known as Auntie Maggie, made family history by broadcasting in *Children's Hour*. She was frail and tiny, but had an enormous and sweet high soprano voice. She had taken singing lessons, and ever after half the audience at local concerts would whisper confidingly to each other that 'of course it's a *trained* voice'. Hearing this, I used to imagine all sorts of physiological stretchings and strainings, rather like the Spanish Inquisition, which Auntie Maggie had endured in order to be able to sing like that.

But if she was the only 'trained' singer in the family, she was not the only one of my relations who sang. They all sang. My mother, who was one of 12 children, kept her splendid, but totally untrained voice, until she was 80. All her brothers and sisters and her parents sang, sometimes in two- three- or four-part harmony; sometimes, alas, in that unbuttoned zealous manner known to the unsympathetic as a 'Methodist shout'.

My father's eldest brother, my real Uncle Tom (as opposed to my famous Uncle Tom Forrest) always insisted, and argued with his sister to her dying day, that his mother was Welsh – 'That's why we can all sing!' Auntie Elsie said she'd never heard her mother say she was Welsh. But she did die comparatively young, of a broken heart it was said, when four of her five sons volunteered for the forces in August 1914. Whether I had a Welsh grandmother or not, all my father's seven brothers and sisters could, and did sing, in choirs and at musical evenings.

Musical evenings were still quite usual until the mid-thirties, when the wireless began to dominate social life. Then they began to fade away when high standards of performance were heard daily in nearly every home. There had to be a piano, of course; and at least one person to play it. In our case there was also a violin. Following her maternal grandfather, my sister had, without noticeable enthusiasm, mastered the basic technique, but suffered agonies I remember with mysteries that sounded horrific to my young ears called harmonics and seventh position. My father made a half-hearted attempt, when he inherited his father's concertina, to learn that instrument; but, largely because of a punctured bellows (in the concertina), it came to nothing. My father painted a vivid picture of my grandfather playing hymns, and swinging the concertina round so that the sound seemed to swell and fade.

The main part of the musical evenings was 'songs round the piano'; and at first I was always in another room with the rest of the under-12s, only appearing, after what seemed an eternity of caterwauling, with the refreshments. The songs that were favoured were ballads. I can see the large-paper white-covered music now – I still possess quantities of it – with names like Clifton Bingham, Theo. Bonheur, May H. Brahe, H. Trotère, Albert W. Ketêlby, Haydn Wood, Eric Coates, Edward Lockton, Edward Teschemascher, P.J. O'Reilly, Wilfrid Sanderson, Hermann Lohr, Guy d'Hardelot and many more. There was an enormous repertoire of such songs available.

At first we did not have a piano; but then, returning home from an eight-week stay in the local isolation hospital after scarlet fever, I saw it: highly polished, challenging and, in the end, heartbreaking.

Nearby lived a widowed shoemaker, with a daughter who gave piano lessons on a very old wooden-framed upright piano. My enormous keenness to learn evaporated in a mist of basic misunderstanding and indulgent but inept teaching. I confused the two clefs with the system of fingering, which was the English not the Continental method, of a cross for the thumb and 1, 2, 3, 4 for the other four fingers. If I saw a cross I put my thumb on middle C. If I saw a 2 I put my middle finger on E. Within three or four weeks, I was totally confused and reduced to tears both by my teacher, who was the mildest of little ladies, so mild in fact that she was almost a non-event, and by my mother, who could not read music herself, but couldn't understand why I was making such heavy weather of things.

The lessons cost sixpence (2½p.) an hour; and, as I was making no progress, such large sums could not be wasted and I faced the ignominy of having failed. Yet there were few things I wanted more than to play the piano, to be the centre of the musical evenings on Sundays, to accompany my sister's violin and my mother's solos or her duets with my father.

Then my sister found a boyfriend in one of the families with whom we shared the rota of musical evenings. He played the piano extremely well, although he was barely 15. And it was he who sorted out my confusion and for over a year taught me the rudiments. Looking back, it was clear that he must have been a born teacher – he is now a free-church minister! Within a few months I could play a whole range of simple pieces, together with a large selection of hymns and various simplified extracts from 'the classics', mainly to be found in the *Golden Treasury for Young Players*.

But my schoolboy teacher was unable to continue helping me: his mother had died, and he was faced with what we now call 'O'-levels. So for a time I went it alone. I enjoyed playing through my repertoire, even though it never grew any bigger.

Then one day I was playing, on a vast grand piano in rented accommodation occupied by family friends, an arrangement of the 'Miserere' and 'Romance' from Verdi's *Il Trovatore* and other extracts, when I heard an Austrian voice saying to my parents: 'Thet poy hass ebilitee . . . I vud laik thet poy!'

Inevitably, after the pleasantries, my parents had to say: 'How much?'

When they were told two shillings (10p.) an hour, the whole deal was off. Eventually, though, after some negotiation, it was agreed that I should have lessons of half-hour duration at one shilling (5p.) per lesson.

So once a week Mr Hillmann came to the house. I was terrified of him. His thick Austrian accent frightened me, and everything else about him. I could not play a simple scale, let alone play it legato, as he wanted it.

'Dornt chump, poy, dornt chump!' But I did 'jump', both with lack of technique and plain fear.

The piano was in the best or 'front' room of the early Victorian house where I was born; and that room was heated only once a week, on Sundays, High Days and Holidays. My lessons were on Wednesdays. In winter it was very cold; and if I became too exasperating, my teacher would knock my hands from the keyboard, exhorting me not to 'chump'. The room was cold, my hands were cold, his manner was cold – and it hurt a bit (but not as much as I made out) when my fingers caught the raised edge of the piano stool.

Mr Hillmann was, I am sure, a very good musician; but he believed in old-fashioned iron strictness. He had been taught keyboard at the console of the organ of Vienna Cathedral by a master who was armed with a cane. He was locked in, so there was no escape, and the cane would come swishing down on his fingers every time he played a wrong note. Such a background did not predispose him to be soft and indulgent with me. Of course he was right in what he was trying to do. All my parents had wanted was to hear me playing hymns and 'little pieces'. In the previous months with my sister's boyfriend as teacher, I had gratifyingly quickly learnt to do so. But I had learnt no formal technique, and very little theory. I couldn't play a simple scale in C major. Mr Hillmann was merely trying to take me apart and re-assemble me as a pianist on sound principles. How much I might have learnt from him in later years when I was not so easily scared! But at the age of 10 or so, I was terrified. The lessons were nightmares, and loomed up each week like ordeals by fire (or during the winter, ordeals by freezing). For the only time in my life I truanted – usually disappearing next door to seek refuge with the Guest family, who of course had no idea I was a fugitive. They had in their house, ironically enough, a superb upright Bechstein which later I frequently played.

Always, as a child, anaemic, I began to worry and lose weight, until my parents finally asked why. I then remember saying: 'If you'll stop him coming to the house, I'll teach myself the piano!'

This was clearly an empty claim; but my terror (of someone who was, I am sure, an admirable if temperamental teacher) persuaded my parents to agree. We struck a bargain. If I could teach myself to play the most difficult piece I then knew, which was L. Ascher's 'The Robin's Return', a great favourite on musical evenings, then I should be given a shilling. More than that I would be deemed to have vindicated myself.

This was the sort of challenge I could never resist. In quite a short time the shilling was presented, with acclaim, and I began to accompany the family and to qualify for membership of the adult half of the musical evenings – and even to an occasional sip of a certain Mrs Gardner's home-made orange or parsnip wine, when the evenings took place at her home.

When we moved to Nuneaton I was involved in the local 'tin tabernacle', a thriving Methodist church. Inevitably, I was called on to play the 'organ' – a harmonium or a reed organ – and when I wrote and produced pantomimes for my contemporaries (I was now 15 or so), I usually played the musical accompaniments, until I promoted myself to playing the lead.

By now I was enjoying playing the piano: from the age of 12 until today it has always been one of the pleasures of life to me. When alone (which is often) I play and sing: if as a writer I have a problem of plot or character, I will rattle through sonatas of Beethoven, Mozart, Clementi or Telemann while my subconscious finds, as it usually does, solutions.

At the University of Birmingham, egged on by one of my close friends, Neville Hill (who won his doctorate and then sadly died far too young), I joined the university choir. I cannot pretend that I was, as most of my colleagues seemed to be, exilerated by singing the bass line of Bach and Handel. I did, of course, join the music society, and still remember with the liveliest pleasure lunchtime concerts, given with an engaging informality by John Waterhouse and Nina Pearson, which fired my enthusiasm for two-piano music.

Following a conversation with Edward Downes about my consciousness of lack of piano technique, he very kindly gave me one or two invaluable lessons: I have only to hear the Presto movement from Beethoven's Sonata, op. 10, no.2 to be transported to that dark little music room in the now demolished Edmund Street buildings of Birmingham University. Ted's strictures on how an apparently simple little movement should be played impressed me so much and were so revelatory, that I remember them still.

Having been allowed to proceed to the Degree Course after my preliminary intermediate year, a very tempting possibility arose: to be allowed to read music as one of my subsidiary subjects. Of course I would have to convince the Professor, Victor Hely-Hutchinson that I had the necessary background (which I clearly hadn't). All I had was an intense love for music, of all sorts; and a growing knowledge of the normal concert repertoire.

I could remember vividly the humiliation I felt when at King Edward's Grammar School, Nuneaton, the maths master (not the music master) had suddenly said to the fifth form, 'Hands up anyone who can tell me the name of a classical symphony.' Not a hand went up. I racked my brains: I could think of pieces by Bach and Handel and Beethoven and Schumann and Scarlatti and Grieg and Tschaikowsky – but, crazily enough, the name of a symphony – 'Pathetique', 'Pastoral', 'London' – just would not come. I had even, not long before, played in an arrangement of the Minuet from a Haydn Symphony in Queen's Hall, London; but my mind went a blank. Then came the scathing comments: 'You barbarians, you uncivilized louts,' etc. all the easy abuse of a schoolmaster who knew he was in the right.

I had, in the intervening years, through radio, gramophone and occasional concert-going, remedied that – though throughout my Birmingham University years I could not afford to go to the City of Birmingham Symphony Orchestra concerts in the town hall just across the road. Instead, I would listen to the half of the concert that was normally broadcast and then meet my friends in Pattisons, Kunzles, the Union or University Club or The White Horse, to discuss the music. Among my closest friends at this time, both in lectures, tutorials and concert-going was Dr Nigel

110

Fortune, a musicologist recently much occupied with the new edition of the musician's bible, *Grove's Dictionary of Music and Musicians.*

It would clearly be highly desirable to study music as a subsidiary subject; so Ted Downes briefed me on how to convince the professor. After informal chat in his room, I was told, he would indicate a piece of music open on his piano. He would then invite me to play it. I was to read through the piece very carefully, noting tempo, key, repeats, accidentals, modulations, and not to be in too much of a hurry to play it, a common mistake. Secondly, I was not to be put off by the fact that I would hear the professor, sitting at his desk behind me, apparently reading the newspaper rather noisily, as if to show no great interest – this was a regular ploy. Ted must also have briefed me on the interview part, too, though after so many years I cannot remember it.

The day came. I went in. Victor Hely-Hutchinson sat there, too human and lively a man to appear as dauntingly professorial as I think he would have liked. We exchanged pleasantries: he asked about my general musical interests and training; and, as predicted, he indicated the music on the piano and invited me to play it.

Ever the actor, I looked a little nonplussed and unprepared, and then sat down at the instrument. Just as Ted had predicted, the newspaper was noisily opened behind me. I read the music. It was in E major, in six-eight, 'allegro ma non troppo' and looked pretty uneventful to me. So I read on, just in case there were any sneaky key-changes or other hazards. The newspaper twitched. I still read on. Then the newspaper gave a great irritated flurry. I looked over my shoulder.

'Everything all right?' enquired the professor querously in his high musician's voice (why do musicians so often have cracked unmusical voices?).

I blandly replied that I was sorry for the delay, but I always believed in reading the music through carefully before playing it. (Pompous ham!) But realizing that I had gone just a touch over the top I sailed into my rendition. I've always been a good sight-reader, and from an early age learned to fudge the bits I couldn't play. To my delight I was accepted.

Offering music at subsidiary level was not quite, as I'd expected, like being paid to eat strawberries. My knowledge of 'strict' harmony and counterpoint was minimal; formal analysis was a mystery to me – but somehow I kept my head above water. I enjoyed two-piano playing in the practice-rooms of the Barber

Institute of Fine Arts, where the Music Department was established. And in the concert hall the following year (when Victor Hely-Hutchinson had been succeeded by Professor Jack Westrup), we had visits from some very great artists. In particular, I remember Benjamin Britten and Peter Pears, Jascha Heifetz, James Blades (in a Bartok and Stravinsky programme) and Gerald Moore.

I was sad to see Victor Hely-Hutchinson go; and sadder still when, three years afterwards, he died at the early age of 46. His spiky sense of humour often crept into his compositions: he was an easy and companionable man: creative and unstarchy: and always very gentle. He was an officer in the Senior Training Corps, and caused considerable flutter on his first appearance on parade in his brand new second-lieutenant's uniform, when it was noted that he was wearing his battledress webbing gaiters not only upside-down, but on the wrong feet. His funny little voice was once heard in the middle of the night by the student on guard, when he and the adjutant were bedded down near to the guardroom, complaining of the cold: 'Felix' said the plaintive academic voice, addressing the adjutant, 'I'm bloody cold . . . !'

There was a pause, and a silence. Then, again: 'I'll go further . . . I'm fucking frozen!'

Thirty-odd years ago the combination of that voice and that sentiment expressed in that way and under those conditions was irresistibly funny. But he was a delightful man. Some years later, over a beer in a Maida Vale pub, I remember happily reminiscing about him with Reggie Smith and Dylan Thomas. Dylan said he'd recently mentioned him to Louis MacNeice, who was equally sympathetic to Victor except in one thing: his fondness for beer – 'He's such a pint-minded man,' Louis had said.

He certainly had an infectious enjoyment of life, though I can remember no mention of beer whatsoever! He was, as I have said in Chapter 1, a delightful pianist; and some of us cherished the picture of him being carried shoulder-high round Oxford in his Doctor of Music robes, having completed a series of recitals in which he played all the Beethoven piano sonatas without a score.

His successor, Professor Jack Westrup, stayed only briefly at Birmingham University. After two years he became Professor of Music at Oxford, succeeding Sir Hugh Allen, who had been killed in a road accident there, and whom I remember for his rivetting personal recollections of Brahms and Sibelius. Jack Westrup and I both moved from Birmingham to Oxford at the same time; and I know that I disappointed him by having very firmly to decline his most pressing and repeated invitation to direct a production by the Oxford University Musical Society of Stanford's *Much Ado about Nothing*. It was in the end directed by a friend whom I recommended, Morton Demmery, who came from a very musical family and of whom I have one rather startling musical memory.

He was no mean violinist, and I sometimes used to accompany him at the piano – just as years before I had accompanied a cellist schoolfriend, Brian Kennett. My father invited Morton and me to play the violin and piano at a political meeting in Nuneaton – at that same Co-op Hall which I mentioned in Chapter 1 where I'd appeared 'in that Greek tunic with all those girls'. The speaker was Aneurin Bevan. It was at that stage of the war when we were allies with Russia; and a Baptist minister friend of socialist leanings had challenged us, in a jokey way, to play the 'Internationale'. Morton and I, blithely and a-politically said we saw no reason why we shouldn't play the music of our country's allies; but I have to confess that when the moment came, we funked it. I wonder what Aneurin Bevan would have thought if we had? We might have warmed up his audience for him; or we might have inflamed them. Either way, it mattered little. I have no special fondness for politicians and hardly any at all for immutable political dogma: in fact I hate the rigidity of party-lines. As a speaker, though, Aneurin Bevan was brilliant. From the piano a few feet away I watched him, literally spellbound. His oratory seemed at times, especially in view of his almost paralysing stammer, miraculous. He was a rabble-rouser; but he was more than that. He was a magician; he was a word-weaver; he was electric. The only other speaker that I found so intoxicating, so persuasive and so apocalyptic was a very different man: Charles Williams, poet, mystic and Christian apologist, whom I entertained on several occasions when he spoke at student societies.

For anyone interested in music, Oxford is almost embarassingly tempting. In term-time one frequently had (and still has) the chance of half a dozen concerts in one day: there are college groups, and university groups, city-based groups and visiting groups. My teaching, archaeological and dramatic activities left me little time for personal music-making during those Oxford years. I especially enjoyed, as I have already indicated, the music in Christ Church Cathedral; and I did, unknown to him, occasionally play Sir Edward Boyle's piano in his rooms in Meadow Buildings through the kindness of a mutual friend! I was also roped in, I remember, to play the piano for rehearsals of the stick dance which David Raeburn introduced into his production of

The Shoemaker's Holiday, and which drew from the critic Harold Hobson the comment that they were as well drilled as the chorus in an American production like *Oklahoma*.

During my student days, the gramophone, oddly enough, did not play as large a part in my life as might be imagined. At Birmingham, though, I remember Ted Downes acquiring an ancient wind-up affair, on which he would occasionally play 78s, especially Sibelius: the seventh and the fourth symphonies, and the quite terrifying 'Tapiola'. I did not spend all my days doing permanent fire-watching. I was rescued by Neville Hill and his family, and given a room and breakfast at a very modest sum in their little house in Handsworth. I shall forever be grateful to them for their kindness and, for accepting me as one of the family. Neville had a large collection of early 10-inch 78 jazz records, together with one or two oddities like Bethove, the French parodist, and Edith Sitwell's first recording of Façade. What little I know of jazz I learnt from Neville – including losing my prejudices about it.

When I later moved out and shared a flat nearer the university, close to the home of Ted Doherty, where there was both a radiogram and a piano, there were one or two much-played records, I remember: Marlene Dietrich singing 'Falling in Love Again', and 'The Boys in the Back Room'; Aaron Copland's 'El Salón México', Brahms's Academic Festival Overture and a Nadia Boulanger performance, or part of it, of d'Indy's 'Symphonie sur un chant montagnard'.

I did not buy my first record-player and long-playing discs until after I came down from Oxford, for the perfectly good reason that LP's were not available until that time. Among my first acquisitions were the Elgar 'Cello Concerto, Vaughan Williams's 'A London Symphony' and Britten's glorious 'Serenade for tenor horn and strings'.

I became interested in the music of Edmund Rubbra, whom I never met, though he was often to be seen in Oxford during my time, and two works became firm favourites. The Fifth Symphony, the slow movement of which was used throughout my *Stories of the Saints* series of plays in *Children's Hour;* and the second string quartet.

The potency of cheap music is, as has been said, strange; but I have only to hear any of half a dozen pop songs of 1950 to send me back in imagination to America: 'Sam's Song', 'Goodnight, Irene', 'She Wears Red Feathers', 'Zena, zena zena,' 'New York, New York is a Wonderful Town' and 'Some Enchanted Evening' which was then brand new, and not yet a standard or a golden oldie.

I ventured more than once into composition. My signature tune for the *Simple Simon* series seemed 'catchy'. One of my life's moments of joy was hearing, some two hours or so after one of the broadcasts, someone (I never discovered who), going off-duty from Broadcasting House whistling it. Composers, the world over it seems to me, must find greater pleasure than almost any other artists when they hear their work sung, whistled or hummed.

It is also, as I discovered, a tremendous thrill to hear a song one has written sung by a superb singer with a large orchestra. I was delighted when, during one of the Simple Simon pantomimes, a love song I had written was sung magnificently by Vanessa Leigh with a splendid orchestral backing.

I suppose my oddest venture into the musical field came during the fifties when, having sung a comic song at a BBC staff revue (in a music hall item, devised, chaired and produced by Peter Dews), I broadcast several times as a singer. I was in splendid and distinguished company, too. I could read a score, which helped; and as some of the pieces in which I appeared were comic operas with spoken dialogue, I was easily cast in character parts. I appeared in *Lionel and Clarissa, Love in a Village* as well as more weighty works like Bizet's *Djamileh* and Martinu's *Comedy on the Bridge*. For the latter, I merely had to read from the full score, not singing but speaking my part as a sentry to exact notation which gave note-values but not pitch. I enjoyed these Third Programme and General Overseas Service productions by Geoffrey Dunn or C. Denis Freeman enormously. The dialogue gave me little trouble, of course, whereas it often taxed the singers; on the other hand, I was, to say the least, apprehensive at having to sing a quartet with Alexander Young, April Cantelo and Bruce Boyce.

I have always admired singers, especially those who take part in opera or indeed any work that is both musical and dramatic. To have to sing as near perfectly as possible, whilst at the same time having all the other problems which a straight actor has calls for enormous dedication and sheer nerve. Contrary to general belief, I have rarely found singers difficult or 'temperamental'. I had great fun working with Dennis Noble, Marjorie Thomas, John Cameron and Nancy Evans, for example.

In the rarely-performed *Djamileh* we were a small cast: Jennifer Vyvyan, Alexander ('Basil') Young, Bruce Boyce and me. I was amazed at the humility of so distinguished an artist as

115

Jennifer Vyvyan, who repeatedly got me in a corner and asked me to go over her spoken dialogue with her and constantly asked for my opinion on her performance, which, I thought, was admirable. She seemed almost unable to believe me when I said how moved I'd been by both her acting and her singing at a London performance of Britten's *Turn of the Screw*.

I was in no doubt at all of my status in these companies. In fact, before the very first performance Leo Wurmser, the musical director, had asked me to sing for him, 'to see if you can manage it . . . if not, we get a proper singer!' Leo had astonished me by accompanying during the staff revue my point number, which was very irregular and *colla voce*, as if we'd been working together for years.

If taking part in broadcast opera was new to me, directing opera in the theatre was not. In 1955 an old university friend, the conductor Brian Priestman had asked me to join him in founding a Midland Opera Company called 'Opera da Camera'. The Earl and Countess of Shrewsbury had expressed interest, and there was talk of starting a kind of Midlands Glyndebourne at their stately home, Ingestre in Staffordshire. It never quite came to that, though we met there several times, especially after John Shrewsbury's illness. In fact the Countess, under her professional name Nadine Talbot, made her debut as a singer (she studied under Maggie Teyte) at an 'Opera da Camera' concert.

Our first productions of Mozart's *Impresario*, Holst's *Sāvitri* and the first performance for many years (possibly the first in England) of Gluck's *L'Ivrogne corrigé*, or *The Drunkard Reformed* in Brian Priestman's version were very well received. That is to say, we had packed houses and local critical acclaim. The result for me was that I was invited to direct for the Arts Council my first full-length opera, Verdi's *La Traviata*.

I revel, when I'm not tearing my hair, in the technical problems of opera, especially the basic questions of positioning singers so that they can see the conductor, and what to do with them during the purely orchestral passages. One of the delights is directing the singers, once the stage movement point is reached, when they are singing in *mezza-voce*, which is to me a magical sound, like fairy music. (I once used the term fairy music to describe something quite different but equally enchanting. With a few of my colleagues I was invited to the agricultural service during the Westminster Abbey millennium celebrations, and one of the items was handbell ringing. The ringers were placed over the screen, and as the great congregation hushed, that sweet tiny music seemed almost to come from another world: magical music indeed!)

In the early sixties I fulfilled a very old ambition, and bought my first harpsichord. I remember how I'd been invited to a 'Shakespearan dinner' at the Gore Hotel by my dear friend, Geoffrey Jaggard, one of the most entertaining colleagues I ever had, and whose claim to fame, apart from his amusing books on P.G. Wodehouse, is that he was a direct descendant of that Isaac Jaggard who printed the First Folio of Shakespeare in 1623.

At the dinner I met John Morley, who invited me to the Morley galleries, where, for the first time in my life, I played a harpsichord. It was like entering another dimension, finding one-self back in a half-forgotten and yet familiar world. The very first music I had ever bought had been the two Augener volumes edited by Thomas F. Dunhill of Scarlatti sonatas, but these, and all the other sixteenth-, seventeenth- and eighteenth-century composers I had played on the piano. How different on a plucked instrument! Leaving a concert in the church of St Bartholomew the Great, I was very irritated to hear a rather arty voice say, 'It's such a gutless instrument, the harpsichord.' It may seem so, if fighting a large orchestra in a vast hall. But in more sympathetic conditions, it reigns in its own right. I agree with George Malcolm that, splendid as it may be to play one of the really enormous organs, the performer can gain relatively as great an exhilaration when changing from a 4 foot to a 16-foot stop on a really good harpsichord.

I could not afford a custom-built instrument, but I remember being slightly nettled when friends would ask, seeing my shining new one, 'And how much did that cost?' I eventually answered the question with, 'Twenty years of hard work and careful saving!'

There have been many days of recording *The Archers* that have begun and ended with my playing at the harpsichord long extracts from the works of John Bull, or favourite pieces from *The Fitzwilliam Virginal Book*.

I had by now moved into the house in Notting Hill Gate of one of my best and dearest friends, Joan Hassall. Joan (and her brother Christopher) had been born in this house where her father, John Hassall the painter and poster artist, had settled at the turn of the century. After his death, Joan – or Joana as she is known to her closest friends – took over the house, and converted it into flats which were to be occupied by friends, or people who quickly became friends. It was more of a club than a converted house: below was Joana herself occupying the ground floor and basement, with Max, the viola player, in her father's old studio which had been built over the garden. Above, was Anne, a painter; above her, Marguerite, a retired principal of a training college; and, above her, John and Joy who were in advertising.

Notting Hill Gate was a good place to live: excellent shopping was nearby in Portobello Road, and the neighbourhood was, in common with so many quarters of London, very much like a village. I could leave the flat on the first floor and be in Studio B12 in Broadcasting House within half an hour – and I frequently was. If I had a free episode or two during *Archers* recording sessions, I could be back at the flat and sunbathing on the balcony before half the cast had got as far as the BBC Club. (This was during the fifteen months or so when we recorded in London.)

Apart from Joan herself, there were other compensations: music. Joana plays piano, organ, concert harp, Irish harp, flute, recorders, and both treble and bass viols. Although we were both supposed to be working – I at a script and she at some exquisite wood engraving, a book illustration or a bookplate for the Prime Minister, – one of us would ring and suggest a 'twenty-minute play'. Then Joan would arrive with the kitchen timer in one hand, music under her arm, and the chosen instrument. We would play K.F. Abel's gamba sonatas, or Elizabethan folk-songs, works by Gabrielli, Marin Marais or whoever. The timer would ping, either or both would cry, 'One more minute'; and then we would return to our work after what Joan often described as a 'very nourishing play'.

Eventually, when the studio became vacant, occasional meetings of the Viol da Gamba Society would meet there. At first, the mere sight of Natalie Dolmestch and some 40-odd viol players (some more than somewhat odd, it must be confessed, though most of them were surprisingly ordinary folk) all tuning to what Natalie called 'an approximate A' was singular enough. There were comic possibilities. But when they found their level and played in unison, I felt the quality of the sound almost unbearably stirring. I think I would have to paraphrase the Reverend Sydney Smith and say that to me Heaven would be eating pâté de foie gras to the sound not of trumpets, but an enormous consort of viols.

Occasionally a few of Joan's friends would be invited to bring their instruments and their music and much musical fun was had by all. After the first of these meetings I couldn't sleep for sheer excitement. The idea of a group of comparative strangers arriving, opening their scores and then just playing, at sight and in harmony was intoxicating. There is, of course, a vast repertoire of suitable music – French, Italian, German, Spanish – which is still available and in print for groups of strings, recorders and continuo. We dubbed ourselves 'The Nottynge Hille Noyse', and if it sounds precious, it wasn't. We weren't trying to impress anybody; we never performed in public: we just wanted to have fun, and thanks to Joana we did.

Joana and I, with a flautist friend, Ian Forsyth (whose wife Peggy sang), did sometimes 'oblige' at local functions, when I would give a reading of verse and prose, interspersed with trios and songs, but that was a different matter. The 'Noyse' was an informal and always varying group of friends invited to Joan's home; one never knew whom one would meet. On one occasion I nervously produced my tenor recorder which I was desperately trying to learn, and had to share a music-desk with Margaret Lane, the novelist, who produced a splendid treble recorder and played it like anything!

Living around the corner in Ladbroke Grove at this time was another musical acquaintance, the soprano Elizabeth Harwood. I had known her through Gwen Berryman, who was a fellow-student with Elizabeth's mother at the Royal Academy of Music. Gwen and I had been invited to appear at a function some years before at Elizabeth's home town, Ilkley, where her father Sydney had been town clerk. We arrived on Friday evening, and on the Saturday opened, and signed autographs at, the event.

The following day, Elizabeth's mother, Connie, said that two old friends of hers and Gwen's were coming over to the house in the afternoon, bringing their little boy, and we could 'have some music'. Connie, who sang and taught singing was also an excellent pianist, and she accompanied the teenage Elizabeth and Sydney. Elizabeth was already 'the perfect English rose': tallish, very fair and with a chocolate box peaches-and-cream complexion: she was delicate and exquisite, and winningly shy. She sang like an angel, even then.

The little boy, who must have been only nine or ten, was anxious to go and play on the swing in the garden; but his mother insisted that he must play the piano for us first. He sat on the stool, his little legs way above the pedals, though he did manage to reach them when necessary. As if it had nothing whatever to do with him, as if he and his hands were not connected, he played with great expression and complete independence of hands, some Bach partitas, finishing with: 'Can I go and play on the swing now?', and before we could draw breath and beg him to play again, he was gone like a rabbit. His name was Michael Roll, who now, having won the First Leeds Piano Contest, is a pianist of international fame. Elizabeth, too, has become world famous. What an extraordinary memory: of two such brilliant children on one summer afternoon.

One other memory remains from that time. Elizabeth was heard asking Connie: 'Mummy, why don't Auntie Gwennie's diamonds sparkle like yours?'

'Because they're real, dear!' came Connie's dry reply, amusing but without the least touch of acid. Connie is one of those comfortable, easygoing people who refuse to be flustered. She had a voice of great quality with a wonderful creamy tone: it was clear to see where Elizabeth's talent came from, with both parents so musical.

Later, when her career really took off and she was living near me in London, we met more frequently. We took a box for her first *Messiah* with the Royal Choral Society under Sir Malcolm Sargent: Elizabeth's parents were there, and I had my mother and my 'radio mother' Gwen with me, not an unusual occurrence at that time. I still have the programme which was autographed 'with love from Elizabeth': it was among my mother's papers when she died.

Occasionally, Elizabeth would ring up in a panic: she was on television with Eric Robinson that night, and the words of one of her songs were impossible: a very bad translation. So round she'd come, and on the piano that once belonged to Arthur Wood, who wrote among so many other things Barwick Green, the signature tune of *The Archers*, we'd work through it, tinkering with the lyric, finding words that were more comfortable to sing in the higher register, like 'ardour' and 'rapture' instead of the wooden and pompous words printed. Inevitably, in the hurly-burly of live television, she sometimes sang a mixture of each at the actual performance, but no-one noticed except Eric, whose encouraging grin grew even wider as he conducted.

It was around this time, the mid-sixties, that Gwen Berryman in one of her delightfully unpredictable vagaries, decided that she would become known for her hats, would drive whenever suitable in a hired Rolls Royce, with liveried chauffeur, and would give little lunch or supper-parties at the Savoy (she had tried Claridges but didn't care for it!).

This phase did not last long, but it was highly enjoyable while it did. She spent Christmas Day one year at my flat, and arrived in the longest Rolls I have ever seen; and it was while being driven back from the theatre on her birthday, 22 November 1963, that the chauffeur told us the news of President Kennedy's assassination.

Elizabeth Harwood was now singing regularly at Sadler's Wells, and so Gwen decided to take a group to her next first night (in the Rolls of course) and then go on to a party for Elizabeth at the Savoy afterwards. Now in those days, Elizabeth was quite unnecessarily nervous about some of her top notes. Unknown to her, I'd crept into the Alexandra Theatre in Birmingham when she'd been on tour with the Wells, and heard her singing Gilda in *Rigoletto* breathtakingly. Afterwards, she had admitted her anxieties about 'the top'. No doubt all her friends tried to convince her that she was worrying needlessly. I certainly tried to.

The first night of the opera that Gwen chose was that of Richard Strauss's *Ariadne auf Naxos*, and Elizabeth was, of course, singing the taxing and showy role of Zerbinetta. For some unaccountable reason, she became anxious, indeed over-anxious, about some of the high notes; but at the performance she began in great style. As one of the group of family and friends in the audience, I watched, as we all did, with bated breath. Then, just when the climax came and we waited for the final top E or whatever it was, she wavered, and with a split second to decide dropped on to an octave below. Only the company, and those of us in the know, and no doubt the critics, were aware of what had happened. She went on smiling and made her exit to the usual applause.

The opera ended, we all gathered at the Savoy. We knew it was foolish to pretend that something hadn't happened; quite clearly it was in no sense a disaster or a tragedy; and yet we knew how poor Elizabeth must be feeling. We made the usual remarks like 'first-night nerves', 'doubt if most people noticed', 'it would be all right at the next performance', and 'anyway, the rest of the performance was magnificent' . . . She smiled bravely and philosophically, and we soon agreed to forget it. The supper-party, went on: there was a cabaret – brilliant dancing and singing received with the usual cabaret-audience lack of enthusiasm: and there was dancing (I remember Fanny and Johnny Craddock gliding around, she a wispy vision in turquoise tulle), but then came the moment that Gwen had planned, and which should have been the high-spot of the evening. In came, specially prepared at enormous expense, a celebratory cake, and on it in icing was the one thing we were trying to forget: the name of Elizabeth's part in the opera, Zerbinetta. We did the only thing possible: we fell about laughing as we ate, and filled up our glasses with champagne as we toasted Elizabeth. After all, we knew that she was a great singer, with a great future. The incident merely proved that she was also – like her parents, like her 'Auntie' Gwen – warm and fallible and human. So what did it matter? But I don't remember Gwen giving another party!

When I left London and moved to the country, I found two musical freedoms: one was that I had at last room for two grand pianos; and the other, which was much more notable, was that my old stone-built rectory in Warwickshire was solid enough and far enough away from other houses in the village for one's playing not to be a nuisance at any hour of the day or night.

One of the most surprising fan letters I ever received began: 'Cleo and I . . . ' It was from Johnny Dankworth who, with Cleo Laine, was at the time a keen follower of *The Archers;* and he very kindly wrote to me to say so. It so happens that I had been a fan of theirs for many years, too. I first realized that Cleo Laine was not just a glorious voice when she took over from Bertice Reading in Sandy Wilson's version of Ronald Firbank's *Valmouth.* She appeared in Brecht, and recorded a set of Shakespeare songs written by John Dankworth, and, in other words, demonstrated that the divisions that seemed to exist in music were artificial and unnecessary. This whole idea of the Dankworths', their 'All music Project' at Wavendon, very much rang my bell. It was as likely to be seen at Covent Garden or the Festival Hall as at any musical comedy or revue, at the Wigmore Hall or the Hammersmith Odeon. And why not?

Over the years I have perhaps grown out of the saccharin harmonies of what is sometimes called Light Music, though I can still enjoy a superb performance; and I have two short suits, Viennese waltzes and Hawaiian guitar music. Otherwise, I can, and do, enjoy late Beethoven string quartets and Ella Fitzgerald: Peter Maxwell Davies and Nat King Cole; Benjamin Britten and Rod Stewart. I like some jazz, though a little goes quite a long way; and I am not always comfortable with the most extreme practitioners of the avant-garde.

One of music's greatest qualities is to me its transcending of all barriers, of race, geography or time. I thrilled when I heard the broadcast of the tumpets of Tut-ankh-amen, sounding again after hundreds of years; my toes still tap to a mediaeval dance; I can droop over the languorous melodies of Rachmaninov; Elgar moves me to near tears; and Rod Stewart, especially in that rich period around the time of the album, *Atlantic Crossing,* has

produced songs with very telling lyrics describing the human condition, movingly at odds with that unique voice. If one is musical,
if one really enjoys music, then surely it is attitudinizing to say: I
only like classical music, or 'I only like Rock'. That may be true of
one or two rare beings. What matters, I believe, is the quality of
the music: to take up a pose, a rigid position, is to deny oneself
access to a wide range of musical pleasures. One of the greatest
differences between Norman Painting and Phil Archer is in musical tastes. Phil is foursquare, narrow and prejudiced; Norman
likes most music.

No-one is more aware than I am of my technical shortcomings
as a pianist, but all my life I have found enormous pleasure in performing. It is true that I play organs in various villages; though I
am not really an organist, but more a semi-self-taught pianist who
obliges. I love playing the harpsichord, and clavichord. Two musical activities give me exceptional pleasure: accompanying singers
or instrumentalists at the piano, and playing two-piano duets.

From the moment I could play a simple hymn-tune on the
piano, I have been accompanying: my parents and various members of a musical family; schoolfriends and then whoever came to
hand. When I first accompanied the singing of Numa Libin I was
moved beyond all imagining by a voice that I thought had got to
be as good as Chaliapin's. Alas! in spite of the encouragement of
his teacher, Roy Henderson (no mean singer himself, but also
forever to be remembered as one of the teachers of Kathleen
Ferrier), Numa never survived his own perfectionism and devastating self-criticism, and is now producing records of extremely
high quality, under the Nimbus label.

I learnt a great deal from the soprano Freda Rollason, who
said, in reply to a chance remark, 'Yes, of course the accompanist
must follow the singer. Sometimes. But equally a singer needs to
rely on a lead from the accompanist on occasions; and sometimes
demands positive support. The timid, self-effacing accompanist,
who always stays in the background, is not always satisfactory.' I
still enjoy accompanying when time allows, and occasionally give
word and music recitals with the baritone Robert Harding, in
stately homes or churches.

Two piano-playing remains largely a private activity, though.
It is not always easy to find players who are not so brilliant they
lose patience with me; but when I do, the time flashes by in unalloyed delight.

As Philip Archer, I have played piano and organ throughout the
whole run of the programme: I even once played both parts

(thanks to double recording) in a piano duet with Phil and his daughter, Elizabeth.

Early on in the programme, the voices of Dan and Doris were frequently heard singing. Harry Oakes, the first Dan, had a fine but untrained bass-baritone: Gwen Berryman is a Royal Academy of Music gold medallist. Extracts from the 'Easter Anthem', which were, though unacknowledged, written by me, were often heard, not to mention 'Down the Vale', 'When we are Married' (which was included on the Pye record we made) and 'All in the April Evening'.

In the latter two, Basil Jones, who then played John Tregorran, added a tenor line. The voices blended well, and letters were received from listeners asking for the piece to be sung again. So towards the end of one episode, a scene was written in which Dan, Doris and John were in full voice, rehearsing, when the door burst open and in came a farm-worker, Len Thomas, with the news that something terrible had happened to little Audrey Atkins, and would they all go and help. Then the signature tune came merrily in, leaving everyone in suspense till next day, when they would learn what actually had happened to little Audrey. Everyone, it seemed, except the aged father of one listener, who wrote in to say how much he enjoyed hearing Dan, Doris, and John singing, with Phil, of course, at the piano, 'but the other night he was so angry when Len Thomas came in and interrupted the singing with the news of little Audrey that he cried out, "Bugger little Audrey", and hit our wireless set so hard he broke it, and it hasn't gone since!'

The folk-songs of Bob Arnold, as Tom Forrest, have always been popular with listeners, and have been sung at intervals, usually with a piano accompaniment from me, throughout the run of the programme. Several were included on our commercial record, which I arranged and played; and Bob and I have on a few occasions performed together at public functions. Bob has also featured on 78s and an L.P.

Latterly, Tom's folk-songs have been over-shadowed by Eddie Grundy's country and western songs, with occasional effects by Shula Archer with guitar.

For Radio Four's visit to the North in 1980, a 'Country evening with The Archers' was recorded in a barn near Leeds. Bob Arnold and Trevor Harrison sang – one of Trevor's songs was written for the occasion by me, pretending to be Eddie – and there was also music by The Oyster Band. At the end of the programme the identity of the 'mystery accompanist' was divulged. It was of course (surprise, surprise!) me!

So, although there may be differences in musical taste between Phil Archer and Norman Painting, they do have one interest in common: they both like playing the piano. But the music they choose to play, like the music they choose to listen to, is rarely the same.

CHAPTER 8

The screen: Painting in pictures

I was, as I have said earlier in this book, radio-struck as a child in the way some people are stage-struck or film-struck. I have always loved radio, and I suppose always will. But when I agreed, so reluctantly, to go on being Philip Archer after the first three months, I made a decision that altered my whole relationship with sound broadcasting. I thought I knew what I was doing: I realized that it was the end of my radio career as a performer, and that the programme might go on for as long as 10 years, although that seemed extremely unlikely. Events have proved that 10 years was nothing! But when, after 30 years, I realized that I was still only halfway through my professional life, I saw that I had to give thought to planning my future. Writers don't retire at 65!

It is true that writing takes the major part of my energy and enthusiasm: but, for better or worse, I cannot suppress that part of me which is a performer. I was, until quite recently, required to be in the studios to record *The Archers* nearly every week. Latterly, that has been changed to two weeks on, and two weeks off; but there still is barely time to rehearse and perform a stage play. One felt in a way even more trapped than in the early days. Then, we numbered our daily audience in teens of millions, and we were very much sought after for celebrity appearances. As time went by the audience dwindled; and our value as 'celebrities' became muted – or rather transmuted: it became slightly different.

At the peak, we appealed to a very wide age-span; latterly, we noticed that it was the middle-aged or elderly who were our real fans, though there were always gratifying and surprising smaller numbers of the very young who followed us.

As the 25th anniversary of the programme approached, and as more and more basic changes were being made in the running of *The Archers,* following the departure of Godfrey Baseley, some of us began to wonder what the future held. I realized that if I was to meet my financial and domestic commitments, I had to diversify.

Then, one of those coincidences, that perhaps aren't really coincidences at all, happened.

It was in Pebble Mill, the new broadcasting centre of the BBC in Birmingham. I had been recovering from the only serious illness of my life so far – that unfunny thing that makes people laugh called mumps – and so had missed the introductory tours of the nearly-finished building which most of my colleagues had found so helpful. I not only did not know my way around the building, but it seemed full of people I didn't know. This was because for some years, various departments of the BBC had been working in different buildings; now at last they were all under one roof.

We had finished a morning recording session quite early, and, fond as I am of most of my colleagues, I still did not feel fit enough for a two and a half hour lunchtime of chat in the canteen. So, untypically, I decided to find out where the BBC club bar was. It was barely noon, and I imagined that it would at that time be quiet. I planned to have a glass of red wine, and then find a quiet corner back in the studios for a nap – I was not fully recovered from what is, I now realize, a very debilitating illness, and I found I tended to run out of steam at the end of a long day in the studio.

As I guessed, the bar was almost empty; but as I bent to sip my wine I saw an old friend whom I hadn't really had a conversation with for over 20 years, Edmund Marshall. Neither of us I imagine guessed what the outcome of that meeting would be: for one thing, he was to introduce me, in a very roundabout way, to the virtues and delights of real ale; and secondly he was to open the door to television and a whole new series of colleagues. More than that, my career would take another direction; and within a few months I would feel that, once more, I belonged: I knew most of the people I saw around Pebble Mill, and they knew me – far different from those days when I felt an outsider.

I had, of course, always had one eye on TV. At the very beginning of my career, at the time when I was a general programmes assistant on three-month contracts, I was applying for jobs in television. But as I always said quite openly that I wanted to be a floor manager, or whatever the job was, in order to learn the business of writing for television, I was passed over with 'Ah! You want to be a writer, not an engineer!' And that had been the end of that.

Again, when it was first mooted that there might be a sound programme called *The Archers* and that, in some capacity or other I might be involved in it, I was assured – we all were – that, in accordance with the published policy of the then Director-

General of the BBC, we would in time become part of 'the marriage of sound and vision'. That marriage never took place: artistically, logistically and agriculturally it would have been almost impossible.

For some years, therefore, the only television appearances we made were in connexion with *The Archers*. I seem to remember that the first time I saw myself on the TV screen (and it was an enormous, projected, public screen) was when Harry Oakes, Gwen Berryman and I appeared at an exhibition at Bingley Hall on closed circuit. Hardly an event: but it whetted the appetite.

For some years, we were merely 'actualities' and appeared in news or magazine programmes. One such was when the cast of *The Archers* presented a calf to the National Farmers Union in the late sixties, when I met for the first time since schooldays Henry Plumb, who by then was vice-chairman of the National Farmers' Union, and his wife, Marjorie.

Our first attempt at appearing on a popular TV show was in fact vetoed by the BBC. At the eleventh hour, a projected appearance on *What's my Line* was not allowed, as we were radio characters and were to be heard, not seen. So the bandleader Cyril Stapleton deputized at very short notice, and we all watched the recording from the circle of the Television Theatre, feeling like lepers or visitors from Outer Space.

Eventually, Harry and Gwen, as Dan and Doris Archer, were allowed to appear; and after that individual members of the cast gradually managed to get into television.

My own first 'celebrity' appearance, on a television panel game chaired by an old friend Don Maclean, the Birmingham comedian, was not a success – at least I wasn't asked back. I don't think I made any crashing mistakes; but, as with so many parts of show business, one can learn more from actually doing it than all the study and theory in the world. I learned enormously from watching the transmission: camera-angles, mannerisms, twitchings and fidgettings. I had understood that I would be taking part in a quiz on topographical questions. When I reached the studio and found that it was partly based on questions about sport, I was lost – in spite of having appeared regularly as an interviewer of sporting personalities in the weekly programme *Sport in the Midlands* years before.

Because of contracts and timings, I was also recording the quiz in between *Archers* recording sessions, so I was slightly under pressure, dashing along from our normal sound studio, to another sound studio which was being used for television in those improvised pre-Pebble Mill days. The panel and quizmaster were given a buffet meal just before the tele-recording, and to my amazement the producer read, at very great speed, all the questions and all the answers out loud to us, as we stood balancing plate and glass. As this was my first experience, I hadn't realized that the show was slightly 'fixed' in this way, or I would have paid more attention. As it was, I found it very exasperating, shortly afterwards on the set, to be asked a question and not be able to remember the answer, even though I had heard it only a few minutes before! It is, incidentally, only fair to say that this procedure of giving the questions and the answers to the team beforehand is not general practice: in fact, this was my only experience of it.

Occasionally, though, things have to be 're-arranged'. I remember when Patricia Greene (Jill Archer) and I were appearing in a quiz called 'I give you my word' from the BBC Riverside Studios in Hammersmith, we won the contest, but had to repeat about four minutes in the middle of it. This was because the Quizmaster made a slip of a type that I soon learnt was dangerously easy: he referred back to a remark one of us had made, earlier in the programme. Or so he thought. The remark had in fact been made not during the programme, but during the rehearsal, and therefore would mean nothing to the viewers. So, although the quiz, which was a kind of Scrabble, was cumulative, we had to repeat a section halfway through. Paddy Greene and I had to act as if we were losing, when we knew that we would, in the end, win.

On this occasion we were representing The Archers against The Dales. The daily serial *Mrs Dale's Diary* had started before *The Archers,* and for a time was written up by the Press as being a rival show. Whenever the two casts met, though, we were as friendly as any two companies of players, without the slightest trace of animosity. But when the actress Ellis Powell was replaced by the famous musical-comedy actress and film-star, Jessie Matthews, after 14 years, an odd thing happened. I am glad that Gwen Berryman herself has now spoken about this, because till recently one kept it unsaid, but the two 'leading ladies' Gwen and Jessie, didn't quite see eye to eye.

At our first joint party, Jessie told the Press that she was a great Archer fan and loved the show. Gwen said that she never listened to The Dales, because she was always too busy doing housework. Now, anyone who knew dear Gwen knew that she was often as surprised as anyone to hear what she was saying, and there certainly was no thought behind her words at all. But she undoubtedly had said them, and much was made of the fact.

When Paddy Greene and I were chatting with Jessie just before going on for our TV quiz, she said again how much she enjoyed our programme, 'But oh dear! your leading lady!' Luckily, I was able to say with honesty that I had listened to The Dales for years, as I knew and had previously worked with so many of the cast, especially Vivienne Chatterton as the grotesque Mrs Mountford and Betty Hardy as the awful Elsie. I also confessed that I had not listened or watched any serial from the time I became a script-writer for *The Archers*, as I was anxious to avoid being accused of putting forward second-hand programme ideas, if, by coincidence there were a similarity of plot lines.

I had another temporary whiff of the air of a television studio when I visited friends rehearsing a TV opera. My involvement as a director in opera for 'Opera da Camera' led to my being invited by the conductor Brian Priestman on to the set of a BBC TV production of Arthur Benjamin's *A Tale of Two Cities*. Brian knew that I would be interested in the technical problems. He was right: I was totally fascinated.

Quality of sound is always difficult in television opera even when produced in a studio and not direct from a theatre, and several ways of avoiding the difficulties have been suggested. What interested me about this production was the fact that the orchestra was not in the same studio as the singers and the settings. It was in fact a mile away, linked by loudspeakers and monitor-screens. The singers could see the conductor most of the time by using carefully placed monitors; but during the crowd scenes this was at times difficult. So Brian, as associate conductor, was dressed in costume like the rest of the French Revolutionary mob, and mingled with the crowd, but always in such a way that he could see the principal conductor, and where the chorus could see him, as he conveyed the beat to them. If by chance he happened to wander into shot, it could scarcely matter, as he was in costume, and with so many arms waving in the air what would an extra one matter?

There were several old friends in the cast: Alexander Young and John Cameron and, I think, Marjorie Thomas. But there were two others that I was delighted to meet. One was the soprano Heather Harper, who at that time had yet to find her greatest success, and had yet to sing the main soprano role in the first performance of Benjamin Britten's *War Requiem*. Not only did I know and admire her work then, but she was a delightful person to meet. When she confessed to being a fan of *The Archers* I was bowled over.

The other person I shall always remember meeting was the

legendary tenor, Heddle Nash. He was playing Doctor Manette, and although by this time his voice had become a ghost of what it had been, and as one remembered it in the early recording of Elgar's *Gerontius*, or in his famous record of the Serenade from Bizet's *Fair Maid of Perth*, the old magic was still there. What astounded me, though, was the blunt North Country accent of the man in normal conversation; and I never quite reconciled the sight of him in his eighteenth-century costume, for years the Crown Prince of English Romantic tenors, sitting in the corner of an untidy television studio drinking a glass of stout. But Guinness, as I have often been told by singers, is not only 'good for you', but it's also 'good for the voice'. Didn't Kirsten Flagstad once sing *Dido and Aeneas* for the fee of a bottle of Guinness a night?

So, as the years went by, my journey into television was slow and tentative. We were interviewed 'in depth' for a feature by Philip Tibbenham on the *Tonight* programme when we reached 21 years of age in *The Archers*; and the programme was re-run at our 21st party. From time to time, for one reason or another, we were interviewed for news or magazine programmes; but that chance meeting in the club bar at Pebble Mill with Edmund Marshall was to lead to my being far more deeply involved in television on my own account.

Edmund and I were – indeed still are – very good friends. We had been introduced by a mutual friend, Ted Doherty, when we were students. Edmund, having been commissioned in the Royal Navy after a wartime short course at New College, Oxford, returned from the forces to graduate in English at Durham University. We met first in Birmingham during his vacations; and when he returned to his home town with a good degree, he, as it were, infiltrated BBC Birmingham. He had had journalistic training and experience before university, and so inevitably was of use to the news people, for whom, as I have already explained, I too was working as a free-lance. Soon he became a familiar, and eventually an official, figure; he joined the staff in BBC News Room, and immediately proved his worth.

Then, without disagreement or argument, our paths diverged, and apart from the occasional 'Hello, how are you?' in passing, we hardly spoke to each other for 20 years or more! I have already said that, before the different parts of BBC Midlands came together in one place at Pebble Mill, they were scattered round the city, and the reason for Edmund and me losing sight of each other was that he went off to pioneer television programmes from

Birmingham. He edited, and in fact presented on screen, the first news bulletin on television from the Midlands. From there, very often inventing ways and means as he went along, he produced, wrote, and directed documentary films. Over the years, he built up a solid reputation, becoming in time the most senior and respected television producer at BBC1 Midlands.

Although I had missed much of his early work and most of his early films through living in London, I had seen one or two of them when they were networked: and his sensitive film about A.E. Housman with an old 'Birmingham Rep' friend Bernard Hepton, playing Housman, and a graphic documentary on the history and topography of Ironbridge, were distinguished work of a very high standard.

So, that day when he strolled into the nearly empty BBC Midland club, we greeted each other as old friends with considerable mutual respect. In response to his question as to what I had been doing recently, apart from the obvious, I said that I had written far too many BBC scripts in far too short a time. He replied that he had made too many BBC television programmes in far too short a time, so we had another glass of wine together and mutually commiserated. Then he suddenly said: 'You know, we ought to do a film together', or something like that. I secretly thought that this was (as indeed it so often is) just a kind of reflex action, the sort of polite remark one makes in conversation with an old friend. But a few days later came a letter from Edmund saying that I had looked as if I hadn't believed him, but he was in fact quite serious, and would I go in one day soon and discuss the whole question in his office?

In that brief meeting in the bar we must have talked about gardens. I no doubt was enthusing about mine: Edmund was not quite so happy about his as it has problems: there is only a few inches of sandy soil over solid sandstone.

In what seemed a very short time, Edmund was phoning me and asking how appalled I would be at the prospect of making not one but two half-hour films on gardens? Was there enough material? I replied that there were enough interesting gardens to make a hundred films. Soon Edmund visited my garden; and I went and saw his and met his wife and children. Before long we had fixed a date for filming, and arranged several dates before that for visiting possible gardens – this is known as recce-ing.

The films were to be called *A Summer of Gardens*, and were to contain filmed visits to four or five widely contrasted locations. There would be room of course for very large gardens in stately homes; but middle-sized and very small gardens would also be of enormous interest to that vitally important person, 'the ordinary viewer'.

Television makes instant experts: you appear on the screen talking reasonably knowledgably about a given subject, and you are at once an expert. I had to make it clear from the beginning that I had not the sort of knowledge that for example, my old friend of many years, Percy Thrower, had. I am, in short, interested in gardens rather than gardening. There was a strong emphasis on garden design and the principles of design in these films. So places like Rousham Park, Chatsworth and Hidcote were obvious choices. It was not easy, at first, though to find suitable small gardens. This is not to say that there aren't thousands of good small gardens in the country: but, schooled by Edmund, I very quickly learnt that the camera eats up images voraciously, and that many delightful little gardens can very quickly show you all the pictures they have to offer in about 50 seconds of film. To find a small garden which was of sufficient interest to fill from four to six minutes was far more difficult than at first appeared: there had to be something special about the design, about the owner (who would be interviewed) or about the plant material, or all three.

I was discussing this with Gwen Berryman when she was on one of her frequent visits to my home in 1975. By this time, her public activities were beginning to exhaust her, and she would often arrive in a state of near-collapse. But after a few days of the peace and calm of our Warwickshire countryside, she would recover miraculously and happily drive herself back home. We were sitting in the garden room, I reading some reference book or other, and Gwen trying to catch up with her correspondence, when she suddenly said: 'I do wish you'd write to this woman. She keeps writing to me. She obviously knows a lot about roses – she's presented a collection of them to Newstead Abbey, Byron's old home.'

It so happens that I had become interested in a rose called Comte de Chambord, which at that time I had never seen. So, taking Gwen at her word, I scribbled a few lines to the lady in question, who was called Viola Barrett (She was named, incidentally, after an organ-stop and not a flower: her father was an organ-builder).

Three days later an odd packet arrived through the post. Inside was a rose-plant, clearly labelled, 'Comte de Chambord'. It was from Viola, and so began a friendship that continues to this day.

Shortly afterwards, photographs of her garden arrived. It was no larger than many suburban plots, but was in the most unlikely and unpromising situation: at the back of the red-brick street in a declining mining-village in Derbyshire, and was almost entirely planted with roses. I could see at once that this might be exactly what I was looking for. When I met Viola — tiny, bespectacled, smiling, enthusiastic and with more than a touch of benign eccentricity, I knew we could make a good item for the film out of her garden and her passion for roses.

Then the blow fell. I received a flow of letters from her, all protesting that she couldn't possibly appear on television as she wasn't clever enough, and suggesting that a friend of hers would do it much better. Then Edmund, who had of course recce-d with me and had been enthusiastic, began to receive letters and phone-calls from Viola. I knew from my experience in radio documentaries that the best participants are nearly always the reluctant ones: those anxious to appear are more often than not damp squibs: awkward and tongue-tied. So I firmly told Viola that we wouldn't film her roses without her.

It was touch and go: but my insistence won the day. Early in July we arrived and found the garden a blaze of colour, with Viola wearing a clean blouse and clean apron, and having obviously been up since dawn, if not before. Then another blow fell: an essential piece of equipment was missing, and we had to wait two hours before it arrived and we could begin filming. By this time my nerves were almost as taut as Viola's; but by lunchtime we had got it: she was fresh, unaware of the camera, direct and endearing. Her friendly voice, peppered with Derbyshire dialect words, produced most acceptable commentary to go behind several sequences of pictures; and in the direct 'to camera' interviews she was completely natural and unaffected.

This was not the first garden we had filmed, so I was beginning to feel a little more at home with the cameras. Some weeks before, Edmund had suddenly said very much as an afterthought that, as we had our first day's filming coming up, he'd better get me to do a camera test. To my protestations that this seemed rather late in the day, he explained that it wasn't the sort of test that one could pass or fail: he was backing his judgment and his knowledge of me as a person, by booking me to make the films anyway. What he wanted from a test was an indication of my general approach, so that he could see how best to direct me, and also, incidentally, he wanted to give me some experience of the general mechanics of this type of location filming to which I was new. So from the first I learnt those little tricks that help so much – like not rushing into action the moment one's cue-word 'Action' is spoken, but waiting for a silent count of three.

The site for the camera test was a public park near Pebble Mill. Edmund asked me to walk into shot and stop at a marked spot – it was marked by a dead leaf – without too obviously looking for the mark. I was then required to talk to the camera on, say, the pruning of flowering shrubs, or the history of the greenhouse, or some aspect of garden design. This I managed to improvise. Keeping himself out of shot, Edmund proceeded to interview me, and I replied on film. Then he asked me to interview him, again addressing the camera and reacting to his out-of-vision replies. Finally, I was asked to hide behind a tree and attempt a comic entry into vision. This, too, seemed to be satisfactory, and we went happily back to Pebble Mill for a cup of tea. The experience had of course been invaluable to me; and it was quite useful to Edmund, too.

I had several other factors in my favour when, a few days later, we started actual filming. For one thing I was an actor who had specialized in 'realistic' not-larger-than-life acting; I had also been taught the technique of interviewing and had had, albeit some years earlier, considerably professional practice at it; again, the subject was one about which I could be genuinely enthusiastic; and lastly, I was working with a director who, whilst being exacting in his requirements, was basically sympathetic and anxious to help me succeed.

I shall never forget my very first day's filming, which was at Rousham Park in Oxfordshire. Although our main reason for choosing this site was the almost unspoiled eighteenth-century landscape garden, we began with some establishing shots in the rose garden. On cue I had merely to approach a half-open wrought-iron gate, shoot an appraising glance at it as I passed through, and then walk up and past the camera, without seeming to be aware of it. We had a rehearsal. And then another one. We then decided to try a take. Whereupon the skies went black with rain clouds, and the light level dropped so low, the director decided we should all stay where we were and wait for a couple of minutes till the dark clouds went over. Out of shot behind a yew hedge, I stood, aware of my heart beating faster than usual, hoping to get it right, and wondering if it could really be true that this was the first step in a new career. I sometimes wonder whether perhaps I have too much imagination: I certainly built up in my mind the significance of what was a simple shot into something of enormous importance. And yet, of course, it was important.

Simple as the shot was, I could have got it wrong, and done something stupid. This might easily have irritated the film crew, to whom I was a complete stranger, and then not only that day, but many subsequent ones, would not have passed so enjoyably.

The very black clouds did pass over, and although the rain was threatening, it was decided to go ahead. I waited for the cue, 'Action'. I then counted three, and did my walk in, stopping to look at the wrought-iron gate, then turning and walking towards and past the camera.

'Cut', said Edmund, and went into a huddle with the cameraman. He then said that although that was satisfactory, we would try another take, mainly for camera reasons – I think he was being kind. But as we were doing it again, could I manage to look a little more appraising of the beauty of the wrought-iron gate and not, as I was in danger of doing, looking slightly surprised.

So back I went behind the yew hedge, and waited for my cue. I was rapidly learning the first rule of filming: don't expect things to happen quickly. The next take was satisfactory, so we moved to another set-up at the far end of the garden for a shot which would follow on from the previous one and get me as far as the dove-cot. Although the skies were lighter, it was now raining quite steadily, but no-one seemed to mind very much. Anorak hoods went up, and an umbrella shielded the camera, but otherwise the rain was ignored.

'Action!'

I was off again, stepping between the box-edged rose-beds with the rain pelting down, trying to look as if it was a sunny summer day.

'Cut! One more time!'

So, heedless of the rain, I strolled through the rose-garden, and was halfway to my destined passing-out-of-frame point, when Edmund's voice said, 'Cut!'

I wondered what I'd done wrong. The answer was, nothing. We had cut because of another basic rule: you only stop for rain when it *shows* – either on the performers or on the lens. The rain had driven directly towards the camera and wet the lens, so we stopped. The final take was made a few minutes later when the rain had finished. The whole crew, the whole garden, and me were drenched; and yet, when the film was transmitted, the processing laboratories had lifted the tones so that it looked as if it had been shot on quite a bright pleasant day.

We had by now been working for an hour, and less than a minute of usable film was in the can. In a whispered consultation with Edmund I asked if I was not doing very well. He dismissed the suggestion, and I learnt that if a day's shooting produced five minutes of film, with only one or two takes per shot, it was regarded as quite successful.

The most critical test was still to come: my first 'piece to camera' with sound. The crew set up near to the dove-cot, and Edmund directed me to walk along a certain line, stop at a spot he indicated and had marked with a small pebble, and then speak to the camera.

We had no script: at our recce we had planned more or less what we wanted to do, but I was largely ad libbing and improvising. So, with his fingers more tightly crossed than he let on to anyone, Edmund gave the cue. I did as requested, spoke to the camera, walked out of shot, and we cut. The director and crew went into a huddle, and then Edmund came up to me and said that we were doing it again for came. a reasons, but I was to keep what I'd said exactly the same, taking care not to 'go over the top at the end', as it was fine. We shot Take Two, with everything as before except my words, which were slightly shuffled around.

'Cut!'

A few more huddles and whispered remarks, and off we went towards the landscape garden. The crew began to chaff each other: the assistant camera man and the sound recordist began to whistle. The unit seemed to come to life, with a spring in its heel. As we moved off to the new set-up, a beaming Edmund said to me: 'You're all right. Jim the camera-man's just said' "This guy's all right!", and they're happy. You can always tell once they start joking and whistling!' And so it was.

I must say, looking back, that the next thing I was asked to do was a pretty tall order for someone doing his first day's filming. But as I didn't know that it was regarded as difficult or unusual, I took in my stride. I had to walk into shot, talking to the camera which was a long way away from me, and describe the whole layout of the garden in relation to the house, and the function of a large piece of formal statuary which was so placed in order to turn the visitor, and draw to his attention the vast view across rolling fields to the 'Eyecatcher', a fake ruin on a far hill.

We did the shot at the first take: no problems with cameras, no problems with sound. Then Edmund explained that what we had just filmed was a kind of matrix: that was the ground plan. Into it, he wanted to add shots of me in close-up, or much nearer to the camera in relation to the statuary, for insertion by the editor later. So these additional shots would be mute, but I would have to mime to the words I had just recorded on the first take, moving my lips, and making the same gestures as previously, but with the camera closer. A wind had sprung up and was making sound-recording difficult, so this solution was desirable if I could manage it.

It was to me just another piece of technical acting. I quite happily mimed to my own voice, adding gestures to indicate the various features I'd spoken of in the first take. It worked magnificently.

Soon it was time for lunch. After barely an hour, eating the first of many ploughman's lunches with the crew, we returned to the garden; but now we were a team, and I, the Unknown Quantity, was accepted. It was exhilarating; it was the beginning of a love affair which is still going on: a love affair with the film camera.

I learnt so much on that memorable day. We spent a lot of time filming, with portable lights, inside the dove-cot, and getting some interesting shots of the revolving 'potence' or 'potent' inside it. The 'potent' was a wooden structure which enabled the nesting-holes to be examined, and I was made to explain its use to the camera, and was then sent gently spinning round, in an out of shot. My place was afterwards taken by the camera-man who filmed what I was seeing, my 'eye-line', and the result when edited was a most compelling piece of film. We also spent an hour or more in an interview with the garden's owner. Neither that interview, nor the fascinating shots inside the dove-cot appeared in the final film! This was not because they weren't usable, quite the contrary, but because every film has a logic of its own, and this one, completed, was far more telling without the two sections I have mentioned. That was another lesson which all who make films quickly learn: so often some of the very best work ends up on the cutting-room floor.

That first day's filming was also memorable because we were rained off before we had completed our schedule. We stopped filming, not because we were all cold and drenched to the skin, oh no! The reason was quite simply that the rain had set in for the day and the light values were so low that the pictures were flat and without colour. So another lesson was learnt: in films things don't happen in sequence. Our account of the Rousham Garden took the form of a conducted tour through it. Thanks to the expertise of the colour-film processing laboratories, and the film editor and director, no-one ever guessed that the first part of our tour through the garden had been filmed on a grey wet day, and the final part six weeks later! It all looked as if shot on the same day.

I soon learned why film people talk so much about 'the rushes'. These are the unedited takes of the film, just as shot. They are always of interest: there is nearly always a difference between what you did in front of the camera and what you thought you were doing. It is sometimes better than expected; usually never quite as good as hoped for. Those first rushes of my first day's filming were a revelation. I saw mannerisms I was unaware of, and learned something of the basic grammar of film-making: clearing a shot – that is, walking out of frame – as quickly as reasonable, not making wide gestures when you're in close-up so that your arms go out of the frame, and equally, not making fussy little gestures when you're in mid-shot where there's plenty of room for wide expansive ones. I also saw all too clearly how close the camera is: the merest flicker of the lips, or turn of the head, is enormously telling. I understood at once why I'd been told to be careful not to go 'over the top'. I'd merely said: 'Let's go and see!' but it sounded more like an invitation to some apocalyptic disclosure, rather than a visit to a landscape garden. Rushes can be embarrassing; they can be disconcerting; but they are the mose effective way of learning I know.

The film-editing process was a new world to me; but as I sat with Edmund looking at the first rough-cut of my first film, so many things clicked into place. All those establishing shots at Rousham, for example. By themselves, they were only of moderate visual interest, but as soon as I came to write the commentary for the sound-track, all became clear: my voice was heard setting the scene in detail, and the two married up perfectly.

Writing film commentaries was something new; and, like all new techniques, it was immediately of absorbing interest because it was, at times, so difficult. Once the film had been assembled into what was regarded as the best visual order – for it is the image, the picture, which is most important – the decision had to be taken as to how much commentary, and where. There were of course, gaps between those parts of the film which had speech on them, either an interview or a piece to camera, and these had to be filled (or very rarely left quite consciously empty) with commentary, with or without the addition of music, and effects.

I later grew to enjoy the use of what is called 'wild-track'. Here, an interview, or conversation or even a monologue is recorded: a series of mute film shots is made; and then the editor marries the two. When we filmed the garden of the Machins, Arnold the sculptor and Pat the painter, we had not only an in-vision interview with them both, we allowed their words to spill over behind

139

views of the garden. But we also filmed Pat doing one of her exquisite flower paintings while a wild-track of her voice seemed to be giving us the thoughts that were passing through her mind. (The words were in fact lifted from an interview I had done with her, with my sparse promptings removed.)

The two films called *A Summer of Gardens* were finally transmitted, and seemed to be very well received. After the first one, I was stopped by people in Pebble Mill, who only a few months before had seemed total strangers, and complimented. Nearly everyone said that they had especially enjoyed the little lady with the roses. Since then, Viola Barrett has become known by many, and has grown to think of herself as 'The Little Rose Lady'. She and her collection of roses – she has over 400 in her closely-planted garden – have appeared in numerous articles, including one by me in a series I wrote for *Popular Gardening*, called 'My gardening friends'.

The films were so well received that one of them (I never understood why only one was chosen) was shown nationally on BBC2. They have both been repeated on BBC1 Midlands.

Among the gardens we filmed for *A Summer of Gardens* was one at Kingcombe, the home of Sir Gordon Russell, whom I'd met with my old friend, Joan Hassall. (Joan had been the first woman Master of the Art Workers' Guild, and Sir Gordon a past Master himself, who installed her in her new office, also made history by making sure she was the first Master to be welcomed to office with a kiss).

Sir Gordon was a personality of such interest that Edmund decided to devote another half-hour film to him, shot at Chipping Campden where he went to school, at his home, his furniture galleries, and at the Lygon Arms, the hotel his family owns, in Broadway. It was called 'Designer's Eye', and I wrote and presented it, directed by Edmund Marshall.

Although this was among the most enjoyable films I have made, it did present Edmund with one problem.

Sir Gordon Russell was very tall, well over six feet (1.83m): I am only five feet six (1.68m). The shots in the streets of Campden, or walking round the furniture galleries or the Lygon Arms showed the two of us together; but close-ups were impossible, as we didn't both get into frame: there was the top of my head and Sir Gordon's chin! So I wore shoes with built-in four-inch lifts, which helped; and for the Chipping Campden shots, Gordon very obligingly walked in the gutter and I on a high pavement, so that our heads were on a level. Much of the rest of the film showed us sitting talking in his garden or living-room; the problem here was solved by taking away the cushion from his chair and giving it to me to sit on, with a couple more to raise me to his level.

The film that has given me the greatest pleasure to make is 'One Man's Warwickshire'. This is a very personal account of the corner of the world where I was born and spent my childhood. When I was planning it in my mind, I felt that it could well begin with a piece to camera from me standing on the steps of our house in Leamington, showing the window of the room where I was born. So, when we were filming in Leamington, we set up our cameras to do this.

Edmund was quite definite that there was nothing illegal in standing in front of a house and filming; but I felt that not only would I like to position myself on the steps, but I was curious to see what sort of people were living in the house now. So I knocked and explained, and was immediately invited in by Mr and Mrs Beck, who had bought the house from my parents back in 1938 and had lived there ever since.

The piece to camera which I did saying 'This is where my life began' was in fact filmed, and did get off the cutting-room floor and into the picture. But not at the beginning! Jean Renoir, the French film-maker son of the great impressionist painter has said: 'A film should have a beginning, a middle and an end – but not necessarily in that order!' I was to learn the truth of that many times. Not only is it uncommon for a film to be shot in sequence, it is often amazing how flexible the medium is, so that individual takes can be used at almost any point in the work.

I was able, both in 'One Man's Warwickshire' and *A Summer of Gardens* to experiment with the commentary. In both I wrote parts of it in verse, to match – or rather complement – the pictures. I even mixed verse with recorded conversation, asking what seemed a rhetorical question in verse on the soundtrack, and having it answered by someone in vision. It was crazily effective.

Some time before I had made my first television film, I had conceived an idea for a series of programmes which I felt was ideally suited to the medium. At that time, though, I had no close contact with anyone in television, and was afraid, as many of us rightly or wrongly are, to put forward the idea for fear of having it stolen – or at least changed a little and put on under a different title. These things can happen.

The idea, which I felt exploited colour and human beings and plants and gardens, was a garden quiz in the manner of the old *Animal, Vegetable, Mineral?* or *Face the Music*; and now that I had worked so amicably and productively with Edmund, I felt able to put the idea forward. It was immediately accepted. It was recorded in the large television studio at Pebble Mill with an audience. For our panel we had Valerie Finnis, a well-known plantswoman and photographer, Percy Picton, an experienced professional gardener and a 'character' (as well as being one of the nicest men you could meet) and David Poole, a young man just setting up in the garden centre business, who specialized in house-plants. I was in the chair.

Our first attempt, which was luckily a 'dry-run' tele-recorded on a closed circuit, was disastrous: the panel all talked at once, there was little humour and the whole thing was undisciplined.

We then, with much apprehension, recorded a single pilot programme; and, in spite of reservations, many of which concerned me, we were given a series later in the year. I had written a signature tune for *The Garden Game* as the quiz was called, and two days before we recorded the pilot I went in to Pebble Mill to record it on a Moog synthesiser. When he saw me, Edmund was appalled and asked what on earth was the matter? I explained that I had been working night and day round the clock for the past couple of months, but especially during the last three weeks, in order to finish my history of The Archers, *Forever Ambridge*. Once the signature was safely in the can, Edmund begged me to go home as quickly as possible and get all the rest I could.

This was not a good start. In addition, we had decided to try to keep the programme fresh by having it totally unscripted. This was in one sense laudable; but in another it was foolhardy. I was new to the intricacies of a modern TV studio – at the time our Studio A was among the largest and most up-to-date in Europe. The only aids I had were a few notes on hand-written cards, and unfortunately my nerves took the form of fiddling with those wretched cards.

My vivid imagination didn't help, either. I wanted the programme to succeed more than anything else in the world and I was only too aware of the thousand and one things that could go wrong, especially if I gave the wrong cue or the wrong lead.

The viewers seemed most enthusiastic, but more than one person inside Pebble Mill commented adversely on my nervousness. It never occurred to any of the critics that most of the people they saw occupying the chairman's place were facing cameras every day. I had done so once only: on the day we recorded the pilot programme. Even when we were given a series of four to do, they were recorded in two days: I then went away and didn't see the inside of the studio for another 12 months!

My shortcomings apart (and they grew less and less as I gained in experience) the programme was one of the most successful in the region. To start with, each programme ended with a celebrity gardener. The very first was my friend and neighbour, Gwen Watford. In the 1976 series we had Percy Thrower, Fred Whitsey, editor of *Popular Gardening* and gardening correspondent of *The Daily Telegraph* and Isobel Barnett, whom Edmund and I visited in her Leicestershire home. Her recent death and the circumstances surrounding it make that a poignant memory. In the studio she was glamorous and radiant; and wrote me a very warm letter of thanks after the programme was broadcast.

The late seventies were times of stringent economies in the BBC, and fears began to grow that *The Garden Game* might have to go for economy reasons. It managed to survive until 1980 before that happened; but I hit upon a scheme to help keep it going. If instead of the star gardener at the end of the programme we had a star garden, we would end up with four transient studio programmes as usual, but also, as a bonus, four filmed garden visits, which could be joined together to make a compilation film not unlike *A Summer of Gardens*. This idea found favour, with the result that not only did each late winter bring a series of four garden games, but in spring, we had 'Gardens of Delight', 'A Prospect of Gardens' and 'The Garden Makers'. Each of these films was shown more than once.

When Edmund Marshall left the BBC for the Central Electricity Generating Board, and broadcasting lost the sort of experience, expertise and judgment it can ill aford to lose, the excellent and likeable John Clarke took over *The Garden Game*. Valerie Finnis, to my personal regret, did not appear again, but her place was taken alternately by Ann Liverman and Tristram Thacker.

I had hoped for some time that the programme might have been seen nationally. It was certainly very popular in the Midlands; and over the years we had hammered out a formula which seemed to work admirably. The use of an automatic cueing system made my task a thousand times easier; and once the heavy burden of keeping the show together had by this one device been eased, I not only enjoyed the programmes in the studio, but appeared on screen, as relaxed as I had so quickly learned to be on film.

There are several of these auto-cueing systems in use now, and they are almost magical. The script is printed on a roll of paper, which is then fed into a machine and optically transferred to a mirror in front of the camera lens. The reflection is then (don't ask me how!) passed on to a glass screen which sits right across the centre of the lens. So one can look dead centre of the camera and yet be reading one's words, which slowly roll away out of sight as you read them, fast or slow depending on the skill and reflexes of the operator. This is how newsreaders can, after a glance at a script, reel off whole lists of facts and figures and difficult names: when they're apparently looking you in the eye, they are in fact *reading* the news!

I was very sad to feel that, having at last ironed out the problems in *The Garden Game*, and having been given the great aid of the automatic cueing system, the programme should be taken off the air. So, too, were very many people who, recognizing me in the street would ask when it was coming back.

That question of being recognized is an interesting one. As Philip Archer, I was for some 25 years a well-known voice, but I could travel anywhere without being spotted. Occasionally, especially on the telephone, someone might recognize my voice; but this was rare.

The moment I began to appear on television all that was changed. Because of *Radio Times* and local press publicity for my first film, it was no secret that viewers were going to see the face behind the voice of Philip Archer. Immediately I began to be recognized. Then I noticed an odd phenomenon: I could almost draw a line around the area where this happened. I was recognized in Nottingham, in West Herefordshire (almost in Wales) and South Warwickshire – in fact all over the Midland region. But after a comparatively short car drive, into say, Oxford, I could wander around quite happily unnoticed.

I found this rather pleasant. There is at first (it doesn't last!) a slight feeling of flattery at being recognized; but as any film or TV celebrity will tell you, it can quickly become a great problem. Personal privacy disappears: whatever you do, wherever you go, is the subject of comment. I quickly adjusted to being stopped in the street, asked for an autograph and given cheerful smiles or words of criticism, when inside that marked area. But I knew that if I wanted peace and privacy I had only to motor a little way to where my programmes were not regularly seen, and I became unknown again.

If this really had been the case, I think I would never have wanted to alter it: I did seem to have the best of both worlds. But one day I was in a music shop in London, looking along some full orchestral scores, when another customer asked: 'Looking for something for next week's Band Concert in Borchester?'

I turned to find a young man in spectacles, whom I had never seen in my life before. It was, though, true that in *The Archers* there was going to be a band concert the following week. I asked if he lived in London. He did. Then how, I wondered, did he recognize me. He replied that over the years he had seen me in various television appearances, and had instantly recognized me. Now, as must be obvious from the early part of this chapter, the number of times I have appeared on national television is not great: but so powerful is the visual impression that only one appearance is long enough for some people.

Since that incident, there have been other appearances, including two in the live and highly successful programme 'Pebble Mill at One',

One television appearance that I enjoyed enormously (once it was safely over!), was by accident and at very short notice. John Clarke had asked me to select a programme of seasonal verse for Richard Pascoe to read in a Christmas programme of words and music called 'Good Company'.

The poems were chosen and approved, and the day before the recording I bumped into John Clarke who said that Richard Pascoe, who was appearing with the Royal Shakespeare Company in London, had phoned to say that he was battling with gastro-enteritis. John asked me to stand by. I had been on the point of suggesting that there was no need for me to be present at the recording, but this changed everything.

Quite confident that Richard would make it, I went to Pebble Mill the next day, and someone said: 'Do you know where that big book is that Richard Pascoe was going to use?'

I said that I didn't. Then I did a double-take: 'What do you mean?' I said, '*was* going to use?'

'Oh, haven't you heard? He's ill. You're doing it!'

The next hour went very quickly, as I was pinned into the turtle-necked sweater chosen for Richard, while the sleeves of the casual jacket which Wardrobe had provided for him were shortened. In something of a whirl, we began rehearsing.

Then came another shock. I had imagined that the reader (not, I had thought, myself) would be seen in his pleasant study-like set, in his carved arm-chair apparently reading from the large book, but that the words would be written up on an auto-cueing device. But no. Inside that property book, each of the poems, typed in Jumbo type, had been stuck; and had to be, quite literally, read from there.

I normally wear bi-focals; but as most of my contribution was going to be in close-up, John Clarke and I agreed that I should on

145

this occasion wear contact lenses. So, after lunch, I put in, with trembling hands, my contact lenses. Before I knew it, we were recording.

I was fairly familiar with the poems I had chosen; and all my professional life I have been reading verse aloud. Never, though, have I been more anxious to read well. Incredibly I got through the long session without a single mistake, though I never let on that I was having great difficulty in seeing the text. There were many changes of lighting, especially at the beginnings and ends of poems; and also when the camera glided off my face on to the wall behind me, which then dissolved giving the illusion that the camera was passing through it to find the choir or the brass ensemble. It was only when I took my contact lenses out later that I realized why it had been so difficult to see. In my panic, I had put them in the wrong eyes!

That experience underlined one thing: the television studio no longer frightened me. Quite the contrary, I really felt at home there, just as much at home as I now am with the film camera. There's little reluctance on my part where facing the camera is concerned; and I look forward to doing so increasingly as time goes by.

CHAPTER 9

The Ambridge landscape: in perspective

I can fully understand why eyebrows should be raised when I describe myself as a reluctant Archer. How can anyone describe himself as reluctantly doing something for well over 30 years? The answer is, of course, 'very easily, because it's true'. Almost from the beginning, I had a love-hate thing about *The Archers*. And it was mainly love.

When, as I have explained, I resigned in March 1951, after the first three months, it was not solely because of inequalities over fees – though if I had been desperately keen to do the job, I doubt if I would have been quite so positive in my actions. I really did want to get out.

Even after so short a time, there had been glimpses of what lay ahead: fan-letters, requests for autographed photographs, invitations to open public functions, the possibility of commercial sponsoring and advertisements. None of this appealed to me in the least; indeed I found the prospect of it distasteful. Not because the possibility of becoming well-known did not appeal to me. To say that would be absurd. But I wanted to be famous for being Norman Painting, not for being Philip Archer. So the main reason for my reluctance was I suppose egotism, not modesty.

It must be remembered that I had made a sufficient living with great variety and enjoyment in it, for nearly two years: that I was writer, actor, presenter, reader, interviewer, researcher, musician – not earning a fortune at any one, but making a good living by gaining a few pounds here and a few pounds there at each. It was a good life; it was an interesting life. Above all, it was Norman Painting's life.

So why, after my resignation and violent argument with Godfrey Baseley, did I succumb? I suppose the answer was vanity. Godfrey – perhaps inadvertently – flattered me, when we had that splendid row in the music studio in Broad Street, Birmingham. He banged the Steinway grand; so I banged the Bosendorfer. I had

147

been incensed because someone had left the bar just before Godfrey and had heard him discussing me, and saying, having taken a drink or two: 'He'll sign when I've finished with him!'

Yet I did sign the contract, knowing that I was committed to no more than a month, in spite of Godfrey's shouting down the stairs after me, 'Silly young fool: you've got a job here for ten years if you want it!'

My decision to resign had not been taken lightly. I had given the matter very careful thought and made three attempts to persuade the BBC that I was serious. I knew that, whereas Robert Mawdesley, for example, could adopt a heavily-disguised voice for Walter Gabriel and still be employed as an actor as much as ever, I could not. The voice I used for Philip was more or less my own natural one. If I went on playing the part, then my career as a radio actor would end very quickly. This was only speculation at the time: but events very soon proved me right. I enjoyed radio acting, and indeed have been performing at the microphone for over 30 years. I was not reluctant about that: I was reluctant to tie myself to one part.

I remembered a story that Dorothy Reynolds had told me about a young actress who from her teens into her twenties played the juvenile lead in an extremely successful West End play. When the play ended, and she was looking for another part, she was asked what experience she had. She replied half-laughingly that she'd played a West End lead for five years; and was horrified to be told that she had played only one part: what other significant experience had she had?

Not that my case would be exactly parallel: at least we had a different script for each episode, so it was not soul-destroying in the way a long run of the same play can be. But it worried me. In spite of Godfrey's talk of ten years, all that was certain was that we knew the programme was planned for three months, terminable at one month's notice; but even for so short a time I was still reluctant to reduce my microphone work to one part.

I have been reluctant ever since, in one respect: public appearances. I had no illusions that I was being invited to functions all over the country because I was a good actor or a good writer or even because I was an interesting person. In fact, Norman Painting wasn't invited at all. It was Philip Archer who was welcomed, whose autograph was wanted and whose hand the fans wanted to shake. I used to have nightmares about it; the sort of dream that all actors have, where you find yourself centre-stage, with a full house, and you're playing the lead and you don't know any of the lines or any of the cues.

I tried, almost from the start, to talk about Phil in the third person at public appearances; or, at the very least, to explain that I was really Norman Painting but if I were Philip Archer I might well say something like this . . . and then I'd lapse into his sort of talk. But that didn't go down nearly as well as when my colleagues appeared in character, both in voice and manner, and spoke in the first person.

I wasn't being bloody-minded about this. Our contracts made it unequivocally clear that the BBC held the copyright of the names of all the characters and locations in the programme. In other words, I was not Phil nor could I claim to live in Ambridge. Indeed for many years, until the recent relaxation of many of the rules and guidelines governing the programme, we were required to get permission to appear at any function. Eventually we were forced in self-defence to indemnify ourselves by getting a signed declaration from organisers that they would advertise and announce us by our real names as well as our character ones.

One more characteristic which Norman Painting has which is not so strong in Philip is the habit of seeing far ahead: and the prospect of becoming well-known solely as somebody else didn't appeal to me at all.

Several other members of the cast felt the same. When the programme was less than two years old, Pamela Mant, who had played Christine from the beginning, and of whom I had grown very fond, suddenly upped and left, as did John Franklyn (Mike Daly). Monica Grey, Grace, had left after one year, saying quite clearly that she had other ideas for her career than a life in a daily serial. It was a very reasonable attitude.

The older members of the company did not quite see it that way. Dan, Doris and Simon all did everything they could to become their characters on mike and off. Gwen even had writing paper printed with From Mrs Doris Archer, Brookfield Farm, Ambridge, Near Borchester at the top of it, which I thought was not within the terms of our contract; but throughout her long stay with us dear Gwen was always a law unto herself. (She's one of my oldest and dearest friends, and I know she won't mind my saying that.)

It may reasonably be asked why, if I was so reluctant to ruin my radio career as an actor, did I then go ahead? Partly because Godfrey, however obliquely and brusquely he put it – and he was oblique and brusque! – had made it clear that I was very much wanted for the part, and would be offered the same fee as the other main performers. (In fact Doris, Chris, and Grace all received a very substantial increase as a result of my demonstration.) I also knew that the programme could be taken off the air after three months.

So my reluctance was not so much allayed as put into cold storage: I was persuaded that if I gave it a further few months' trial, I could still pull out. That of course was the deciding factor: three months later it seemed too late. I had stayed in the cage. I was trapped! The programme's rise to popularity was so rapid, so heady, that I was swept along with it. My old friend, Jack May, who had done much to persuade me not to persist in my wish to leave the cast saw my playing Phil as an occupation of two and a half days, in which one could earn enough to live on. In the rest of the week, he said, I could 'write my masterpieces'.

It wasn't like that, as I had foreseen. Success brought with it the sort of public interest I have mentioned, with the result that there were few days in the week that weren't in some way taken up by the programme: interviews, photo-calls, personal appearances, charity work, commercial sponsorings. The writing of the 'masterpieces' was postponed indefinitely. I remember meeting some years later John Chandos, a writer and actor with whom I had, years before, had many conversations about our mutual writing ambitions, and he said, quizzically, 'No time for Tragedy?' That touched a nerve.

I hope this does not give the impression that I am misanthropic and ungrateful for the life that being in *The Archers* has given me. Whenever I have tried to explain my reluctance, I have always prefaced my words with the fact that I realize how fortunate I am to have been in steady work as an actor all my professional life, even though it was not the life I would ever have imagined for myself.

My life as a writer, as I have shown in Chapter 6, has by no means been an idle one. I have to admit that my output has been enormous; but it has been mainly writing that does not require weeks of isolation to prepare, and mainly commissioned work, not writing that I was burning to do on my own account. Before the pace became too hectic I wrote a couple of 'well-made' plays. Also, encouraged by Tony Cornish, in the early seventies I managed to get down on paper the first draft of a theatre play in a form which appeals to me enormously. It was called *Portico in Paradise* and is written for open stage.

More recently, I wrote, as a vehicle for my friend Trevor

Harrison and myself, what may prove to be the best thing I have yet done for the stage, a play called *Squat*. But that, like *Portico in Paradise* has yet to be put on. Both were written at white heat in a very short time: there has been no opportunity in over 30 years to set aside a few weeks or months for the natural gestation and parturition of a work written with heart and soul. My whole life seems to have been commissions and dead-lines. I'm certainly not complaining; but one of my hopes for the future is that there may be more time to write what I believe is still to be written. My ambitions are, if unfulfilled, curiously unchanged from what they were 30 years ago.

It would be less than honest to say that there have been times when my frustration almost turned my reluctance into positive resentment. By the early Sixties I began to feel that unless I got out and let someone else take over I would do something drastic. But then two factors weighed heavily: the team-spirit of the whole Archer company, which for many years was an almost tangible thing; and a (possibly misplaced) sense of loyalty to the listeners. (It is only recently that Phil has become a less pleasant character: before, although he was big-headed, over-confident infuriating and as often wrong as right, he was always likeable. If his character continues to deteriorate into smallmindedness and misanthropy it may well be that soon his departure from the programme would be welcomed by most of the listeners, as opposed to that minority which hates every character, however popular.)

For a time I accepted my fate, and for 10 years threw myself into playing Phil with gusto and enthusiasm. The character was so three-dimensional, and so different from me, apart from superficial similarities, that it was both challenging and enjoyable. Perhaps it was 'delusions of indispensability' which made me cling to the part, but cling I did. Then something else happened, and the reluctance returned. Towards the end of his all-too-short life, Geoffrey Webb and I grew closer to each other. I never quite understood why this was so, and the only reasons I have managed to find have been regarded as so esoteric as not to be convincing to the generality.

When, in another book of mine, *Forever Ambridge*, I suggested that my early scripts for *The Archers* were influenced by the departed writer from another level of existence, one of my new masters was so pontifical in condemning the suggestion as nonsense that I knew him to have the closed mind I had always suspected. His line was that if I so much as suggested that our lives could be influenced by forces other than those which were material and could be measured, then I was putting myself out of court where ordinary reasonable people were concerned. If that is the case, I am out of court, and no ordinary reasonable person need read on.

It has to be said somewhere in a book which claims to be a self-portrait, that I have a very firm belief in re-incarnation, and am aware of other states of being, of other levels and planes of consciousness than the mere material one. Mal-functioning of the brain, or irregular coherence of its lobes, may 'explain' such feelings as *déjà vu* or 'I have been here before'; But no such 'explanation' can account for, say, the genius of a prodigy, or my friend Joan Hassall 'remembering' how to use a wood graver the first time she picked one up.

I try never to inflict my religious views on anyone, nor to dissuade anyone from beliefs firmly held: they are the rafts that keep us poor humans afloat. No good is served by telling a fellow-survivor that there is hole in his lifeboat: if he thinks it's keeping him afloat, why argue? We can suspect much: we can believe much, we can wonder much. Sometimes, in a small corner of our lives, we can say with complete confidence, in spite of all the reason, the logic, the ridicule of others, 'This is what I know.' *Know*. Not suspect. Not believe. Know. I know what I know.

Geoffrey Webb died, and half the writing-team of *The Archers* died with him. There is no doubt in my mind that the ideal number of writers for serials is one. But the strain is too great. The next best is two writers; and that is what *The Archers* had through its early, golden years. As I write these words there is almost a score of writers currently producing scripts for the programme. That in my opinion is about ten times too many. A 2-horse coach is easier to drive than a 4-horse one: an 18-horse coach is in my view virtually impossible.

When Geoff Webb died, there were murmurings in the cast. I was known to be a writer: my scripts were (as they continued to be for the next 15 years or so) constantly broadcast. Why didn't I ask if I could write *The Archers*?

Now I really was reluctant! If my ambition as a radio actor had never really included acting in a daily radio serial, there was no doubt that I had no wish to write a daily radio serial. Other works for radio, yes. But not a serial. And that was the end of that.

David Turner, a one-time fellow-student of mine, joined Ted Mason in writing scripts. He, like so many of the programme's current writers, showed quite positive writing skill, producing some interesting, if controversial, scripts; what he essentially did not produce was Archer scripts. They were, unmistakably, Turner scripts.

Many developments in recent years have hurt and annoyed me. But the one which has caused me most pain is the suggestion that the scripts which I eventually wrote were not only stereotyped, hidebound and old-fashioned, but that that was all I was capable of. That is to mistake my intention. I was deliberately writing in a precise convention.

Classical forms are strict and rigid: diversions from them may be entertaining, but they are not the Thing Itself. Many newcomers have tried to throw over the accepted conventions of the programme, just as politically some of them would like to throw over the present structure of society. Neither undertaking is easy. In order to be accepted as a serial writer you have to be prepared to write as part of a team, to a strict formula. Many otherwise good writers fail to write good serial scripts because they hold the mistaken view that in some way by doing so they compromise their own integrity. This is not the case, as I was to discover.

But that discovery did not come for some time. I was by now (1962) inured to the fact, however reluctantly, that I was saddled with playing Philip Archer for the foreseeable future. My main concern was trying to carve out of each week enough time to meet the deadlines of various writing commitments that came my way. Life was only slightly less hectic than it had been at the peak period of the mid-fifties. We still found ourselves opening fêtes and bazaars, shops and festivals. The only difference was that in the early days, it was 'The Archer Family' that was asked, as a unit, to appear. Gradually that had dwindled to single appearences, or with one's partner possibly because a realistic fee was now payable. Thus, for example, Ysanne Churchman and I, as Grace and Philip were invited together, or Dan and Doris. One was even invited to appear with someone not connected with the programme. For example, at a fête in Warwick Castle, I was invited, through my friend Geoffrey Jaggard (to whose grandson, Christopher, I am a highly inefficient godfather) to appear with the Roman Catholic Archbishop of Birmingham and Vera Lynn! I very much enjoyed meeting both of them, but especially Dame Vera (This was in fact many years before she was appointed DBE) because of her completely unaffected and warmly gentle manner. Her husband and daughter were with her; and I silently much admired the way that Vera did not indulge the little girl in demands for extra spending money, once the agreed allowance had been spent. I also remember this occasion for another reason: it was one of my first appearances in public wearing the rather primitive contact lenses of the period. They were far from comfortable to wear at times; and one or two of the photographs taken on that occasion show me looking unusually squinney-eyed.

John Keir Cross took over from David Turner as second scriptwriter to Edward J. Mason in 1962, and for the next four years there was no question of my fellow-actors, or anyone else, suggesting that I should consider writing *The Archers*. This was the time when I was writing so happily for Tony Cornish, so the question did not arise.

Then, in 1965 it became increasingly clear that John Keir Cross's health was beginning to fail. I was asked (along with several other writers though nobody told me that till some time later!) if I would consider submitting five trial scripts for *The Archers*. I did so. It may be asked why. If I say I can give only part of the answer it is not because I am trying to avoid the truth. One can only ever tell a part of the truth; and no-one, but *no-one*, ever does any single thing for a single motive. I must admit that in agreeing to consider writing for *The Archers* I certainly had an ulterior motive: it may have been fully understood, or may have been lurking somewhere in my subconscious, but it did seem to offer a way out.

I would be dishonest if I did not admit that most of the cast had felt that none of his successors had really matched the quality of Geoffrey Webb's scripts. He and Ted Mason had been perfectly paired; and since his death, Ted had not found either the complementary balance or the stimulation which Geoff's scripts had given him.

One of the factors which drew me to attempt to write the trial scripts was the possibility, because of my involvement in the programme from its beginnings, that I might do better. Another factor was one that I have already touched on: I am always fascinated by a new writing technique. I had never written drama for so small a canvas before: I was rather curious to see whether I could master the technique of moving some 20 or so characters around convincingly in a script of less than a quarter of an hour's duration. It was rather like a novelist attempting for the first time to write short stories.

But the unspoken thought at the back of my mind was that if I could by some miracle write good Archer scripts, there was at least a chance that I might be able to release myself from the treadmill of playing Phil, and earn my living as a writer. It very nearly happened.

My trial scripts were approved, indeed applauded. Then I was told to wait until called. The wait lasted from October 1965 to 8 June 1966. Then the telephone rang, and I was told by Godfrey Baseley to stand by, as John Keir Cross was in hospital. On 28 July 1966 my first three scripts, as Bruno Milna, were recorded in Studio B12, London. By the end of the year I had written 27 episodes. When John Keir Cross died in January of the following year, I had a meeting as the heir apparent, with Godfrey Baseley and Ted Mason. It was clear that Godfrey was anxious for me to become the second half of a scriptwriting team of two, with Ted. Ted had misgivings, feeling that both writing half the programme and playing one of the main parts was likely to prove too much. His own health was beginning to give him trouble at the time, and no-one knew better than he did how easy it was to over-work. I said I was sure that I could do it; and then Godfrey spiked my guns completely by saying 'But there's to be no nonsense about Philip. We still want you in three or four episodes a week!'

So my plan, at least for a time, was thwarted. I have to confess that having once written a few scripts and heard them broadcast I had no reluctance at all about writing *The Archers*. I loved it. It was difficult, so difficult it hurt in some ways, especially trying to keep one's requirements within the budget allowed. I suddenly realized that I was doing something I had always wanted to do: be a writer in residence for a company of first-rate actors. The only thing that was different was that I'd always imagined writing for a theatre company, not a radio one.

The great discovery about writing *The Archers* was how little I had to compromise. Once one accepted (and as I have said it is essential to do so) the rigid conventions of the programme, then the writer was free (within those conventions) to say anything he wanted to. Clearly what happened had to be possible, indeed likely, in a village like Ambridge. And, obviously, the right characters had to express the right views in an acceptable way. We could talk about junkies, for example; but the young characters would express a very different viewpoint from Doris, and in very different language. But otherwise, the writer was free.

Soon, far from being reluctant, I was eager – as a writer that is. The more I wrote, and the more time I spent with the (then) extremely small creative team, the more I was able to promote my view that the character of Philip was dispensable. Soon I had convinced Godfrey and Ted that the spotlight would fix on the next generation, and skip Philip. Tony Archer was to be the bright young farmer, full of the very latest farming ideas, while Phil would move to the periphery, as a good and successful but no longer a pioneering farmer, while Jill, Shula and the rest of the family could be heard taking their normal part in village life.

Soon, I was pleased to hear Godfrey explaining the policy to the programme heads: 'We shall miss a generation, and build up Tony.'

It was not long after this that Godfrey half-whispered another idea he had had for some time for Doris to die. The rest of us were horrified; and we made sure it didn't happen. This was yet one more thing that I was unable even to hint at in conversation with my friend Gwen.

Gwen and I had become close friends very early on. The moment I had heard her infectious laughter as she entered the studio for her audition as Doris Archer, I realized I was about to meet an old friend for the first time! So it has proved.

There is no doubt, as time eventually made clear, that she was an excellent choice for Doris Archer. There was, however, one snag, caused by something which no-one noticed during the ambition. Although Gwen was always as she has said, 'a fat girl', and looked comfortably rounded and homely, her voice was, like her singing voice, a high soprano. When we came to record the programmes, not only did she not sound her age, she also had a close similarity to Pamela Mant, who was playing her daughter, Christine.

Godfrey Baseley, who produced the programme for the first few weeks, with Tony Shryane at his elbow, was insistent and relentless. 'Too high', he would call, over the talk-back loudspeaker. 'Bring it down. Make her older! Use your lower register.'

Gwen was at first worried. Then discouraged. Then desperate. More than once, she was reduced to tears. Then she was forced to a ploy she was to use very effectively over the next 20 years or more, of threatening to 'Hand me notice in!'

Several of us always tried to comfort her; but I in particular seemed to have the knack of making her laugh. After the first three months she said to me, as she later said to many other people, often in the course of giving public talks, that but for me she would have given up. Odd that the only person at the end of that three months who was *really* trying to withdraw from the programme, was me, the reluctant Archer.

Gwen and I became close personal friends, spending holidays together, and seeing each other at least one evening a week in addition to recording sessions. I moved to London in the late fifties; and Gwen moved there, too, within a year or so. When I later moved out of London back to the country, Gwen too moved back to the Midlands. We were very good friends: we had few secrets. But then, suddenly, I was part of the inner group that planned and ran *The Archers*. I tried to explain to Gwen, and she, I know, tried to understand, that there would have to be some questions from now on that we could never discuss. Loyalty to a friend had, in this case, to give way to loyalty to the programme. This punctiliousness on my part now seems very old-fashioned; but I felt that unless I could demonstrate that I was capable of keeping professional secrets, then I could not expect to be party to them. This sort of feeling is now, of course a thing of the past: some of us in the cast are not only uneasy when we find newcomers privy to what ought to be, in my view, the programme's secrets, but annoyed and uncomfortable when details of the programme are leaked to the Press. Annoyed, because the element of freshness and surprise which as actors we try to create is destroyed; and uncomfortable because of the unsettling effect of not knowing who the 'mole' is among us. We all have ideas as to who he, she or they are: but this feeling of uncertainty does not help to create an atmosphere of harmony in the studio.

There was only one time, in our 29 years association, that I was unable to make Gwen laugh. She had been feeling increasingly low: we had all tried to persuade her to use every ounce of energy she could find to stay with the programme until its 30th birthday. One day, she felt she was at rock bottom, and telephoned to say she was too ill to make the short journey from the hotel where she was staying to the studio. But she arrived. But then a tactless and ill-timed remark completely, as Gwen used to say, 'knocked her bow off!'

I offered to take her back to the hotel. At first she sat silently beside me in my car. Then she suddenly said: 'I shan't come in tomorrow morning!'

'Oh, yes, you will,' I said. 'You're a pro and you've signed a contract.'

Then I used one of those silly names, which, like a friendly cuff, mean the opposite from what they seem.

She didn't laugh. She didn't answer. Two huge tears rolled silently down her cheeks, and I knew that this time there was no chance of raising a laugh. She was disenchanted. She felt that, as she was not taking part (mainly at her own request) in so many episodes, she no longer knew everybody. Gone were the days when she had her own chair and woe betide anyone who dare sit in it. Gone were the days when she was Queen of *The Archers*, as absolute monarch. She now hated the studio. She was ill-at-ease with those in charge. She did not like the changes that were being made both in the scripts and the staff. Her great friend and ally, Tony Shyane, had retired. She was utterly demoralized.

She did struggle to the studio the next day. But it was for the last time. She retired to Torquay, rarely venturing very far from the nursing home where she lived, apart from one memorable visit to Buckingham Palace by ambulance to receive the decoration of MBE from Her Majesty the Queen. So Gwen, too, in those latter days, was a reluctant Archer.

I also was to find myself feeling reluctant again, on several occasions, for rather different reasons than the previous ones.

Although *The Archers* were radically and often ruthlessly updated from time to time throughout its first 21 years, the departure of Godfrey Baseley, its creator, prime mover, promotor and defender, changed the programme quite basically. It is no secret that I was uneasy about his leaving; and I became extremely unhappy while working under his successor − purely for professional reasons: I had no personal disagreements. Then he left.

Under Charles Lefeaux's editorship I was at first equally unhappy and reluctant to continue until his manner towards me changed from frost to sunshine. But now that the programme is so much altered from its original specification, my reluctance has returned. I merely state, with malice towards none and with criticism of none − for only time will show how right or wrong the changes have been − that I found that I was no longer enjoying writing the scripts; and I am frequently unhappy about playing the part.

I say that only time will show: but even that is far from certain. When value judgments are made one quickly becomes involved in imponderables: what would have happened if this had been done, or had not been done, are questions impossible to answer.

The surprise to me had been that once my natural reluctance had been overcome, I discovered, as I have tried to explain earlier in this book, that I was caught up as an actor in the excitement of the thing. As a writer, too, I was enormously switched on by the realization that I could air views on, for example, conservation, the use of the land, modern farming methods, both arable and with stock, and many other important issues. Both sides of the case had to be given of course − and if I received as many letters complaining of bias as praising the script I felt I'd got the balance correct! − but at least, in the long early tradition of that programme, I was writing of serious matters that were in the public interest. Not that one was allowed to be solemn: and my most successful efforts were always those which, again, were in the programme's tradition of treating serious issues with humour (but not facetiousness).

I have withdrawn from the writing team; and the possibility is also open to me of withdrawing from the cast. As an actor one has to be prepared to perform whatever part is offered: my problem is that I feel that the character I have played for so many years has changed arbitrarily and not, as up till now, gradually, naturally and organically. It is not that one is unhappy about playing a mean-minded penny-pinching misanthrope. Quite the opposite: most actors agree that the baddies are much more fun to play than the goodies. The key factor is that the actor must believe in the character himself. My old reluctance has returned because on so many occasions in recent years I have been asked to play a part that is so changed I cannot believe in it, and to deliver lines that, in spite of whatever skill the experience of so many years has brought me, still seem out of character and lacking in credibility.

Yet there is no such thing as half a performance: once the cue light shines, the adrenalin flows and like all actors I can give no less than my utmost. That happens, anyway; there is no choice; it is like the act of love.

And there is another consideration, and mentioning it may take us dangerously near to pomposity: loyalty. If it were decided that I should, for reasons of plot or policy, be removed from the cast, then I would bow to that decision without demurring. What else could one do after such a record-breaking run? But as for resigning, for withdrawing from the cast on my own initiative, that is a different matter. It would seem disloyal and I would feel, would you believe, a certain reluctance to do it!

CHAPTER 10

Framed portrait: warts and all

Now we are approaching varnishing day. The rough outline of this self-portrait has been sketched in, but, as with all self-portraits, the final picture is bound to differ in some way from the accepted view: the world sees from without, the painter from within.

I have put in some of the warts: but with painter's licence. I have missed out one or two lines and wrinkles. There are omissions for various reasons: space, narrative shape, diplomacy, the wish not to offend, and the simple inadequacy of the painter's memory. And just as many portraits are of head and shoulders, so this concerns itself with little below the neck: there are few details of the subject's digestive process or sexual appetites, habits of diet or hygiene, or other such matters which belong perhaps more to pathology than portraiture.

This portrait should show very few lines of resentment or malice or discontent: there have been disappointments, failures, times of depression and misery; but they have been outweighed by other moods. The few, most unwelcome, spells of indolence and apathy have been overwhelmingly outnumbered by cheerfully industrious activity.

But how good a likeness is it? I have tried to be as accurate as I can, but I must confess that in writing much of this book, and especially now in touching-in the final little lines and details, I have been aware of one great drawback: most of the time I cannot really believe that anyone will want to read it. Why should anyone be interested in me? Yet, there are times when I myself am irritated or dismayed when people I meet expect me to be quite different from what I am. So I have attempted the almost impossible and tried to tell at least some of the truth about myself. For anyone who spends any time in the public eye there is always the question of 'image' to be reckoned with. It would be disingenuous to pretend that I have not spent some 30 years as a public person, to a greater or lesser extent. I have grown to describe myself as a'mini celebrity'. Most people who have heard me in *The Archers* have naturally assumed that I have a great deal in common with that imaginary, but still very real, person who shares a voice with me. The truth is, as readers of this book will by now be aware, that Philip Archer and Norman Painting have very little in common. Our material conditions are not entirely similar, nor have they ever been. Philip was born on a farm, the same farm where he now lives; he went to the village school, then to the local grammar school, and on to a farm institute. His parents were never very rich, until perhaps in recent times when they were, at least on paper, comparatively affluent. Norman Painting's parents on the other hand were always far from affluent. Norman's father was a railway worker, one of a large family, the son of a railway inspector. Norman's mother was one of 12 children of a Staffordshire coal-miner. Philip was born in Ambridge; Norman was born in Leamington Spa. The course of Philip's life was in a sense preordained; it was fairly predictable. It is true he was something of a rebel, and a tearaway, but this was not untypical of young men of his background. After sowing many wild oats, he eventually 'settled down', married the boss's daughter, and to no-one's surprise took over his father's farm.

The predictable course for Norman Painting might easily have been to have left school at 14 to have found work in a local factory or even to have followed his father on to the railway; to have married and produced a family and lived contentedly but unremarkably in a Midland town. But one quality which Norman shared with Philip was that of rebellion; the predicted course was not for him. It is true that family circumstances forced him to leave the grammar school in which he had found a place by means of a scholarship, when he was only 15 years old. But by dint of effort and an unwillingness to be deflected from his chosen course, he broke away from the tramlines that stretched before him into a more adventurous and more hazardous career.

There are those who speak of one's life as a work of art. Such people mark their development into maturity by asking, 'Who am I' and then proceed to ask, 'What do I want to do?' Norman Painting's problem was that he knew quite clearly what he wanted to do long before he had any clear idea of who he was. It is, paradoxically, true to say that it was not until he was confronted with an *alter ego*, that he was forced in self-defence to discover at least something of his own identity. When *The Archers* began, most of his colleagues, who were in the main much older than he, eagerly chose to take upon themselves the characteristics of the characters which they were called upon to play. Norman Painting, almost from the beginning, decided that he was *not* Philip Archer, nor would he allow himself to be smothered or overlaid by his fictional creation. But Philip gave Norman social and sexual advantages. The steady income earned by playing Philip gave Norman a slowly improving life style. And the inevitable complication which a real wife and real children might have brought into his life was evaded by accepting the two wives and the four children which the programme gave to him, vicariously. The best of both worlds.

It must never be forgotten that *The Archers* was not Norman's only means of livelihood. When recently one of the late-coming officials in the programme accompanied a very new young actor in *The Archers* through the spacious gardens around Norman's country home and said, 'See how rich you can become by being in *The Archers*' he was telling less than the truth. As this book shows, from the time Norman left Oxford, he had worked extremely hard as a free-lance writer and broadcaster, researcher and reporter; and the not inconsiderable income that he thereby gained did not come entirely from *The Archers*. It is not generally understood how, over the years, the amount of an actor's time required to record *The Archers* has slowly decreased, until it is now at most six days a month. This leaves ample time for other work.

In Norman's case this has been filled with making several series of television films (most of which have been seen only in the Midlands) writing books, articles, plays and radio scripts and in doing a great deal of public work. Philip Archer, it is true, is a JP. He has also in the past been active in the National Farmers' Union and in the Scout movement. He also plays the organ in the village church. Norman, on the other hand, has spent a great deal of his leisure time in a wide variety of public work. There has, inevitably, been the usual number of requests to make public appearances. But increasingly, especially since he began to appear on television, Norman has been invited to launch large-scale appeals, to sit on committees and commissions, to be a vice-president, a trustee, a chairman of a trust and so on.

I have dwelt at such length on the difference between Philip Archer and Norman Painting merely to emphasize their dissimilarity. Painting this portrait of Painting seems to be moving step by step further away from the expected to the unforeseen. And it's still an unfinished picture. I recall a snatch of conversation that happened many years ago in the early days of the *The Archers*.

We had just finished the week's recordings in Birmingham one wintry wet Saturday evening and Jack May (my old Oxford friend, now known to *Archers* listeners as Nelson Gabriel) was talking to Mary Wimbush. In the manner of young actors they were discussing the sort of life-style they wished they had. Jack said: 'What I would like to do now, is to drive to my comfortable house in the country, have a hot bath, pour myself a whisky and soda whilst I waited for a delicious dinner to be served!'

Mary and I eagerly agreed.

Jack continued: 'The person nearest to doing that is of course Painting!'

I was still living in my country cottage near Oxford, and it was by no means the luxurious country home Jack conjured up. Nonetheless, I cannot deny that the thrust of my ambition has been towards a comfortable lifestyle in order to provide the conditions in which I can write at my best. Starving in a garret has never really seemed an attractive prospect to me, and I know from experience that the flame of my inspiration, if that is the word, never burns brightly enough to warm and brighten basically uncongenial conditions.

It was to be some years after that conversation with Jack May and Mary Wimbush that, having lived in London for some 10 years, I acquired a comfortable home in the village of Warmington, in the very south of the county where I was born. The story of finding that house, the making of its garden and tales of my four Cavalier spaniels is told in my forthcoming book, *Gardens and Cavaliers*.

My main motivation has always been to try to enjoy the good things of life, and to be prepared to work extremely hard in order to pay for them. Through the same lack of confidence I mentioned at the head of this chapter, however, I failed to seek the publicity which some of my colleagues found and revelled in. My excuse was that I was too busy, and there was, for most of the time, some truth in this. My output of talks, serials, plays and books based on my radio programmes, was considerable. But the real reason was that I was shy. People who don't know me very well find it hard to believe that I am as timid as I say. It is nonetheless true. It's the ice-breaking that's so difficult. I hate new places – hotels, pubs, offices. But having crossed the threshold, having got there, I am completely at home within seconds – just as I was in Christ Church Hall at Oxford, once I had overcome my initial timidity.

The problem is that I seem to see imaginary barriers; but, imaginary or not, they are to me all too real. Now, after many years of soul-searching, I am convinced that, without intending it, I erect an impenetrable wall of glass between myself and strangers, even strangers that I would very much like to meet. As a private person, that is; as Norman Painting. Philip Archer has none of these problems. When I'm 'on duty', being a Public Person, I can talk to anybody and everybody, and I do. But when I am alone in a strange town, I am quite capable of spending days without saying a word to anyone, except waiters and bus drivers and so on. But this is in no sense the desire to be standoffish. Most of the time I am longing for company. I just seem to lack the knack of making friends, or of meeting any stranger on a personal and not a formal level.

I am also an inveterate 'looker forward'. Only rarely do I enjoy looking back (which is why writing this book has been at times so traumatic). I believe that reminiscence and nostalgia should be severely rationed. On the other hand, I sometimes look too far forward. I've always assumed that I shall marry some day, but I never seem to have got round to it! In fact, on two occasions, the girls I might easily have married went off with someone else before I even got as far as declaring that our friendship was something special – at least to me. (It's now clear that one of those marriages would almost certainly have been a disaster; but the other might well have worked.)

Another wart on the portrait – or is it a wrinkle? – is my absentmindedness. I once broke off from brushing my shoes to check how much butter I had in the larder. When I went back to my shoes, the shoebrush had disappeared. I found it the next day, with the butter in the larder.

Twice I have shot off a whole reel of film with odd results. On one occasion, the owner of a herd of pedigree cows drove me round and round them in his landrover, manoeuvring to give me the best angles and so on. On another occasion I spent an hour or so with Tony Cornish and his wife Linda, photographing their baby son, Simon: laughing, not laughing; with his father, with his mother; with both, with neither; standing on his head, falling asleep. The results of both these exercises were that I produced not a single photograph either of pedigree cattle, nor of the Cornish family. The reason was simple: I had forgotten to put a film in the camera . . .

Once, motoring to the Birmingham studios from London, with three short plays I was writing very much in my head, I went right round a traffic roundabout instead of turning off, and suddenly found myself on the way back to London.

And yet, for certain things, I have an extremely good, but very erratic memory. I was once being shown around Nottingham Police Headquarters by the then chief constable, one of the most colourful and certainly the most delightfully named in the country: Capt. Athelstan Popkess. I several times referred to things I had seen on a previous visit some years before. He exclaimed, with admiration, what an incredible memory I had. Yet I couldn't remember what I had done the day before! I hoped that no misdemeanor caused by forgetfulness would ever bring me on the wrong side of him: he would never believe me if I said I'd forgotten!

I arrived for Tony Shryane's wedding wearing my gardening shoes; and once, throwing a few things into an overnight bag I arrived at my destination amazed at how heavy it felt. When I looked inside, I had brought the wrong bag, and was carrying several reels of recording tape, a microphone and two or three heavy reference books.

I'm very much like a squirrel in many ways: I carefully put things in a very safe place, and then forget where. I seem to spend half my life looking for things which very often turn up exactly where they ought to be. (I secretly think that Gremlins move them.)

Merely to keep ticking over takes every ounce of self-discipline I can muster (and during the years when I was writing well over 100 scripts a year, I found reserves of industry and self-discipline I didn't know I had).

I write shopping lists, and leave them at home; and notes for speeches are sometimes in the pocket of my jeans and not the suit I'm wearing.

My sister once asked me the time, and I consulted my watch and told her. It was only when she could restrain her laughter no longer that I realized that my hand and watch, were under water in the ornamental fish-tank: I'd seen a little alga and was busy removing it!

Apart from the occasions I have mentioned, I normally do manage, miraculously, not to be late, nor indeed to miss appointments altogether. But the effort and organization and safeguards involved are considerable. I am amazed therefore when told that I project an image of prissiness, over-correctness, orderliness, conformity, and sober-sided seriousness; in other words I appear quite different from what I am. I was delighted to learn that J.B. Priestley had the same problem: inside his rotund dependable-looking, down-to-earth exterior, there was, he suggested, a skittish gazelle skipping about lightheartedly and irresponsibly.

There is one matter on which I am prepared to be charged, by some people, with prissiness: that corrupt area of showbiz that takes in the bar and the casting couch. If it is prissy to want to feel that you have been cast for a certain part, invited to write or present a programme, because you are judged to be the best person available, rather than knowing one won it by buying certain people drinks, or going to bed with them, then I'm prissy. It is, though, a question of confidence, not necessarily morality. I need to know I've been chosen for my ability, not for any other attributes, otherwise I lack the confidence to perform the part, direct the scene, or write the script. It seems to me that only the moderately talented and the insecure put their professional, and also their personal, dignity at risk by selling themselves or by trying to buy favours. An artist's first duty is to believe in himself.

It is a source of constant wonder that my inner feelings and my outward expression are so often contradictory. I was once travelling home on a tube train late at night when the only other person in the compartment was a middle-aged man who was extremely drunk. I looked at him, trying to understand the reason for his pitifully inebriated state. I was thinking his lack of merriment suggested that he was desperately unhappy and had been driven to seek refuge from his problems in alcohol. My thoughts were of compassion and fellow-feeling; 'There but for the Grace of God . . .' that is what I felt. What I must have transmitted to him was very different. He suddenly fixed me with a rolling glaring eye, wagged an accusing finger at me and said 'It's all right for the likes of you, sitting there all smug as if butter wouldn't melt in your mouth. You don't know what some folks have to put up with, do you?'

My compassion had been interpreted as disapproval. Do I really seem on such occasions to be 'Holier than Thou?' I never feel like that. I once bought a comic birthday card, finding it amusing. I have it still, because I can think of no-one to send it to. The reason is that it applies more to me than to anyone else I know. It says quite simply on the front of the card: 'I may look like a Sunday-school teacher . . . .' and inside it says: ' . . . But I have Saturday night ideas!' Those who do not know me very well find it almost impossible to believe that I have Saturday night ideas at all; the truth is I have Saturday night ideas nearly every day of the week. But most of the time I'm too shy to do much about it!

I suppose this impression of conformity, even conventionality, is a hangover from my mother's attempt at impressing me with middle-class values. All those things which were to her so important, which were so necessary in order to 'get on,' in order to 'Better oneself', have turned out, of course, to be worth nothing at all. But in spite of myself, I still cling to them, on occasion. The casual clothes in which I normally live (I never wear a tie wherever possible), complete lack of shoes (I spend days on end in the summer walking barefoot through my house and garden) – all these things give way when I go into the public eye. This I am sure is, if not a mistake certainly a shortcoming. But during my lifetime the conventions of society have changed so radically, and in so many directions, that it is sometimes difficult to know which image to project or indeed which image one is projecting. It may well be asked, 'Why so self-conscious? Does one have to project an image at all?' The point is that anyone who is exposed in any way to the public gaze for any length of time will soon find himself categorized and typed by the media whether he likes it or not, sometimes to his disadvantage.

I am not a joiner of societies, and certainly not a founder of them, but if I were I would certainly found the Anti-Tie Club. Men's fashions, although showing signs of becoming more imaginative, seem to have become fossilized at the neck. There are still occasions (and regrettably there are still restaurants) where a necktie is a curious talisman which alone gives admission.

It is not many years ago that after an hour of hesitation I finally plucked up courage to go to the theatre without a tie. Once there I found it impossible to find any other person wearing one!

I suppose the most comfortable costume that I know is jeans and a leather jacket. But to wear this particular combination of clothes is really to court the most extra-ordinary demonstrations of prejudice imaginable. Thus attired not very long ago I went with one of my closest mates of the last few years, a highly successful newcomer to the cast, Trevor Harrison, known to the world as the awful Eddie Grundy, into a local country pub, which was empty. It was ten minutes to two in the afternoon: the owner had decided to close, and only grudgingly agreed to serve us. When in addition to ale we asked for food, and the juke-box and the space-invaders (they'd already been switched off), the publican said with some vehemence: 'I can do without people like you in my pub!'

This was not only the statement of a bad businessman, it showed almost unbelievable prejudice. If we had been dressed nattily or sportily or obviously expensively, I doubt if his tone would have been so hostile in response to our mild approach. By 'people like you' he meant people dressed informally. Little did he

167

know that Trevor, dressed in exactly the same way, was appearing that night on TV with Terry Wogan, helping to raise money for charity; or that I would be chairing a meeting of trustees concerned with conserving old churches.

There are occasions when, like many people, I love dressing up in formal clothes for an evening function; but equally, I insist on being free to wear what I like at other times.

It is rare at my social level (whatever that is) to be asked to wear formal dinner-clothes at small dinner-parties. It never happens in my house! My problem is usually to get guests out of the kitchen. The idea of drinks and 'nibbly-bits' in the drawing-room is rarely put into practice. What is sometimes a planned meal degenerates (or perhaps blossoms) into a continuous improvisation of pâté and red wine and garlic butter and whatever else comes to hand. Now that so many of society's rigid rules have been relaxed, it seems foolish not to enjoy our freedom: freedom to choose the long dress and black tie, the costume ball, or the sweater and jeans party.

Another snobbism which I hope I don't have is coyness about money. At Birmingham University, where I spent so many of the happiest days of my life, I exhibited my poverty to the public gaze by working in the refectory. Nobody minded, least of all me: it was honest toil! Sentimental proletarianism is as distasteful to me as ostentations of newfound wealth. And I learned things by being poor I might otherwise never have known. For example: I had tutorials with a parson's son, a delightfully easy-going student called Mike, who spent as much each week on beer as I did on feeding myself. Yet every Thursday I would lend him 'half a dollar' (12½p.) and every Friday he would pay it back.

Later in life when I was beginning to be known as a broadcaster, I received one of the most distressing letters I ever had. It was from a much older man to whom I owed an enormous debt of gratitude for all his help with applications for grants, writing testimonials, and so on at a time when I had been most in need of them. With the letter, which contained flattering references to my success and greetings from his wife and daughters whom I barely knew, came a request and a 'note of hand' for the loan of what was then a large sum of money. It was Gwen Berryman who helped to deal with that. She advised me to do what her father always did in such cases: to send a small gift, but to refuse a loan. Her father argued that few beggars would ask twice; and this proved to be the case here. I knew the poor man had a drink problem and that my very small gift would disappear quickly; yet I owed him more than any money could pay. I learnt

168

much about values by such experiences. I still find begging letters more hateful than abusive ones; and pompous old Polonius had something when he advised his son to be neither a borrower nor a lender. The genuinely deserving rarely ask. And those who think I am a soft touch are usually disappointed.

Another manifestation of the misleading image which I seem to project is the hardest to understand. I have always had a great interest in English village church architecture. I also love the language of the Authorised Version of the Bible. It is to me a great pleasure to play an organ in a church or chapel, in such a way as to encourage a congregation to sing with greater gusto and expression than it thought itself capable of. All these activities are to me pleasurable, and I see no reason therefore to deny myself access to them. But they do contribute to a very misleading impression of what I'm really like! I have even on more than one occasion preached sermons (usually for personal friends whom I haven't wanted to offend – I have many friends among the clergy; my life has been bedevilled by parsons!) The content of my sermons has been extremely carefully chosen, though, because I am in no sense a conformist in matters of religion. I belong to no sect, and no denomination. This fact alone very often surprises people.

As a child I was sent to chapel on Sundays two and sometimes three times, so it is scarcely surprising that I broke away at the age of 15. At Oxford I went to the college chapel and may have appeared to the world to be an Anglican. The attraction for me was the superb architecture and the beauty of the service, especially the singing of the choir.

Later still, as I told in Chapter 6, I wrote a series of radio plays on the lives of the saints. My interest here was a dramatic, not specifically a religious, one. But the churchy, parsonical image persists. I inaugurated, and conducted for a year, the Morning Service for primary schools in the BBC schools programmes, though I was chosen because I didn't sound parsonical!

Not that I am in any sense irreligious. Far from it. Religion in its widest sense is never far from my thoughts. What I rebelled against, as a child onwards, was the strictness of a system of any religion which narrowed an impoverished life. Most things in this world can be regarded as God-given gifts: food, sex, alcohol, the Pill, some drugs and medicines. The evil comes in with the way these gifts are used. In human relationships, too, I found it difficult to accept strictures which, it seemed to me, reduced rather than increased the enjoyment of living. Today we see in such manifestations as the 'open marriage' and similar relationships, a pinpointing of the weakness of an accepted convention which narrows rather than broadens life. Marriage, indeed any relationship, should be an enrichment, and enlargement of life, not as it so often has been in the past, a restricting strait jacket with 'Thou shalt not' written across it like the motto on a T-shirt.

How far all this is from the predictable conformity of Philip Archer! How zealous, too, has been my own search for independence. From the time I was in my early teens, I longed to be independent and self-sufficient. Leaving school at 15, I was able to make a contribution to my upkeep. As I have said in Chapter 1, I bought my own clothes, made my own bed, was capable of cooking all my meals and, when necessary, the meals for the rest of the family. I have little patience with people, male or female, who are unable to fend for themselves in the basics of life. I suspect that P. Archer depends more on his wife than he often admits. Could Philip make a bed, or a pie or a speech at a Women's Lib. Meeting? I doubt it!

This portrait of Painting would be incomplete if I did not mention three hates. Unlike those of my friend Phil Drabble, they don't begin with 'P': they end in '-ism'. They are ageism, sexism and racism, three things so beloved of the media ('Indra Abani (43), dusky cast-off wife and mother' etc.).

I have never been interviewed for the Press when almost the first question has not been, 'How old are you?' Some reporters have apologized, saying 'My editor insists', but it irritates me beyond measure (especially, as with the report of my visit to the Palace for the Investiture, there was a misprint and they added six years to my age!). Those ages in brackets are a silent, often mischievous, comment. The utterly blameless, even noble, Dame Margaret Rutherford was reported as leaving for a tour of Scandinavia with another performer, an actor many years her junior. Both their ages appeared, accusingly in brackets after their names, and Dame Margaret's innocent reply, 'Of course we're friends' was so placed that there was totally unwarranted innuendo in it. Age is a mirage: some people of 18 are as foolish as they will be at 80; and some as wise. A gap of 40 years between lovers is in reality as little an obstacle as one of four years, all other things being equal. Why (to ask an ageist question!) is it that the middle-aged are so obsessed with age? The very young and the elderly are rarely so much concerned about it.

Sexism, too, in its discriminatory modes is a constant source of irritation to me. The subject is so well worked over that there is no need for me to repeat all the arguments here. I do think, though, that we have not quite got the divorce laws right yet: and passionately as I feel about the equality of all human beings, I find over-reactions like 'Ploughperson's lunch' absurd. Sexual equality has anomalies in both directions. If a man is knighted, his wife is given the title 'Lady'. The husband of a 'Dame has no such honour. But basically, I feel strongly that many women have been over-exploited, and many under-exploited through history; and one of the excitements of living in British society today, is to see the ferment of change slowly having its effect, in spite of attempts by some men to entrench their position, and some women to over-state their case.

Racism may be more controversial; and, because of pressure groups, may too often get submerged in other issues. I think I first encountered the phenomenon directly at Oxford. Richard Atkinson, whom I mentioned in Chapter 2, had invited me to join an archaeological dig he was organizing, and when I went to discuss details with him, I found him furious. One of the would-be helpful people in the town where the dig was to take place, who was arranging for us students to be billeted on friendly residents, had said: 'I see you've got a jew-boy in the party. Don't know where I'm going to put him! Does he *have* to come?' I imagine my reaction was similar to most other students: 'How does he know he's Jewish? And anyway who is it? Anyone we know?' It was a revelation to me then to know that having a Jewish name, as was the case here, was sufficient to provoke discrimination, prejudice and hostility. Richard Atkinson dealt with his objector quite admirably: 'Of course he has to come on the dig. If he is excluded, the dig will be cancelled!' The dig, of course, took place. I was fascinated to discover that, without knowing it, I had a number of Jewish friends; I was as interested as when I discovered that I seemed to count a number of Roman Catholics and atheists among my acquaintances. It seemed an unsuspected enrichment in my circle of friends. How could any reasonable person see it as in any way an embarrassment?

Another quirk of mine is a curious vagueness about social class. I hope I have never been so foolish as to pretend that my origins are other than they are; but equally I find myself little in sympathy with the self-consciously proletarian. My early years as a BBC writer-producer sent me searching for good broadcasters through the whole fabric of society. I met nature's gentlemen at the bottom of the social scale, and many a boorish philistine with a title at the top. The worst snob I met was the principal of a university; and the most dyed-in-the-wool capitalist was the unlettered self-important chairman of a large working-men's club. One of the few points on which I agree with D.H. Lawrence (who was, I feel, several sorts of snob, and who rarely managed to get much of his undoubted genius into his written works) is 'how beastly the bourgeois is! Middle-class morality' though, and middle-class social *mores*, as John Betjeman has so often shown, can be highly amusing, so long as they are not taken seriously.

I may be painting the most telling stroke in this whole portrait, if I say that one of the remarks that pleased me most, and which I have never forgotten, came years ago from Shirley Williams. We had lingered over a typical student meal in the Tackley Restaurant in the High at Oxford, and the question of class came up. Then, responding to a hint from me, Shirley said: 'You know, I've no idea what your background is.' I quizzed her: 'Terraced house? Suburban villa? Mining village? Country town? Industrial city? Stately home on its own estate?' She said she had not the faintest idea. If that was the case, then I had in a sense succeeded in neither claiming a status for which I didn't qualify, nor flaunting sentimentally a milieu that I was only too happy to escape from. I have no nostalgia for Tuesday's hash, the ice-cold bedroom and the always empty money-box. If I was a little self-conscious about all this, it is because I never forgot a tutorial with John Waterhouse, when we discussed Keats and Shelley, the son of a baronet and the son of livery-stables keeper. One was a snob: and it was not the son of the baronet. The tone of some of the letters of Keats to Shelley is uncomfortably patronising. I resolved never to emulate it. So here is one more characteristic to be included in the self-portrait: classlessness – or at least the wish for it.

I have mentioned my need for friendship and my difficulties in making personal friends. But along with that goes the fact that, in limited amounts, I enjoy my own company. At least two thirds of me is a writer; and the writer's dilemma has always been that he needs both the market-place and the ivory tower. He needs the peace and detachment of the ivory tower in which to commit his writing to paper; but if he lives there the whole time, he has nothing to write about. Even Proust, alone in his cork-lined room, was feeding on memories of previous times when he was not so confined. I set out, following my years at the university, to become a writer. But, as I also had experience as a performer I felt that I could help to support myself in that way, by acting, whilst I wrote the works I wanted to do. I got it wrong, though! The performing, and its attendant activities, took up so much time and energy that, as I have explained, there was little left for masterpieces. Even if my swans turn out to be geese, I would like to try for them. There *will* be time; and I must learn, as all who try to serve the Muses must, to find a lifestyle and a work-style that combine the social with the solitary, the forum with the sanctum.

In his discomfortingly perceptive book, *Enemies of Promise*, Cyril Connolly touches the sensitive spots of those of us who battle with a public life on the one hand, and who need solitude on the other. He really enquires into the problems of how to write a book that lasts ten years: and among the pitfalls that await a writer of promise he lists politics, journalism, daydreams, conversation, drink, sex, ties of duty and domesticity, worldly success and promise itself! Young writers, he says, need from three to seven years to live down their promise. I have yet to live up to mine!

This portrait of Painting would be skimped if it were not admitted that the only enemy in Connolly's list I haven't wrestled with is politics. Perhaps that is yet to come. My father constantly annoyed my mother by devoting to politics and public work the time and attention she felt should have been hers. And yet she never forgave him for withdrawing from local politics a couple of years before, according to unwritten custom, it was his 'turn' to become mayor!

Both my parents were much occupied with causes and committees. My father was involved with the National Council of Social Service, the St John Ambulance Association, the Citizens' Advice Bureaux, the Rural Community Council, as well as being an unpaid Labour Party agent, and secretary of his local branch of the National Union of Railwaymen. My mother, too, was to be found on almost any committee that was going, usually, in those sexist days, in the 'women's section'; but she was chairman (yes, not chairperson, I'm glad to say) and president of this committee or that until late in life; as well as an enthusiastic singer in choirs, and founder of one.

Inevitably, having returned to live in the county where I was born and grew up, I have been drawn, sometimes unwillingly, into public life. And yet not always unwillingly. I am sometimes surprised to find in myself this curious urge to serve the community, to be of some service, however vague. I make only one stipulation: I never agree to serve on any committee unless I am prepared to go to the meetings and support whatever functions are involved, unless I am genuinely unable to. So for three years I served on a working-party at the Arthur Rank Centre at Stonleigh considering ethical, moral and religious factors in modern farming; and I am a trustee (and for three years was chairman) of the Warwickshire and Coventry Historic Churches' Trust; and a vice-president of the Friends of the magnificent collegiate church of St Mary, Warwick.

Some 15 or so years ago when, almost for the first time in my life, I felt I had a little spare cash, I bought four things: a picture I'd long wanted, life fellowship of the Royal Horticultural Society; and life membership of the National Trust and the Council for the Protection of Rural England.

The honour that touched me most, after, of course, the OBE, was being made on Lord Netherthorpe's suggestion, an Honorary Life Governor of the Royal Agricultural Society for '25 years' service to agriculture in the United Kingdom'.

So, after so many years, I am nearly a famous person. I'm not sure I know what being famous is or what it means. The most famous lawyer in the land may be unknown to the most famous stockbroker: the name of the most distinguished surgeon may mean little to the most famous soldier. Society is rather like a layer cake, and in each layer there may be a dozen really noted people, who count for nothing in the layers above or below. The really famous person is the one who is a household name: a name that is known in every layer of the cake.

I am not speaking of worth, or the value of the person's contribution to the good of mankind; but rather of that new class of person, the celebrated. Fill a room with these celebrities and probably their only feature in common is their celebratedness.

The really famous person, as opposed to the nearly famous person, is instantly recognized by name, by voice and by appearance; is in *Who's Who*; has been on *Any Questions?*, *Desert Island Discs* and *This is your Life;* has honorary degrees from several universities, whether an old student or not. None of these things I claim; but I happily enjoy my life as a mini-celebrity.

My home, untidy and unsmartly 'lived-in' as it is, gives me constant pleasure, and the company of friends and visitors to the gardens, when they are open, is a source of great enjoyment. Only sometimes, especially in winter, when a promised visit from friends is cancelled, or heavy snow cuts me off from the world, do I feel lonely. Often I am alone, and happy to be so. There are those times when the unsuppressible thought insists on asserting itself that if, so many years ago, I had married, or at least found a life-long companion, then there might be two less lonely people in the world, . . . But then friends arrive, or I see at close quarters the misery of an unhappy marriage, with two otherwise excellent people eating themselves alive, and a glow of contentment arrives. Perhaps as Pope said, whatever is is best.

My present, compared with the lot of so many, is good: and, what gives me the greatest satisfaction of all is knowing that, in spite of enormous help and encouragement from so many people, the impulse and the effort were my own. My house and garden and pool and greenhouse and barn and orchard are *mine*: I earned them, and no-one can easily take them away.

I have little in common with Winston Churchill; but there are two things we share. One is our pride in the fact that we earned our much-loved homes by the use of our pens. And the other is the feeling that a day away from the home we made is a day lost.

There have been shadows: I have wandered the dark corridors, the lower depths and the sub-basement below sub-basement of depression and the despair of the valley of the shadow of suicide. There are no regrets there for a thing not done; but I hope never to be so close to the edge again. I do not wish to over-emphasize this; but the shadows in a portrait give modelling to the features, bring out the depth and give another dimension to the figure. A succession of predictably sunny days can be boring and monotonous, as we discovered in that brilliant, but to me gruesome, summer of 1976: it was ironic that a time of such personal honour and success in such glorious weather should for me have been the nadir of my life. I hope, and in fact I firmly believe, that I shall never let events or people pull me down in that way again. My eyes are on the mountain-tops, looking for the first glimpses of the new dawn.

There are many compensations in leaving youth behind. So much that was strange and unknown is now familiar: so many people who were daunting and intimidating have turned out to be paper-tigers, who don't scare you any more. The transiently powerful people don't have to be placated any longer: you know their little day will soon be over, and they, with all their threats and their self-importance, will be on their way.

The time comes when reluctance must become resolution. When one is a beginner it is hard to refuse offers that have some tempting qualities in them, even if one can also see dangers. But I am no longer a beginner: I have worked hard, some of my friends think too hard, for many years. I have been lucky, and I have been careful. There is no longer so great a need to work quite so desperately in order to survive. The time is overdue, long overdue, for me to spend more time doing my own thing.

And what is my own thing? It comes in many forms. Almost from the time I could write, I have written verse. I must do more of that. I would love to be a visiting professor, or a writer in residence. There are plays to be written, and directed, and acted in. There is the whole world of film, a promised land whose borders I have just crossed but whose interior I have only so far penetrated a little way. There is so much more of the world to visit, too. So many more books to write. And so many more things to do in television, before the camera, as well as behind it.

I have had for very many years one particular theatrical ambition: to play the Shakespeare clowns at the Royal Shakespeare Theatre – Dogberry, Launcelot Gobbo, Speed and even, possibly, Peter Quince, and so many others.

For a greater part of my association with *The Archers*, I loved it almost beyond reasonableness. Even when I resented it most for taking so much of my energies as writer and performer, when, in a word, I was at my most reluctant, I still gave to it, as we all did, every ounce of effort I could find. Even now, when there are days when I have to steel myself to go to the studio at all, I know that, once there, I shall give it everything I have. No performer can give less; your name is in the cast list; you are as good as your last performance.

Unlike the Beatles I do not believe in yesterday. Tomorrow is what matters. If I invoke yesterday in these pages, and speak of what might have been it is merely to justify my times of reluctance. Not to say, 'Look what I might have done, if I had not spent half my life and energy in *The Archers*'. Far from it. On the contrary, what I am trying to say is: 'There were always these alternatives; there were always so many other things to be done.' This is not to say, 'Now, alas, it is too late!' No. The exact opposite. My sword is still bright, my will as keen as ever. I say with Browning, 'The best is yet to be.'

St Teresa of Avila completed the autobiography that she was ordered to write with the suggestion that she was now past middle age and her work was over. She was not to know that her real work, for which she would be remembered, was yet to begin.

I am no saint; and I have enjoyed my life so far as much as most, and a great deal more than many. It has, in fact, been so good that I can barely wait to start the next phase of it. Without any reluctance whatsoever.

Pendent to the Portrait

At this point, the original manuscript of my book was felt to be complete. I then returned to my normal busy schedule, quite unaware that the succeeding days would lead me closer and closer to death.

Having completed the book at 2 a.m., I embarked the same day on a difficult journey to Oxford (it took two hours rather than the usual 45 minutes because of traffic congestion provoked by a rail strike) to meet my oldest Italian friend, Professor Giorgio Mazzotti, poet and painter, and four other old friends: Judge Saró Barone (one of the youngest judges in Italy) and Rita his wife, my friend Sonia (who may well be a judge herself one day) and her friend Barbara.

I was weary from the abnormally long journey and would have welcomed a rest; but my friends had not received the telephone message saying I would be late. So, with five Italians piled into the car, I turned round at once, instead of resting, and headed for home. After an improvised meal, I took them to Warwick, then for a swim. After dashing against the clock to see the sun setting over the exquisite cottage garden of my friends Betty and Stephen Baum Webb, before a flying view of Compton Wynyates house and windmill, we went home for a meal. All very merry and enjoyable; but, unawares, I was approaching disaster with every minute.

The next morning, another lightning tour: Stratford-on-Avon, then Oxford. After their taxi had finally whisked them away, I battled with the traffic home, and found myself too exhausted even to swim.

I inflict this cautionary tale on my patient reader to show how dangerous 'showing a stiff upper lip' can sometimes be. If your body tells you it is utterly exhausted, believe it.

But there was to be no rest for me. The following day was our village fête day, when my house is taken over by the village ladies and teas are served on terraces and courtyard. That evening once again found me so exhausted I couldn't even walk to the pool, let alone swim in it.

Next day, Sunday, was not a day of rest: after I had visited gardens and a flower festival in the village church at Combroke, who should arrive unexpectedly but two of my dearest friends, Jack May and Trevor Harrison?

The next three days in the recording studio culminated in a

meeting of the Warwickshire and Coventry Historic Churches Trust.

I woke the next day with the same unrelenting weariness of limbs that had prompted me, two weeks before, to cancel my trip to see Gwen Berryman in her Torquay Nursing Home and then attend the funeral of Edgar Harrison (*Dan Archer*) on the way back.

On Friday morning my old friend Edmund Marshall and his son Sebastian arrived and we set off on one more sentimental journey to Oxford, this time taking all day, seeing most of the major sights as well as Edmund's old college, and mine.

That evening was relaxed but, for me, weary: I had no pain, merely this debilitating aching exhaustion. Next morning I dragged myself up with great difficulty for a gentle stroll to our excellent local inn, The Plough.

Within minutes my muscles were wracked with a severe, indescribable pain, at that time totally new: it was to become all too horribly familiar.

At five o'clock I dragged myself to the house to feed my Cavalier spaniels, Flora, Nimrod and Mina, before sinking, in pain, into a chair. I had never felt so ill, nor so frightened: yet there was no grasping hand of pain in my chest that I had so often read about.

That night was one of doubt and sorrow, fear and loneliness, and agony; the spasms increased after shorter and shorter intervals, until, at 8 a.m., I telephoned the local surgery.

Soon I was in the Intensive Care Unit of the local hospital, and once attached to the electronic machinery my pain and my fear subsided. How was I to know that I was on the point of death? Nonetheless, at precisely 11.45 a.m., my heart went into a rhythm called 'ventricular fibrillation', a condition which does not sustain life. I was unconscious, but resuscitated my means of electric shocks of 100 joules which restored the heart to normal rhythm. Technically, for some moments, I had been dead.

Once securely alive again with no bones broken and with no recollection of the incident, I had plenty of time to think over my life – that life which had so recently ended, if only momentarily.

I thought of what I had managed to get into this book; but my main thoughts were rather of what I'd omitted. It is not overstating the case to say that I came back from death to write these final pages.

Most of my childhood has been missed out, for that is in my head as a separate book. But perhaps I didn't sufficiently emphasize, during my account of student days, my growing delight in

Gothic architecture on foggy mornings in Birmingham, or the months when, earning an honest crust as night porter at the University Overseas Club, I literally lived in a cupboard! (It was a stationery cupboard with a ceiling sloping beneath the eaves and a garret-window view of what I tried to persuade myself could be Paris or Heidelberg, rather than the much maligned Birmingham).

If much has been left unsaid of my Birmingham undergraduate days, even more has been perforce missed out or truncated of my Oxford years. Days in the Bodleian (among the most wonderful interiors in the world); days running along towpaths; snowballing at Headington; nights of lamplight in the Radcliffe Camera (to me the centre-piece of the most satisfying group of buildings in the world); evenings at the theatre, the Cinema Club; or dining guest speakers like Gillie Potter (a humourist and eccentric far too soon forgotten), or Sir Nikolaus Pevsner.

And I have said too little in this book about some of my hilarious foreign travels, including my passionate affair with Italy, the Italians and most things Italian.

Only some of the highlights of my musical life have been touched on, and a whole new recent venture as theatre director barely even mentioned.

As for my years in London and my 15 mainly idyllic years in the South Warwickshire village of Warmington – they must wait for another occasion.

I've assumed throughout this book, almost casually, that most creative people don't retire but continue till they dry up or die. And as my professional life began in my early twenties, I took it for granted that I was about half-way through, and that the second half would automatically follow. Recent events have taught me otherwise. I am assured that there is every chance that I shall fairly speedily make a complete recovery to first-class health; and that the anticipated second half of my life may well follow.

One of the great consolations, looking back after that Sunday afternoon when my life momentarily ended, was realizing how few regrets I had, and those few were more for things not done than for actions I now wished undone.

Reluctant Archer?

As I hope this book has shown, my only real reluctance has been that, giving up so much of myself to *The Archers* has so far left all too little time for many other desirable things. But there *will* be time. How could anyone who has survived as I have, be reluctant about any part of life? Reluctance has turned to eagerness. I am eager for life, the more so for having been so near to losing it.

179

Index

INDEX

181